ADVANCE PRAISE FOR
The Positive Parent: Raising Healthy, Happy, and Successful Children, Birth–Adolescence

"A vital, comprehensive parenting manual to guide and support parents through the complexities of 21st century parenting. *The Positive Parent* is an invaluable, urgently needed resource."

> —**Katharine Bensinger**, Parenting Education Program
> Director, Community Counseling Centers of Chicago

"The age-old complaint is that children don't come with instruction manuals. Now they do. *The Positive Parent* provides a comprehensive navigation aid for anyone concerned about raising well-rounded kids. Don't guess. Don't lose sleep. Dr. Alvy provides the tools needed to identify and solve those vexing issues faced by parents everywhere."

> —**Paul Petersen**, Child Advocate,
> President and Founder of A Minor Consideration

"Dr. Alvy draws on his rich professional and personal experience in this engaging text for parenthood. He offers depth for professionals with practical advice and techniques for parents. Parent educators will welcome this book."

> —**Jack C. Westman**, M.D., President, Wisconsin Cares, Inc., and
> Professor Emeritus of Psychiatry, University of Wisconsin Medical School

"A wonderful resource for all parents. Dr. Alvy's respect for parents and children is evident in every chapter, and his tips are helpful and easy to read. He does a terrific job of taking complicated research and presenting it in every-day language. What a comprehensive, easy-to-follow book!"

> —**Jody Kussin**, Academic Chair,
> Clinical Psychology Doctoral Program, Phillips Graduate Institute,
> author of *Catch Them Being Good: A Guide to Positive Parenting*

"Dr. Alvy does it again. With *The Positive Parent*, Kerby raises our awareness of parenting in the new century and challenges us to invest in our country's future while focusing on the most important job we will ever have: parenting all of our children. Thank you Dr. Alvy."

> —**Anne S. Robertson**, National Parenting Education Network (NPEN)

"*The Positive Parent* is an outstanding resource for raising healthy, happy, and successful children in 21st century America. It is *practical* because it offers solutions to common parenting challenges *and* special parenting issues. It is *informational* because it offers lists of educational resources and programs parents can trust. It is also *inspirational* because the author has taken the initiative to spearhead a national campaign to motivate parents and family professionals to make a commitment to effective parenting . . . and invites each reader to join him in this important cause.

—**Jody Johnston Pawel**, LSW, CFLE, parent educator, nationally recognized parenting expert, and author of the award-winning book, *The Parent's Toolshop: The Universal Blueprint for Building a Healthy Family.*

"A comprehensive, readable, wise, and informed book. A guide for parenting in the 21st century."

—**Duane Champagne**, Native Nations Law and Policy Center, University of California, Los Angeles

"Kerby Alvy shares his encyclopedic knowledge of parent education in an easy-reading resource. Guaranteed you'll learn 'stuff' that helps your work with parents—a recommended desktop reference."

—**Don Dinkmeyer, Jr.**, Professor of Counseling and Student Affairs, Western Kentucky University, Co-author, *Systematic Training for Effective Parenting* (STEP) Programs

"Parenting has become increasingly difficult in a world where commercial media competes with parents to shape a child's values and behaviors. Alvy's book provides many practical parenting tips and ideas to help make parents more confidant and effective in shaping their children's growth and development."

—**Karol L. Kumpfer**, Professor, Department of Health Promotion and Education, University of Utah

"In *The Positive Parent*, Dr. Alvy has given the context, the circumstances, and the course that leads to raising healthy, happy, and successful children. With meticulous care, insight, and skill, the ingredients that are necessary for rearing children are delineated in all of their variety. Most important, the numerous parenting effectiveness programs that Dr. Alvy presents are practical models to equip parents of all backgrounds to be successful at what is considered to be the toughest job you will ever love."

—**William S. Epps**, Editor of the *National Baptist Voice* Magazine and Pastor of the Second Baptist Church of Los Angeles

The Positive Parent

Raising Healthy, Happy, and Successful Children,
BIRTH–ADOLESCENCE

KERBY T. ALVY, PH.D.

Teachers College
Columbia University
New York and London

Center for the
Improvement of Child Caring
Studio City, CA

Published simultaneously by Teachers College Press, 1234 Amsterdam Avenue, New York, NY 10027, and by the Center for the Improvement of Child Caring, 11331 Ventura Blvd., Suite 103, Studio City, CA 91604-3147

Library of Congress Cataloging-in-Publication Data

Alvy, Kerby T.
   The positive parent : raising healthy, happy, and successful children : birth–adolescence / Kerby T. Alvy.
     p. cm.
   Includes bibliographical references and index.
   ISBN-13: 978-0-8077-4808-4 (pbk. : alk. paper)
   1. Child rearing. 2. Parenting. 3. Parent and child. I. Title.
   HQ769.A49 2008
   649'.1—dc22   2007028591

ISBN 978-0-8077-4808-4 (paper)

Printed on acid-free paper
Manufactured in the United States of America

15 14 13 12 11 10 09 08   8 7 6 5 4 3 2 1

To the three women I adore:
my wife, Mary, and our daughters, Lisa and Brittany.
They bring me great pleasure and their interactions are
joyous to behold.

Contents

Acknowledgments

A work of this nature places unique pressures on the family. My family has had to deal with my physical and emotional unavailability for long periods of time, as well as with my constant cycles of anxiety and elation over my own assessment of the value of what I have written. Well, they have been great—especially my wife and life partner, Mary. She has not only been emotionally supportive but also a valuable critic. Drawing on both her experiences as a parent, including being an avid consumer of parenting books and programs and her experiences in relating to hundreds of other parents in her work over the years as both a kindergarten and special education teacher, she has provided excellent suggestions for improving what I have written and a good deal of praise.

I would also like to acknowledge Gary Oltman, from the Center for the Improvement of Child Caring. Gary also has provided helpful suggestions, especially in terms of assisting in a clearer expression of ideas with which I have struggled. He not only brought his experiences in working at CICC to bear, but also those of a loving father.

Marie Ellen Larcada at Teachers College Press has been a fine editor, supplying timely feedback and guidance. I appreciate all she has done to make this book as helpful as possible to our fellow parents. Also of importance in shaping the book has been the trenchant critique and helpful recommendations of Wendy Schwartz from Teachers College Press.

CHAPTER ONE

Introduction

There is no one in the world who can influence the life and future of your children like you can. You, the parent, are your child's first teacher and guidance counselor. How you treat your children, and the examples you set in your behavior, educates them about life. No matter how old your children, there is real power in being a parent!

If you do not use this power, or if you misuse it, children can feel worthless, insecure, and not able to learn and achieve their full potential. Then their attitudes and behaviors will work against their education and their success in dealing with life.

Yes, it's true—you are not the only force that shapes your children's lives. Their own biology has a lot to do with how they grow and react, and they are under other influences all the time. But you can have a say about how these other forces affect your children. You can help them understand and evaluate the people they meet. You can guide them in analyzing what they see and hear on television, at the movies, in songs, and on the Internet. You can also manage their exposure to such forces in such a way that it supports rather than detracts from the quality of life you want in your family.

You can also help your children with the second most important influence in their lives—their school. You can prepare your children to take advantage of what schools have to offer. You can work in partnership with their schools so your children get the best possible education—which gives them the best preparation for life.

In the second chapter of this book, you will learn more about the challenges of raising children in the 21st century. Many of these challenges are by-products of the high cost of living, and of high divorce and remarriage rates. Other challenges have to do with the AIDS epidemic and an explosion of sexually transmitted diseases. And, as has been indicated, some of the challenges that you face in your parenting emanate from children's exposure to television and films, and their use of the Internet and other technological advances. In addition, pressures to use tobacco, alcohol, and other drugs pose special challenges and risks. Many of these are of a life-threatening nature.

In Chapter 3, you will learn the reasons why most people become parents and you will see if these motivations and circumstances match your own. You will also gain a fuller appreciation of all you do for and on behalf of your children. Chapter 3 also includes what research studies with parents and children from all backgrounds have to say about what is helpful and what is harmful in raising children. In addition, this chapter describes two of the major ways that parents influence children, through modeling and through the use of consequences. You will be able to use this knowledge to help you understand your current situation with your children and to enact changes or improvements in your relationships with them.

In Chapter 4, you will find 16 guidelines for raising healthy, happy, and successful children. Many of these guidelines emerge from the research on effective parenting and address the realities and challenges of raising children in contemporary times. Each guideline contains examples of the skills and practices that are involved in carrying them out with children.

These guidelines work with all children of all races, in all places. Take them to heart. Apply them to your own parenting. Your power as a parent will help your child become the best that he or she can be.

Chapter 5 provides an opportunity to learn more about understanding and parenting children with special needs and disabilities. It begins by answering the question "What is a special need?" Here you will learn the definitions used by health professionals who have the responsibility of helping special needs children and their families. The areas of child development on which they focus and the value of accurate diagnoses receive coverage, as does the importance of identifying and helping these children as early in life as possible. The officially recognized types of special needs and disabilities are listed and briefly described, with three types receiving more extended coverage: autism, attention deficit, and learning disabilities. A major resource for learning more about special needs children and how best to manage the childrearing challenges they present is also provided.

Chapters 6, 7, and 8 are devoted to the community, Internet, and other resources and services that are helpful to all parents. Chapter 6 provides practical information about how to use and advocate for the best parenting and family skill-building programs for your community.

These are the modern ways of learning how to be the best parent possible, as they teach the skills that research has found to be helpful in successfully raising children.

Chapter 7 describes a sample of the best programs, so you will know what to expect when you take advantage of what they have to offer. In Chapter 8, you will learn how to easily access a myriad of other helpful community services, as well as how to make good use of television, parenting magazines and newspapers, and the Internet.

In the concluding chapter, you will learn that your power as a parent, when it is used wisely, not only benefits you, your children, and your family, but also society as a whole. You will also learn about an exciting National Effective Parenting Initiative (NEPI) in which you, your family, and your community can play significant roles.

In writing this book for you—my fellow parents—I am drawing upon my more than 30 years of experiences as a clinical child psychologist and as the founder and director of one of our country's most influential parenting and parenting education organizations, the nonprofit Center for the Improvement of Child Caring (CICC). Those experiences have included conducting psychotherapy with children and families in affluent communities and within inner-city settings, such as at the community mental health center that serves the Watts area in south Los Angeles. There and at CICC, it has been my pleasure to have created many parenting education programs and classes and to have seen hundreds of thousands of parents enrich their own and their children's lives through participating.

I am, of course, also drawing upon my experiences as a parent. For over 20 years, my wife, Mary, and I have had the privilege of raising our daughters, Lisa and Brittany (and facing all of the challenges of being parents in the current era of AIDS and technology). What they taught us about the realities of their lives in the middle- and upper-middle-class communities where our family has lived, and how they reacted to our love, commitment, and parenting practices—all have influenced what I believe, know, and teach about raising children.

Lisa and Brittany are doing marvelously in all phases of their lives, and have been considered by their teachers and peers to be good and kind people. They have also excelled in many ways, and continue to do so in their early twenties. Mary and I are very proud parents, and how we brought the girls up had something to do with that. So you know you are reading the work of someone who has dedicated his life to studying the art of parenting and a person who loves children.

A previous version of many of the ideas and guidelines of this book appeared in a booklet I wrote called *The Power of Positive Parenting.*[1] The thousands of parents who read that booklet and shared their reactions with the researchers found it to be very helpful. Some indicated that it was the manual that should come with each child, a mini-bible for parents, and that it changed their entire approach to raising their children. Others believed it confirmed and reinforced what they were already doing with their children, and they appreciated knowing that they were on the right track.

I hope that your response to this book-length version will be equally as illuminating and reinforcing!

CHAPTER TWO

Parenting in the 21st Century

Parenting in the 21st century can be the most challenging and the most fulfilling job that anyone can have. Parenting challenges us to be self-sacrificing and involved with children on a daily basis. It calls up all of our insecurities as we try to meet the evolving and often emotionally charged needs of children.

On a day-to-day basis, parenting can provide us with numerous little joys that come just from being in the presence of children, and from seeing and feeling how much they need and love us. It can also provide the deepest personal satisfaction for having successfully met the needs of children, and, in so doing, for having successfully guided another human being to adulthood and maturity.

Parenting in the 21st century is different in a variety of ways. Many of these differences have to do with the composition of today's families and with the time and energies that today's parents have available to carry out their responsibilities. These types of differences are due to changing attitudes and decisions about the types of relationships within which people are choosing to raise children, or in which they are finding themselves compelled to raise their children. The high cost of raising children is also a major influence on the time and energy available for rearing children these days.

RELATIONAL CONTEXTS FOR RAISING CHILDREN

Data from the U.S. Census Bureau indicates that there are 73.5 million children in America.[1] They are being raised within three major types of relational and family contexts:

- Two-parent families (married or unmarried)
- Single-parent families (created out of choice or due to circumstances such as divorce, death, incarceration, and so forth)

- Blended families (created through remarriage or through becoming a reconstituted family without remarriage)

These relational and family types have, of course, always existed. It is the changing numbers within each family type that make parenting today so different. For example, in 1970, 9% of children lived in single-parent families. By 2000, 28% were living in single-parent households.[2] In addition, because 50% of marriages have been ending in divorce and because the majority of divorced parents eventually remarry, more children than ever before are being brought up in blended families and are experiencing frequent changes in the composition and organization of their families.[3]

The most traditional relational context is the married, two-parent context. Large numbers of people today still strive to raise their children that way.

There is a great deal of research evidence to indicate that raising children in a two-parent context is a worthy goal for the partners and for their children, if the marriage partnership itself is a healthy one.[4] Healthy marriage partnerships, as well as any other healthy partnerships in which children are being raised, are characterized by both partners being committed to the relationship as a life-long undertaking, and striving to be emotionally supportive of one another and to meet one another's needs for intimacy and respect. These healthy partnerships are also free from partner or domestic violence, as healthy partners know and use nonviolent means of addressing and resolving the inevitable conflicts that emerge from living and raising children together.

In terms of the research evidence about the benefits of healthy marriage partnerships, the U.S. Department of Health and Human Services reviewed a wide range of studies where comparisons were made between the impacts of healthy versus unhealthy marriage partnerships.[5] The studies showed that, for example, women from healthier relationships were healthier both physically and emotionally, were wealthier, and had better relationships with their children. Men from such relationships lived longer, were also healthier physically and emotionally, were wealthier, and had more sexually satisfying relationships. The children from healthy marriage partnerships were also found to be emotionally and physically healthier, to have fewer behavior problems at schools, to be more likely to succeed academically, less likely to abuse alcohol and other drugs or to commit delinquent acts, and more likely to attend college.

These impressive findings confirm the wisdom of people striving for healthy marriage partnerships. They also have implications for any type of partnership in which children are being raised.

The findings clearly show that children and youth do better in nearly all spheres of life when they are raised by partners who take good care of their own relationships. Everyone benefits from a healthy relational partnership. The importance of the quality of the relationship between parenting partners is one of the main reasons why this book includes parenting guideline 15 in Chapter 4 about nurturing the relationship within which children are being raised.

The importance of the quality of the relationship between parents and children, regardless of whether the context is a two-parent married context, a single-parent context, or a blended-family context, is what all of the other guidelines are about. And those guidelines apply to relationships between straight parents and their estimated 59.5 to 69.5 million children, as well as to the relationships of gay and lesbian parents and their estimated 4 to 14 million children.[6]

ECONOMICS

The direct money costs for raising children are not only substantial; they are increasing. In 1960 the total direct monetary expenses for raising a child from birth through age 17 was estimated to be about $129,000, based on reports from the U.S. Department of Agriculture (USDA). By the year 2001, the total estimated costs rose to nearly $197,000.[7]

The direct costs upon which these USDA estimates were based include seven types of expenses:

1. *Housing*—Includes shelter (mortgage interest, property taxes, or rent; maintenance and repairs; and insurance), utilities (gas, electricity, fuel, telephone, and water), and house furnishings and equipment (furniture, floor coverings, major appliances, small appliances). These housing expenses are underestimates, because they do not include mortgage principal payments, which the USDA considers to be part of savings.
2. *Food*—Includes food and nonalcoholic beverages purchased at grocery, convenience, and specialty stores, including purchases with food stamps; dining at restaurants; and household expenditures on school meals.

3. *Transportation*—Includes the net outlay on the purchase of new or used vehicles, vehicle finance charges, gasoline and motor oil, maintenance and repairs, insurance, and public transportation.

4. *Clothing*—Includes children's apparel such as diapers, shirts, pants, dresses, and suits; footwear; and clothing services such as dry cleaning, alterations, and repair; and storage.

5. *Health Care*—Includes medical and dental services not covered by insurance, prescription drugs and medical supplies not covered by insurance, and health insurance premiums not paid by an employer or other organization.

6. *Child Care and Education*—Includes day-care tuition and supplies; babysitting; and elementary and high school tuition and supplies.

7. *Miscellaneous*—Includes personal care items, entertainment, and reading materials.

In terms of the costs per year for these basic expenses, the latest USDA reports show that they vary as a result of realities such as the age of a child, a family's total before-tax income, and whether a child is being brought up by a husband–wife team or by a single parent.

Depending upon the age of the child, total yearly direct monetary expenses range from $7,040 to $8,070 for families of the lowest income group; from $9,840 to $10,900 for families in the middle income group; and from $14,470 to $15,810 for families in the higher income group.[8] These figures also show that expenditures for children are generally lower during the younger years, with this being true across income groups.

Other data from the same USDA report also showed that these expenses varied by the region of the country where a family resides. Expenses were highest for families in the urban West, followed by the urban Northeast and urban South. Families in the urban Midwest and in rural areas have the lowest childrearing expenses.[9]

However, all of these figures are underestimates of the current costs of raising children, as they are derived from what the dollar could purchase in 2001 and inflation has decreased purchasing power since then. Many expenses—such as those for child care, housing, and transportation—have also increased since 2001. In addition, these direct parent expense cost figures for raising children do not include parental expenses for children older than 17 or the costs for a college education.

More importantly, in terms of coming to grips with the total costs of raising children, these figures do not show the indirect costs of raising children by parents. These include the time costs for raising children for which parents are not paid, the earnings that parents forego when they care for children instead of working, and the career opportunities that are missed or deferred while devoting time to raising children.

Taken as a whole, these direct and indirect costs are truly substantial, and they certainly should be carefully considered before assuming the job of parenting. In addition, such cost considerations need to play a role in how parents go about raising the current generation of children. These are some of the reasons why guideline 12 in Chapter 4 addresses the role of parents as financial mentors for their children, and the importance of children being financially successful and giving.

These economic realities and considerations are also why guideline 16, about setting a good example of life-long learning, includes the recommendation that parents pursue their own financial literacy education through learning more about saving, investing, and making good consumer decisions. There is much evidence to indicate that most of today's parents could benefit from this type of education. Consider the following:

- Only 27% of parents surveyed in 2003 by Fleet Boston felt well-informed about managing household expenses.
- Fewer than half of those surveyed felt they were good role models for their children regarding saving and spending.
- In 2004, the average credit card debt among 25- to 35-year-olds, including parents, was $5,200, which was nearly twice what it was in 1992.
- Over 60% of families pay the minimum amount on their credit cards, creating a continuous debt situation.
- 79% of high school students have never taken a course on personal finance.
- 94% say their parents are their primary teachers on financial matters.[10]

Also, while the median family income has increased by 5.8% between 1990 and 2005, the costs for sending students to college have skyrocketed, according to the College Board. Over that time period, the total costs for sending students to public colleges and universities, which the majority of students attend, is up 63%. The cost of private colleges and universities has increased by 47%.[11]

Another important family-related expense that is on the increase is the cost of retirement. With people living longer and health care costing more, plus inflation and the possibility of decreased Social Security benefits, the costs to retire are now at their highest levels. These economic realities are further reasons for parents to become as financially educated as possible and for them to include being financial mentors for their children as a basic parental role and responsibility.

The economic realities of modern life are also the main reasons why we now have so many parents in the workforce, including both parents from dual-parent households. It used to be that one parent, usually the mother, stayed home to care for the children, while the other parent worked to generate the income to pay for the family. This possibly ideal situation no longer is the norm for two-parent families. Now the majority of both parents are working full- or part-time to generate the needed family income.[12]

Finally, it is very much worth noting that economics plays a major role in how available and nurturing parents can be. Having ample financial resources allows parents greater freedom to be physically and emotionally available to children. Not having ample resources means having to devote a great deal of time and energy to just being able to survive, which detracts from the physical and emotional availability of parents.

It is an unfortunate and often tragic truth that millions of children in our country are being raised in families without adequate resources. For example, in 2006, as many as 13.5 million of the 73 million children aged 18 or younger were living at or below what the federal government considered to be the poverty threshold at the time ($20,000 for a family of four, $16,600 for a family of three, and $13,200 for a family of two).[13] This enormous number of children is at the highest risk for nearly all health hazards, as well as being at the highest risk for being abused and neglected by their parents. So, as we continue our journey through the 21st-century childrearing terrain, it is meaningful to realize that literally millions of American children are being raised under conditions that are shameful and abuse-promoting.

PARENTING-ON-THE-RUN

Many of the realities of modern family life that have been mentioned thus far contribute to a situation that I refer to as "parenting-on-the-run." This is a situation where parents spend a great deal of time and energy having to coordinate and balance family and work responsibilities that often conflict, and consequently are stressed out and fatigued a good deal of the time.

Think about a parent, or two parents, having to get up early to prepare children for child care or school, and to prepare themselves for their jobs. Then they have to get everyone to where they belong for most of the day and work long hours. Then they pick up the kids after work, get home, obtain food at a fast-food restaurant or prepare dinner, have dinner, supervise homework, regulate TV and computer usage, and possibly have to prepare for a morning job meeting, and so on. Add to these responsibilities the need to have some children spend time during the week or on weekends at the home of other parents, which is what happens regularly with divorce arrangements and blended families, and modern family life becomes even more pressured. Then place on top of all of these types of activities the basic household tasks of shopping, cleaning, and repairing. It is this "parenting-on-the-run" that began to characterize most family life toward the end of the last century and that now is characteristic of so many families at the beginning of the current century.[14]

It is because of this type of stressful situation that taking good care of one's health becomes so important. Indeed, attending to one's personal health-care needs, which is another issue that is addressed within the guidelines for effective contemporary parenting, is truly a necessity for being able to cope with these "parenting-on-the-run" stresses.

CHILDHOOD OBESITY AND OTHER EATING DISORDERS

These stresses very well may be one of the major contributors to what at the beginning of the 21st century became known as the epidemic of childhood obesity. Health authorities noted that over the past 3 decades, the childhood obesity rate had more than doubled for preschool children aged 2–5 and adolescents aged 12–19, and that it had more than tripled for children aged 6–11. Thus, at the beginning of the present century, approximately 9 million children over 6 years of age were considered obese.[15]

Obesity is usually defined by use of the body mass index (BMI) charts developed by the Centers for Disease Control and Prevention (CDC) and is indicated when children and youth between the ages of

2 and 18 have a BMI equal to or greater than the 95th percentile of the age- and gender-specific charts.[16]

In our society, where a trim body is so highly valued, the problems for children and youth that accompany being obese include social and emotional problems as well as physical health problems. The social and emotional health problems that are often consequences of being obese include being socially stigmatized and marginalized, negatively stereotyped, teased, bullied, and discriminated against; and having a negative body image and low self-esteem, and becoming depressed.

The negative physical health consequences of obesity are equally as devastating. They include glucose intolerance and insulin resistance, type 2 diabetes, hypertension, sleep apnea, menstrual abnormalities, impaired balance, and orthopedic problems.

Obesity itself is basically an energy imbalance problem where the calories consumed are far greater than the calories expended. Put simply, obesity involves eating too much and not moving enough. The rise in childhood obesity is probably due to a complex interaction of social and environmental forces that influence eating and physical activity. Over the decades, these have collectively operated to create an adverse overall environment for maintaining a healthy weight. This environment, as described by authorities at the Institute of Medicine, is characterized by:

- Urban and suburban designs that discourage walking and other physical activities;
- Pressures on families to minimize food costs and acquisition and preparing time, resulting in frequent consumption of convenience foods that are high in calories and fat;
- Reduced access and affordability in some communities to fruits, vegetables, and other nutritious foods;
- Decreased opportunities for physical activity at school and after school, and reduced walking and biking to and from school; and
- Competition for leisure time that was once spent playing outdoors with sedentary screen time watching television or playing computer and video games.[17]

Many of these realities of modern life are under the control or influence of parents, especially those that have to do with eating and exercising. As a result, guideline 8 in Chapter 4 stresses parental vigilance and intelligence in these critical health spheres.

These are, of course, the same matters that influence or determine a parent's ability to keep up with the pace of modern family life. More parents themselves are obese these days than ever before, which underscores the importance of not only promoting and shaping a physically healthy lifestyle for our children, but also for us.

One of the main pressures that contribute to the psychological problems associated with obesity also contributes to other eating-related disorders. Specifically, the value that our society places on a trim body influences an alarming number of people, children and teenagers included, to engage in restrictive eating, some to the point of starvation and even death. Anorexia Nervosa and Bulimia are the most prevalent.

Anorexia Nervosa is a serious, often chronic and life-threatening eating disorder. It is defined by a refusal to maintain minimal body weight within 15% of an individual's normal weight. Other essential features include an intense fear of gaining weight, a distorted body image, and, in women, an absence of three consecutive menstrual cycles. Bulimia is marked by a destructive pattern of binge-eating and inappropriate behavior to control one's weight.[18]

A combination of environmental and biological factors predisposes people—mainly girls and women—to develop these disorders. In addition to our culture's current obsession with thinness, these predisposing factors also include a family tendency toward obesity, low self-esteem, social isolation, perfectionism, compulsivity, as well as the presence of certain predisposing neurotransmitters.

As many as 0.5 to 1% of females in the United States develop Anorexia Nervosa. Of that group, 90% are adolescents and young women. In addition, males and children as young as 7 have been diagnosed. Bulimia also tends to begin in adolescence or early adulthood and it, too, mainly affects females. An estimated 2 to 3% of young women develop Bulimia.[19]

The signs to watch out for and some suggestions for dealing with these serious problems will also be addressed in guideline 8 in Chapter 4.

CULTURAL DIVERSITY

The United States in the 21st century has become more culturally diverse than it has ever been, and it is likely to become even more diverse as time progresses.[20] This means that today's parents must prepare their children to become productive participants in schools, colleges, workplaces, and communities that are composed of more different people and groups than most of them were exposed to when they were growing up. Success in these settings now requires the ability to get along with more people from different racial and cultural backgrounds than ever before.

The cultural diversity of so many settings in our society also means that we now have unprecedented opportunities to expand our understanding and appreciation of the uniqueness and beauty of different cultures, as well as to expand ourselves as human beings. These realities propel us to look at and overcome centuries of misunderstanding and intolerance. These are some of the reasons that guideline 9 is devoted to orienting parents to teach their children about their own and other cultures and about tolerance.

Let's take a look at the population in the United States at the beginning of this century and how it has become so diverse. The Census Bureau indicated that the United States was composed of 281.4 million people in 2000.[21] By 2006, that number had reached 300 million, which represents an increase of 100 million people since the mid-1960s.[22] That phenomenal growth, which has made the United States the third most populous country after China and India, was greatly a result of immigration. About 53% of the 100 million additional Americans since the 1960s are recent immigrants or their descendents.[23]

The newcomers have transformed an overwhelmingly White population of largely European descent into a multicultural society that reflects every continent on the globe. Some arrived as war refugees. Most, like the waves of White immigrants who journeyed to the United States early in the last century, came in search of better opportunities in a country that has strong civil liberties and a stable economy. The most recent immigrants have been from Latin American countries such as Mexico, Puerto Rico, Cuba, and Guatemala, and from Asian countries such as Korea, Japan, Vietnam, and Cambodia. Immigrants from Middle Eastern countries such as Iran and Iraq have also increased recently.[24]

The exact numbers and percentages are hard to determine, as the Census Bureau now allows people to designate themselves as part of more than one category of race or ethnic group. In addition, the federal government considers race and Hispanic origin to be separate and distinct categories. There is also great geographic variation in diversity, and there is now one state, California, that is no longer predominantly White.

Regardless of where parents reside or move, they and their children will have to become comfortable and skillful in relating to more people from cultures that are different from their own if they want to be as successful and neighborly as possible. As mentioned above, guideline 8 provides assistance in this regard.

THE MEDIA AND TECHNOLOGY

Family literacy regarding reading and writing has long been recognized as being fundamental for productive civic participation. Now literacy regarding the uses and challenges of modern technologies such as the computer and the Internet has become equally as important. Both types of literacy are needed in order to prepare children for school, college, and workplace demands and success.

But computers and the Internet are not the only technological advances that are of importance to families and to the quality of family life. New telephone and communication advances, and a new intermingling of technological advances with the entertainment media are also of increasing importance to family life and the futures of children.

Let's take a look at some of the benefits, challenges, and uses that families are making of technological advances. This will also give us a glimpse into how the latest technologies and the updated versions of earlier technological advancements such as the telephone, television, radio, and films are becoming increasingly merged.

Benefits and Uses of Technologies

The extraordinary educational and business usefulness of computers and the Internet is reflected in the fact that more and more schools are requiring students to use both of these technologies in order to master more and more subject areas. Using computers to access the Internet opens students to a world of information that was once only available through spending months in the largest libraries. Some preschools are now also using the computer and the Internet for such educational purposes.

Today, college and university success is grounded in the ability to effectively use computers and conduct research over the Internet. Job market success, whether at entry or higher levels, increasingly requires computer and Internet competencies. As a result, *77% of the 46 million children 7 to 17 years of age now live in households with personal computers, and the majority of those households are Internet connected.*[25]

Other technological advances, which are fusing information and entertainment, speak to another major reason why family literacy in regard to technology is a modern necessity. Computers, cellphones, CDs, DVDs, iPods, and TVpods are now capable of providing games, music, films, and television programs at a moment's notice. Television and radio themselves, while certainly not new technologies, are taking new and more varied forms, with the proliferation of cable and satellite channels to supplement traditional local and national programming. The spectrum of adult and child films available today is also much wider and more varied than ever.

Nearly every family has telephones, television, and radios. These are household staples. And, as indicated, the majority of households with children have their own computer with Internet connections.

Today's children and youth are making extensive use of these multiple means of entertainment and communication.[26] For example, the latest studies show that each day today's 8- to 18-year-olds spend:

- 3 hours and 51 minutes watching TV (TV/videos/DVDs/prerecorded shows),
- 1 hour and 44 minutes listening to music (radio/CDs/tapes/MP3s),
- 1 hour and 2 minutes using a computer (online/offline), and
- 49 minutes playing videogames (console/handheld).[27]

One of the primary reasons that today's youth are making such extensive use of computers and phones is for socializing, friendship, and dating purposes, through direct calling, e-mails, instant messaging, and blogging.[28] One website that fosters these types of communication for teenagers and college students worldwide, Myspace.com, now has more than 100 million members![29]

Many of today's youth are also making simultaneous use of different technological advances, talking to friends, surfing the Net, playing videogames, watching television programs and films, and doing homework all at the same time. *Multitasking* has become the norm for hundreds of thousands of youth.[30]

Challenges and Hazards

Clearly, these technological advances can serve many positive purposes for families and can improve the lives and futures of children and youth.[31] They also carry with them numerous challenges and hazards. One such threat includes privacy concerns where personal information that is shared online can be turned against families in terms of identify theft. Other threats include online sexual predators pursuing children, and youth exposing themselves for sexual purposes, as some are currently doing on Myspace.com and on their own websites, using their webcams to show themselves in sexually explicit poses and actions. Gambling, cyberbullying, and online addiction are also part of the darker side of these technological advances, as is the exposure to hate on certain websites.

Some 1- and 2-year-old children are now spending sizable amounts of time before screen media such as televisions, computers, and videogames.[32] This is a source of concern in relation to the obesity and health issues previously mentioned because it shows that even the youngest of children are being oriented to sedentary habits that promote unhealthy weight gain. In addition, time spent before screens substitutes for interaction with parents and other humans, for manipulation of environmental elements (e.g., blocks or sand), and for creative problem-solving activities. These types of experiences are critical for brain development, and their minimization when infants spend time before screen media raises questions about these uses of technology hindering children's neurodevelopment.

Nearly all technological advances are driven by commercial purposes and are subtly seducing children into being avid consumers at younger and younger ages.[33] The content of what children see and hear on television, films, the Internet, music, videos, iPods, and videogames often includes stereotypical depictions of women and minorities, and provides unhealthy doses of violence.

The exposure to violent content on television has long been recognized as stimulating aggressive thoughts and actions in children, and therefore is of special concern to parents.[34] But now, violent media exposure is becoming more common and pervasive. Television no longer consists of the seven or eight channels that were available when the parents of today's children were growing up. Cable television has proliferated hundreds of new channels, including more that showcase violent and sexual content. These types of programs are now becoming available over the Internet and through cellphones and TVpods. The content of many of the videogames that today's youth are playing has become extremely violent, and recent studies indicate that playing such games can heighten aggression.[35] In addition, the lyrics of many of the most popular songs that youth hear on the radio and through their iPods now contain a great deal of violent content, as do many music videos. Never in history has so much violent content been available to children and youth through so many easily accessible venues.

This extensive multitasking use of technology and media has begun to be recognized by family life experts as a threat to family bonding and family functioning. Such concerns are now being expressed to large audiences, as a 2006 cover story of *Time* magazine reflected.[36] That story asked and attempted to answer the question, "Are Kids Too Wired for Their Own Good?" The story drew on the research currently being conducted by anthropologist Dr. Eleanor Ochs, the director of UCLA's Center for Everyday Lives of Families. Dr. Ochs shared the following observations about the impact of absorption with technology on family life interactions:

> We saw that when the working parent comes through the door, the kids are so absorbed by what they are doing that they don't give the arriving parent the time of day.[37]

Ochs's studies showed that the returning parent, usually the father, was greeted only about a third of the time, usually with a perfunctory "Hi." Most of the time, the children ignored the parent, and the parents learned not to approach their children when they were absorbed, retreating from making contact.

In addition, concerns have also been expressed by neuroscientists that the rapid multitasking that children and teens are doing may be corroding their ability to give the concerted attention that is needed to understand complex academic issues.[38] Here's an example from a 15-year-old girl: "I'm always talking to people through instant messenger and then I'll be checking email or doing homework or playing games AND talking on the phone at the same time." Through this type of multitasking, this child and yours may be getting into habits that undermine the ability to concentrate, reflect on, and fully understand complex issues and topics.

Finally, the impact of the easy availability of all of these technological advances, which as we have just seen often result in family members receding into cyber-cocoons for sizable amounts of time, raises several serious questions.[39] Is their availability and extensive use undermining the quality and importance of family interaction and communication? With so many families today so strapped for time together due to multiple work demands, do these advancements make it even harder to connect face-to-face with each other? Are these advances hindering family bonding and cohesion? Indeed, in those families with only one computer or television, fighting with one another for access is not uncommon.

So it is of special concern to today's parents that they become aware of these potential hazards and that they address them as creatively as possible. Here is a listing of the potential media and technology hazards:

- Commercialism
- Cyberbullying
- Family life disruption
- Gambling
- Identity theft
- Interrupted infant development
- Sexual exposure
- Sexual predators
- Stereotyping
- Hate
- Violence promotion
- Weight gain

Guideline 13 in Chapter 4 provides some ideas about how these hazards and challenges can be addressed.

AUTISTIC AND OTHER SPECIAL NEEDS CHILDREN

Childhood autism is characterized by serious problems in getting along and communicating with other people; for example, problems in the social, emotional, and communication areas of development.[40] Toward the end of the 20th century, children with these types of developmental problems were becoming more apparent because more were being diagnosed. Not only that, but there was an emerging professional consensus that there were several varieties of children with autistic characteristics, which resulted in a more accurate depiction—children with Autistic Spectrum Disorders.[41]

These disorders are part of a much larger range of childhood difficulties that now fly under the heading of childhood disabilities and/or children with special needs. These include children with problems in other areas of development, including motor development (e.g., children who have problems walking and manipulating objects), sensory development (children with hearing and vision problems), and children with problems in the spheres of cognitive and language development (children with thinking and speaking problems). These children are often considered mentally retarded, emotionally disturbed, learning disabled, and visually, speech, and/or hearing impaired.

Altogether, it is estimated by professional groups like the American Academy of Pediatrics that 12 to 16% of the 73 million children under age 18 in the United States are children with these characteristics and special needs.[42] It is also widely known that only a fraction of these children are being identified early in their lives, which means that they and their families cannot benefit from the early intervention programs and services that are known to be extremely helpful for these children to reach their full potential. For this reason, there is a guideline about being alert to special needs in Chapter 4. In addition, the large numbers of children with special needs warrant greater coverage, and Chapter 5 is devoted to them.

TOBACCO, ALCOHOL, AND OTHER DRUGS

Another parenting challenge that became salient in the second half of the 20th century, and which continues to require parental vigilance, has to do with the use of tobacco, alcohol, and other drugs, such as marijuana and cocaine. These often health-compromising substances became more available to children and more children began experimenting and using them during the 1980s, resulting in what was referred to as the War on Drugs. It is a war worth fighting.

Consider the following facts about the actual and potential harmful consequences of the use of legal drugs such as tobacco and alcohol and their currently illegal or illicit counterparts. This information is drawn from such authoritative sources as the National Clearinghouse for Alcohol and Drug Information, and the National Youth Anti-Drug Media Campaign.[43]

Tobacco: Cigarettes and Other Nicotine Products

Nicotine is one of the most heavily used addictive drugs in the United States. Cigarette smoking has been the most popular method of consuming nicotine since the beginning of the 20th century.

In 1989, the U.S. Surgeon General issued a report that concluded that cigarettes and other forms of tobacco, such as cigars, pipe tobacco, and chewing tobacco, are addictive and that nicotine is the drug in tobacco that causes addiction. In addition, the report determined that smoking was a major cause of stroke and the third leading cause of death in the United States.

The Environmental Protection Agency (EPA) has concluded that secondhand smoke causes lung cancer in adults and greatly increases the risk of respiratory illnesses in children and sudden infant death.

In terms of the numbers of persons who smoke, in 1998 it was estimated that 60 million Americans were current cigarette smokers, which is 28% of all Americans aged 12 and older. Of that total, 4.1 million were children between the ages of 12 and 17, which represents 18% of the youth in that age bracket.[44]

Thus, multiple millions of American children are being exposed in their families to role models who smoke and also to the impact of secondhand smoke. In addition, more than 4 million children are smokers themselves.[45]

Alcohol

Health hazards associated with the excessive use of alcohol or with alcohol dependency include dramatic behavioral changes, retardation of motor skills, and impairment of reasoning and rational thinking. These factors result in a higher incidence of accidents and accidental deaths for those who use alcohol than for nonusers.

In a 2001 national survey conducted by the U.S. Department of Health and Human Services, approximately half of Americans aged 12 or older reported being current drinkers of alcohol (48.3%). This translates to an estimated 109 million drinkers.[46]

Approximately one-fifth (20.5%) of persons aged 12 or older participated in binge drinking at least once in the 30 days prior to the survey. Heavy drinking was reported by 5.7% of the population 12 or older, or 12.9 million people. The highest prevalence of both binge and heavy drinking in 2001 was for young adults aged 18 to 25, with the peak rate occurring at age 21.[47]

In terms of the data on underage and illegal use of alcohol, the survey indicated that among 12- to 17-year-olds, approximately 17% had used alcohol in the month prior to the survey. Of those users, 10.6% were binge drinkers and 2.5% were heavy drinkers.[48]

So, here again, as we saw with tobacco smoking, multiple millions of children are being exposed to adult models who regularly use potentially harmful substances, including millions of models who are alcoholics and binge and heavy drinkers. In addition, millions of youth are drinkers themselves, including youth who are binge and heavy users.

Illicit Drug Use

The use of illicit drugs usually causes the same general type of physiological and mental changes as alcohol, although frequently those changes are more severe and more sudden. Death or coma resulting from an overdose of drugs is more frequent than overdose from alcohol, but, unlike alcohol, abstinence can lead to the reversal of most physical problems associated with drug use. Here are some examples:

> *Cocaine.* Cocaine is a stimulant that is most commonly inhaled as a powder. It can be dissolved in water and used intravenously. The cocaine extract (freebase) is smoked. Users can progress from infrequent use to dependence within a few weeks or months. Psychological and behavioral changes resulting from the use include overstimulation, hallucinations, irritability, sexual dysfunction, psychotic behavior, social isolation, and memory problems. An overdose produces convulsions and delirium, and may result in death from cardiac arrest. Discontinuing the use of cocaine requires considerable assistance, close supervision, and treatment.
>
> *Amphetamines (speed, love drug, Ecstasy).* Patterns of use and associated effects are similar to those of cocaine. Severe intoxication may produce confusion, rambling and incoherent speech, anxiety, psychotic behavior, ringing in the ears, hallucinations, and irreversible brain damage. Intense fatigue and depression resulting from use can lead to suicide. Large doses may result in convulsions and death from cardiac arrest or respiratory arrest.
>
> *Heroin and Other Opiates.* These drugs are usually taken intravenously. "Designer" drugs similar to opiates include Fentanyl, Demerol, and "China White." Addiction and dependence develop rapidly. Impaired judgment, slurred speech, and drowsiness characterize use. Overdose is

manifested by coma, shock, and depressed respiration, with the possibility of death from respiratory arrest. Withdrawal symptoms include sweating, diarrhea, fever, insomnia, irritability, nausea and vomiting, and muscle and joint pain.

Hallucinogens or Psychedelics. These include LSD, mescaline, peyote, and phencyclidine (PCP or "angel dust"). Use impairs and distorts one's perception of surroundings, causes bizarre mood changes, and results in visual hallucinations that involve geometric forms, colors, and persons or objects. Users who discontinue use may experience "flashbacks," consisting of distortions of virtually any sensation. Withdrawal may require psychiatric treatment for the accompanying persistent psychotic states. Suicide is not uncommon.

Solvent Inhalants (glue, lacquers, plastic cement). Fumes from these substances cause problems similar to alcohol. Incidents of hallucinations and permanent brain damage are frequent.

Marijuana (cannabis). Marijuana is usually ingested by smoking. Prolonged use can lead to psychological dependence, disconnected ideas, alteration of depth perception and sense of time, impaired judgment, and impaired coordination.

Damage from Intravenous Drug Use. In addition to the adverse effects associated with the use of a specific drug, intravenous drug users who use unsterilized needles or who share needles with other drug users can develop AIDS, hepatitis, tetanus (lockjaw), and infections of the heart. Permanent brain damage may also result. The use of alcohol and many other drugs causes birth defects of a very serious nature.

Numbers of Users. In terms of usage of illegal drugs, it was estimated that there were 5.7 million American illicit drug users in 2000, with 76% using marijuana either alone or in combination with other illegal substances.[49] Marijuana's effects on the user depends on its strength and potency, which is related to the amount of THC it contains (THC, or delta-9-tetrahydrocannabinol, is the main active chemical in marijuana). The THC content of marijuana has been increasing since the 1970s, which means that marijuana is a much more potent drug today than it was when so many of today's parents and grandparents were using it in the second half of the 20th century. In terms of children's use of marijuana and other illicit drugs, 3.8% of youth aged 12 to 13 reported current use in 2001. Among youth aged 12 to 17, 10.8% were illicit drug users in 2001.[50]

So, once again, millions of American children are being exposed to potentially very harmful habits in their homes, and sizable numbers have adopted these habits before they are even old enough to vote.

Large numbers of America's parents are setting poor examples and creating other forms of havoc in the home because of their own use and abuse of these and other substances. And, just as clearly, all children themselves are in need of home guidance away from abusing such potentially unhealthy substances. Hence, guideline 10 in Chapter 4 provides a variety of strategies for helping parents do a better job.

HIV/AIDS AND OTHER STDs

Guideline 11 in Chapter 4 helps parents deal with the many health hazards that now exist when children engage in behaviors of an adult sexual nature. Today more young people are having oral sex and sexual intercourse at earlier ages than in the past. For example, a 2003 study conducted by the National Campaign to Prevent Teen Pregnancy showed that approximately one in five adolescents had had sexual intercourse before his or her 15th birthday.[51]

The health hazards of sexual intercourse, on top of the possibility of becoming pregnant or getting someone pregnant, include contracting HIV/AIDS and other sexually transmitted diseases (STDs). Let's look a little more closely at these diseases, their health hazards, and the numbers of adults and adolescents that are known to be involved. We will rely on information provided by the Centers for Disease Control and Prevention (CDC) in the U.S. Department of Health and Human Services.[52]

HIV/AIDS

HIV (human immunodeficiency virus) is the virus that causes AIDS. This virus may be passed from one person to another when infected blood, semen, or vaginal secretions come in contact with an uninfected person's broken skin or mucous membranes. In addition, infected pregnant women can pass HIV to their baby during pregnancy or delivery, as well as through breast-feeding. Some of these people will develop AIDS as a result of their HIV infection.

At the end of 2003, an estimated 1,039,000 to 1,185,000 persons in the United States were living with HIV/AIDS. In 2004, the largest estimated proportion of HIV/AIDS diagnoses were for men who have sex with men (MSM), followed by adults and adolescents who were infected through heterosexual contact. In 2004, almost three-quarters of HIV/AIDS diagnoses were for male adolescents and adults. Also during that year, there were 42,514 deaths attributable to AIDS, of the total 529,113 AIDS deaths noted since the first charting of this epidemic.[53]

Children and adolescents who engage in adult sexual behaviors are putting themselves in harm's way by increasing their chances of contracting AIDS and living with or dying from it.

Other Sexually Transmitted Diseases

Children today are also much more likely than prior generations to contract common STDs, like Chlamydia, Gonorrhea, Syphilis, and Herpes. And, by doing so, they are at least two to five times more likely than uninfected individuals to acquire HIV if they are exposed to the virus through sexual contact.[54] In addition, if an HIV-infected individual is also infected with another STD, that person is more likely to transmit HIV through sexual contact than other HIV-infected persons.

These other STDs are much more common than most people realize. According to recent estimates, there were about 19 million new STD infections in 2000. *Of those, about one-fourth of the infections were among teenagers.*[55] In addition, these diseases, which can cause infertility, are usually difficult to detect in their early stages. This means that most teenagers and their families are unaware that they have the disease until it is too late to reverse permanent damage. As a result, children who engage in adult sexual behaviors find themselves and others in the path of initially invisible, then ugly health problems, and even death.

Sexual intercourse among children and teens, and alcohol and other drug use are interrelated. Sex is more likely to occur when children are high on these substances.

GANGS AND VIOLENCE

Gangs, crime, and violence are not far behind, as the sale of illegal drugs is the main way that gangs support themselves. Gangs are often highly violent groups because they have to fight to maintain their place in the illegal drug-selling market in their areas. Drive-by shootings and other deadly violence is all too common in these areas.[56]

All of this has contributed to making childhood a more dangerous time, especially in communities where gangs operate. Today, gangs are in existence in both urban and suburban communities, with the movement to the suburbs and to more rural areas fueled by a lesser police presence, lower housing costs, and the lure of unclaimed gang territories.

An example of these 21st-century realities at a local level was conveyed in a 2006 article in the *Los Angeles Times*, "As L.A. Violent Crime Drops, the Desert Becomes the Hot Spot." That article reported that as gang- and drug-related crime in the city of Los Angeles was on the decrease, it was increasing in the surrounding suburban, rural, and desert areas.[57] Part of that increase was due to the existence of many illegal methamphetamine-producing laboratories in the outlying areas, where that drug is apparently more popular than in urban areas. The increase was also accounted for by the migration of gang members to those communities.

In terms of communities nationwide, the U.S. Office of Juvenile Justice and Delinquency Prevention, in its Highlights of the 2001 National Youth Gang Survey, indicated that 100% of cities with populations greater than or equal to 250,000 reported gang activity in 2001, and that in 20% of the smallest cities with populations between 2,500 and 24,999, gang activity was also in existence. In addition, 69% of cities with populations of at least 100,000 reported having gang-related homicides in 2001, and 37% of cities with populations between 50,000 and 99,999 reported having gang-related homicides that year.[58]

Clearly, the existence of gangs and their drug dealing has made childhood a very dangerous time for many children in our nation. Children who join gangs or are coerced into joining them are at the greatest danger. Many times, they join because their families and parents do not or cannot supply the support and security they need.

CHILD MALTREATMENT

It is an unfortunate and tragic fact that for far too many children, the dangers of childhood do not just emanate from drugs and gangs and the other sources already mentioned. Numerous children from all communities throughout our country are also endangered on a daily basis through the abusive and neglectful actions and inactions of their own parents and other caregivers.

The parental maltreatment of children is a serious and widespread problem in and of itself.[59] It is a problem that is influenced by the previously mentioned problems, as many abusive and neglectful parents are also substance abusers. It is also a problem that produces other problems, as children who are abused and neglected are the most likely to engage in self-dangerous behaviors, including becoming sexually active very early, becoming substance abusers or gang members, as well as being more likely to abuse their own children when they become parents.

There are several forms of child maltreatment:

- Physical abuse includes physical acts that cause or could cause physical injury to the child.
- Sexual abuse is the involvement of the child in sexual activity to provide sexual gratification or financial benefit to the parent or other adult, including contacts for sexual purposes, prostitution, pornography, or other sexually exploitative activities.
- Emotional abuse is defined as acts or omissions that cause or could cause conduct, cognitive, affective, or other mental disorders.
- Physical neglect includes abandonment, expulsion from the home, failure to seek remedial health care or delay in seeking care, inadequate supervision, disregard for hazards in the home, or inadequate food, clothing, or shelter.
- Emotional neglect includes inadequate nurturance or affection, permitting maladaptive behavior, and other inattention to emotional/development needs.
- Educational neglect includes permitting chronic truancy or other inattention to educational needs.

It is impossible to know for sure exactly how many American children are maltreated in these ways because most of these abuses occur in private. Those that become part of the public record by being reported to official groups such as law enforcement and child protective service agencies are not the whole story, as there is the matter of unequal reporting based on how exposed a particular family is to public scrutiny, with families who rely on public assistance and families living in poverty being the most exposed. These are also the families who are most likely to become abusive and neglectful because the stresses that accompany a life in poverty make it especially difficult to be attentive and nurturing.

It is generally assumed by those professionals who work in the fields of child abuse and neglect that for every reported instance, there are at least three others that go unreported.[60] Thus, for the 3 million cases that have been reported annually over the last few decades, another 9 million are probably not brought to public attention.

About two-thirds of the reported instances of child abuse receive official investigation by law enforcement and/or child protective service professionals. In approximately half of those cases, it is determined that legally defined child abuse and/or neglect has taken place.[61]

By figuring that there are 12 million reported and unreported instances of child maltreatment annually and that two-thirds are investigated with half of those being confirmed, *it can be reasonably estimated that as many as 4 million children a year have been abused and/or neglected in the United States for the last 20 years or so.* The vast majority of those children are abused and/or neglected by their parents, fathers and mothers alike.

What Are Some Consequences of Child Maltreatment?

According to various authorities, including the Centers for Disease Control and Prevention, there are numerous negative consequences to the children and to the community for these acts of violence toward children.[62] Here are some of the negative outcomes that have been noted:

- Children who experience maltreatment are at increased risk for adverse health effects and behaviors as adults, including smoking, alcoholism, drug abuse, eating disorders, severe obesity, depression, suicide, sexual promiscuity, and certain chronic diseases.
- Maltreatment during infancy or early childhood can cause important regions of the brain to form improperly, leading to physical, mental, and emotional problems such as sleep disturbances, panic disorder, and Attention-Deficit/Hyperactivity Disorder.
- About 25 to 30% of infant victims with Shaken Baby Syndrome (SBS) die from their injuries.[63] Nonfatal consequences of SBS include varying degrees of visual impairment (e.g., blindness), motor impairment (e.g., cerebral palsy), and cognitive impairments.
- Victims of child maltreatment who were physically assaulted by caregivers are twice as likely to be physically assaulted as adults.
- Direct costs (judicial, law enforcement, and health system responses to child maltreatment) are estimated at $24 billion each year. The indirect costs (long-term economic consequences of child maltreatment) exceed an estimated $69 billion annually.[64]

Clearly, the problem of parental maltreatment of children is one of the most serious and costly problems that we as a society must face. Our fellow parents who are the offenders often have backgrounds and live in situations that make their destructive behaviors more understandable, and also provide cues as to what we can do to turn this unacceptable situation around.

Here are some of characteristics of an abusive parent that have become known through various research studies:

- Had an unhappy childhood
- Was mistreated or abused as a child by parent(s)
- Had parents who failed to provide an adequate model of good parenting
- Is socially isolated from family, friends, or neighbors; has few outside contacts of an intimate nature
- Has low self-esteem; perceives self as inadequate, unlovable, incompetent, or worthless
- Is emotionally immature; may be considered an adult child emotionally; has a dependent personality
- Sees little joy or pleasure in life; may be clinically depressed
- Holds distorted perceptions and unrealistic expectations of children
- Is adverse to the idea of spoiling his or her child; strongly believes in physical (corporal) punishment as a means of teaching children and helping them learn family patterns; practices an authoritarian childrearing style; displays minimal nurturing behaviors to child; displays frequent outbursts of temper
- Has severely limited ability to empathize with others, particularly with his or her children; displays a general insensitivity to the needs of others.[65]

One or more of the 16 parenting guidelines in Chapter 4 relate to one or more of these types of characteristics. Thus, the array of guidelines can be considered a blueprint for preventing child maltreatment.

Now, let's take a closer look at what moves people to become parents in the first place, what parents do for and on behalf of their children, what the research on parenting has to say about the better and poorer ways of raising children, and what influence processes parents use in raising children. Knowing how these influence processes work allows for a more educated approach to childrearing.

CHAPTER THREE

The Job of Parenting

As we have begun to look at what parenting is like at the beginning of the 21st century, we have already touched upon many of the responsibilities that make up this job. We have also noted how difficult and challenging parenting is, especially given the conditions and situations in which most of today's parents are raising children.

MOTIVATIONS FOR PARENTING

Why would anyone take on such a demanding and nonpaying job?

Well, people have been doing it for as long as human beings have inhabited the planet, and most people on earth today continue to seek out and assume such duties and obligations. Of course, without people being willing and able to take on this job, our species could not continue.

But it is doubtful that such motivation is the only reason for becoming a father or a mother. Indeed, as with most pivotal and life-shaping decisions, there are likely to be many reasons and some of those reasons may not be consciously admitted.

Here are some reasons that have been suggested over the ages that may help you understand your own motivations for becoming a parent. See whether they have meaning to you in your own situation.

- *Parenting as a social obligation.* This motivation comes closest to parenting in order to continue the species and it emerges from a sense of social obligation to our fellow human beings.
- *Parenting for God.* Here the motivation is shaped by a sense of religious duty and obligation.
- *Parenting for our people.* This motivation has to do with deciding to parent out of a felt obligation to continue one's ethnic, cultural, religious, or racial group.
- *Parenting for our family.* Here the motive is to ensure the continuation of the family or the family name.

- *Parenting for generativity.* This motive assumes that parenting is a phase of human development where becoming a parent fulfills a basic human need to impart one's experience and wisdom to the next generation.
- *Parenting for self-fulfillment.* The reason for parenting here is that becoming a parent serves to further fulfill and actualize one's potential.
- *Parenting for the love of children.* This reason emanates from a deep and genuine love for being in the presence of children and guiding their development.
- *Parenting for proving masculinity or femininity.* The force operating here is to demonstrate that by becoming a father or mother, one is a complete man or woman.
- *Parenting for economic purposes.* This motive has to do with the expectation that children will be a financial asset to the family or the group.
- *Parenting for assistance in the older years.* Here a person has in mind that his or her children will take care of him or her when the person is no longer capable of doing so him- or herself.
- *Parenting to obtain a spouse.* This motivation emerges from an assumption that being willing and able to have children will influence or determine that someone will want to marry you.

PARENTAL FUNCTIONS AND RESPONSIBILITIES

Different motivations for becoming a parent may influence how much one becomes involved in the day-to-day activities of raising children. But those daily activities must be carried out in order for children to survive and grow.

Many of those activities have been mentioned as we have explored what it is like to be a parent in the 21st century. Now let's put them all together in a more systematic fashion to gain an overall appreciation of what modern parents do for and on behalf of their children.

Parenting is the process of raising children, and it covers a broad range of activities. These activities can be viewed as consisting of five interrelated functions and their corresponding responsibilities.[1]

Resource Provision

These functions include providing the whole spectrum of resources that are necessary to sustain and maintain a home and family. They include material resources (housing, clothing, appliances, furniture, toys, games), nutritional resources (food, drink), utility resources (gas, water, electricity), service resources (physical, dental, and mental health services; educational services), community resources (parks, stores, churches), cultural and recreational resources (films, music, art), and communication resources (television, computers, telephone, radio, newspapers).

The education, occupation, and income of parents greatly determine their ability to provide these resources, and this ability, in turn, has repercussions on their other functions. Where the ability to provide is great, there is greater opportunity for cultivating the other functions. Where the ability is limited, there is less opportunity.

An important aspect of resource provision covers the consumption priorities of parents. Do they choose to purchase or rent housing in a more prestigious and safe area at the expense of vacation and clothing luxuries or necessities? Do they choose to purchase an expensive car or customize a car at the expense of educational materials for their children?

Another aspect of resource provision has to do with the relationship between what most parents must do in order to provide the resources—work outside of the home—and what they do in the home. The challenge of balancing work and family responsibilities is greater today than ever before, because the vast majority of parents are in the workforce.[2] Who stays home when the kids are sick? Whose career or job is more important? These resource provision–related questions and challenges are part of nearly all parents' lives these days.

Caring for the Home

These functions include basics such as home maintenance (cleaning, painting, gardening, plumbing), clothing maintenance (cleaning, washing, ironing, sewing), nutrition maintenance (shopping, cooking, dishwashing), and car maintenance (cleaning, repairing). Caring for the home also involves the budgeting, management, and investment of monies. This includes the day-to-day management of funds as well as speculative investments and gambling and giving to charities, causes, and disaster relief.

Protecting Children

Parents are the persons who are usually responsible for protecting family possessions and resources. They are also responsible for protecting the family's physical, psychological, spiritual, ethnic, and cultural integrity from threats from the natural environment and from other persons, groups, and institutions.

Some of the threats from which parents protect children are:

> *Threats of bodily harm.* These include threats to a young child's existence that occur because the child doesn't appreciate the threat, such as sticking hands into fires or running into streets. It also includes threats to children of all ages from other persons, such as physical assaults and rapes, as well as threats from tobacco, alcohol, and other drugs. And, as we have already seen, parents today must be particularly vigilant about protecting children from the life-threatening HIV/AIDS and other predisposing STDs, and from becoming obese.
> *Threats of psychological harm.* Encompassed here is the devaluation of a child's capabilities, characteristics, and appearance by other people inside and outside of the family.
> *Threats of peer harm.* These entail associations with antisocial peers and peer groups (gangs) for which parents must also be more watchful these days.
> *Threats of social harm.* These include discrimination against children of different genders in social institutions, including the school.
> *Threats of racial, ethnic, cultural, and spiritual harm.* These consist of protecting children from the harm that accompanies the demeaning of the values and customs of one's ethnic, cultural, or religious group.

Harm to children in one area has repercussions in others. An infant who sustains head or brain injuries may become psychologically incapacitated and develop with a restricted or retarded range of intellectual abilities. A child who is harmed because his ethnic or religious group is demeaned may be unable to separate himself from the social, political, and economic causes of discrimination and develop a low sense of self-esteem.

Protective functions are carried out through a parent's management of the physical, social, and psychological environments to diminish and buffer the encounters that children have with potential harm. Child-proofing the kitchen, restricting access to unsafe play areas, controlling access to certain people, and influencing how children relate to potentially harmful people and institutions all fall within the realm of child protection. This includes how parents orient children to understand the commercial and often violent images to which they are exposed through television, films, the Internet, and videogames.

Parents differ greatly in how they carry out these protective functions and the degree to which they are involved. Parents who cannot afford optimally safe living conditions and who are themselves victims of discrimination are by necessity very much involved. In unsafe buildings where lead-based paint chips are available for children to eat and where drug trafficking occurs outside of apartment doors, parents have to be especially vigilant in protecting children. When a parent and child's racial, ethnic, or religious group is subject to prejudice, discrimination, and stereotyping, parents must work hard to buffer and protect children from these types of psychological and physical hazards.

Parental violations or negligence in carrying out these protective functions are child abuses. Parents who beat and burn children are engaging in physical child abuse. Sexually abusing or exploiting children inflicts often irreparable psychological harm, as does the use of verbally and emotionally abusive comments and put-downs. Parents who are not concerned about their children's whereabouts or do not know how to supervise from afar are putting their children in harm's way.

Child Guidance

This function involves the use of physical and psychological methods to guide all aspects of the child's development. These include the child's motor, sensory, perceptual, physical, cognitive, linguistic, social, emotional, moral, spiritual, sexual, cultural, educational, and economic development.

Physical caregiving refers to activities such as feeding children, cleaning and dressing them, attending to their health needs, administering medical assistance, taking them to doctors and dentists, and attending to their rest and sleep needs.

Psychological caregiving consists of nurturing children and providing them with warmth and acceptance, disciplining children and helping them learn the social appropriateness of behavior, grooming children to make them presentable, orienting children to appropriate gender functioning, teaching children about the world, assisting children with their formal education, managing the crises that occur when children are hurt or disruptive, providing information and guidance about sexual functioning, and enculturation (i.e., inculcating moral, religious, ethical, and cultural values in children).

The distinction between physical and psychological caregiving is not meant to indicate that they are separate and unrelated processes. For example, the manner in which infants are fed can greatly influence the child's sense of acceptance. If feeding is done warmly and with careful attention to the child, the child is likely to feel more accepted. If it is done matter-of-factly or mechanically, the child is more likely to feel rejected, even though the child's physical needs are being met. Thus, the more focused activities that are part of physical caregiving are also activities through which parents can help meet a child's other needs.

Parents vary widely in how they physically and psychologically care for children. This variability is a function of many factors, including the child's temperament, health status, personality, sex, and stage of development; the parent's temperament, personality, health status, sex, and stage of development; the presence and influence of other family members; the family's socioeconomic resources; external stresses on the family; and the total community and societal context for child care. In regard to enculturation, some parents are extremely involved and very conscious of how and what they teach their children about their own cultural group. Other parents are less aware and enculturate their children simply by the way they relate to them.

There is also variability in terms of those aspects of child development that parents feel a responsibility for guiding. For example, some parents do not see it as their responsibility to guide their children's religious or spiritual development. There is also variability that results from ignorance. For example, a parent may feel responsible for helping a child with her/his sexual development but may not know how to introduce or carry out this kind of guidance.

Indeed, many parents undoubtedly turn away from attempting to guide various aspects of their children's development because they just don't know how to do it. And they don't know how to do it because no one ever taught them. The guidelines and resources in this book are provided, in part, because so many parents find themselves at this disadvantage.

Connecting and Advocating

Children, particularly young ones, need to be represented before various groups and institutions because they do not have the status or capabilities to do so themselves. It is an important part of the job of parenting to connect children to these groups and individuals and to advocate on their behalf.

Parents are the child's link to numerous groups, beginning with connecting them to their family of origin and the extended family. Parents continue this function by also linking children to the worlds of child care and education, to health-care professionals, to tradespersons, to transportation systems, and eventually to the world of work. Parents may physically link their children to these persons, groups, or systems, such as when they personally transport them back and forth, a rather common occurrence in what we have termed parenting-on-the-run. Parents also serve to link their children to the outside world by providing access to television, telephones, and the Internet.

This linkage responsibility also includes making sure that the child receives adequate care and attention from health professionals, child care personnel, educators, and other persons who have responsibilities for children. Getting children to these places and people is only part of this important parental networking task. Parents have to speak with and relate to these institutional representatives and ensure that the best interests of their children are upheld.

As with the other four functions, parents differ greatly in how they carry out these advocacy and connecting responsibilities and which ones they consider to be appropriate. Here again, a reluctance to get involved may have to do with not being educated about how to be involved. For example, a parent may shy away from engaging a child's school officials because the parent just does not know what the ground rules are for parental involvement.

Overriding these five parenting functions is the ability to organize and manage all five of them at the same time. As would be expected, parents differ greatly in how they accomplish this overarching and potentially overwhelming feature of parenting.

In carrying out these five functions, families are organized in a variety of ways. In many families, the functions are shared by two parents, with one parent responsible for one set of functions and the other for a different set, or, in other cases, with each parent sharing in carrying out each function or different aspects of each function.

There are families where the parents contract for the assistance of others to carry out certain functions. There are families where persons other than the parents fulfill some of these functions, such as grandparents, older children, relatives, friends, or even the state. And, as we have seen, there are large numbers of single-parent families where one person fulfills all of the five functions, and more and more families, reconstituted because of divorce or separation, where more than one set of parents are involved in carrying out these functions—and where the sharing and organization is an extremely complex matter.

These are, of course, not the only things that parents do. In order to carry out their resource provision function, most parents today have to work. Their vocation or career not only brings them into contact with people and institutions that may influence their parenting, but it also engages them psychologically in terms of career aspirations, disappointments, and achievements. These personal aspects of work also can influence their parenting by affecting their moods and availability.

In addition to work relationships, parents often have friendships and civic and religious associations that require energy and cultivation. They also have their relationship with one another, or, if they are a single parent, with a lover or significant other. And more and more parents have emotionally draining relationships with their elderly parents. These intimate relationships can greatly affect how they carry out their parenting responsibilities.

Finally, parents have relationships with themselves. They may be embedded in a network of family members, friends, religious and work associates, but they are unique individuals. Cultivating their own uniqueness within this rich relationship matrix can be just as challenging as carrying out their array of responsibilities.

Clearly, the task of parenting itself is an enormously difficult one, and a task that is embedded in a variety of other relationships and societal demands. It is a complex undertaking that calls for education and training to carry it out as successfully as possible.

It is also an endeavor that deserves to be informed and shaped by the best available research on the best ways to carry it out. Fortunately, there is a great deal of solid research to help chart a successful journey.

GOOD PARENTING

From the 1960s onward, there has been an explosion of research on child development and parenting, conducted by our nation's top psychologists, anthropologists, and sociologists from our finest universities, colleges, medical centers, and independent research organizations. For example, there now exists a five-volume *Handbook of Parenting*, compiled by Dr. Marc H. Bornstein of the National Institute of Child Health and

Human Development, that presents and discusses the results of hundreds of such studies and that is over 1,800 pages in length.[3] There have also been extensive reviews of such research that have been published in professional journals and in a variety of other handbooks on child development and research on parent–child relations.[4]

In addition, government and university groups that focus on pressing problems such as child maltreatment, substance abuse, juvenile delinquency, and gangs have researched and reviewed numerous studies that explore the parenting causes and contributors to these serious and costly matters. We had a glimpse of this latter work in the previous section on child maltreatment.

What we will look at right now are the results of a series of studies that point to a particular pattern of parenting that has been shown time and time again to be associated with children developing into healthy, confident, and successful adults. We will also review the results of studies that point to parenting patterns that have been found to promote substance abuse and other serious problems among children and youth.

Patterns of Parenting

One of the earliest of these studies explored the parenting contributors to children developing a sense of worth about themselves and their abilities. These were conducted by Dr. Stanley Coopersmith, a psychologist, and were published in his classic book, *The Antecedents of Self-Esteem.*[5] He found that children who valued themselves as individuals, and whose high self-esteem was verified by their teachers, were personally effective, poised, competent, and capable of independent and creative action. They were relatively unaffected by personal difficulties, gravitated to positions of influence and authority, and were more likely to achieve academic and social success. Their low-self-esteem peers were powerless and felt isolated, unlovable, and incapable of expressing themselves. They expected to be failures in social and academic situations and to be rejected by others, and thus were less likely to achieve social and academic success.

Parents of the high-self-esteem children were themselves high in self-worth. They approached their children with a great deal of warmth and acceptance. They also set very clear limits on the child's behavior and were vigilant about enforcing family rules, thereby establishing the authority of parents and providing standards by which the child could judge his or her competence and progress. They demonstrated a great deal of regard for the personal rights of the child, seeking out the child's views, respecting their opinions, and granting concessions where warranted.

Parents of low-esteem children, on the other hand, had few and poorly defined limits and used harsh and autocratic control measures. They were dictatorial, rejecting, and uncompromising.

Based on the fact that there were no consistent differences in self-esteem among children from different social class backgrounds, Coopersmith concluded that it was the quality of home life and parenting, rather than a family's economic resources and place in the community status hierarchy, that was most influential in children developing a strong sense of personal worthiness.

Dimensions of Parental Behavior. Eight years after *The Antecedents of Self-Esteem* appeared, Dr. Barclay Martin published an insightful survey of 250 research studies in the prestigious *Review of Child Development Research.*[6] He observed that the functioning of all parents varied along two major dimensions for parental behavior—a *Feeling Dimension* that encompassed love and affection and a *Control Dimension* that was concerned with influencing children to behave in socially appropriate ways (see Figure 3.1).

FIGURE 3.1. Dimensions of Parental Behavior

THE FEELING DIMENSION	
Warmth/Acceptance	*Rejection/Hostility*
1. Satisfied with child, child's abilities, and characteristics	1. Not satisfied with child, child's abilities, and characteristics
2. Seeks out and enjoys the company of the child	2. Does not seek out and enjoy the company of the child
3. Provides much positive reinforcement	3. Does not provide much positive reinforcement
4. Sensitive to the child's needs and viewpoints	4. Is not sensitive to the child's needs and viewpoints

THE CONTROL DIMENSION	
Permissive (Lax)	Restrictive (Firm)
1. Does not clearly state rules or the consequences for violations	1. Clearly states rules or consequences for violations
2. Does not firmly or consistently enforce rules	2. Firmly and consistently enforces rules
3. Is likely to give in to child's coercive demands	3. Rarely gives in to child's coercive demands

Copyright CICC.

At one end of the *Feeling Dimension*, parental functioning is characterized by parental warmth and acceptance, which was defined as responding sensitively to children's needs and viewpoints, being satisfied with children's characteristics and abilities, providing much positive reinforcement, and seeking out and enjoying children's company. On the other end of this dimension, parental actions reflect psychological rejection and hostility, which was defined by the opposite characteristics and attitudes.

The second important dimension along which the behavior of parents were shown to differ, the *Control Dimension*, consisted on one end of parental restrictiveness that was defined by clearly stated family rules along with consequences for violations. These rules were firmly and consistently enforced and parents rarely gave in to coercive demands made by the child. The other end of this dimension was characterized by permissive or lax parental control, which was just the reverse of the restrictive approach.

Martin noted that whether parents were warm and accepting, hostile and rejecting, and restrictive or permissive contributed significantly to whether children behaved in a dependent manner, whether they internalized standards of cooperation to guide their behavior, whether they acted independently, whether they achieved academically, and/or whether they engaged in problematic aggressive behavior or became withdrawn and neurotic. *The pattern of parental functioning most often associated with positive child behavior was one where there was a great deal of demonstrated parental warmth and acceptance coupled with moderate to firm restrictiveness.*[7]

Love-Oriented Discipline. Martin also identified a *love-oriented approach* to discipline that seemed to be part of this parenting pattern. In this approach, the parent clearly describes what is expected, explains why a family rule should be obeyed, and points out the long-term consequences, including negative consequences to others. This warm, restrictive pattern with its love-oriented approach to discipline is very similar to that which Coopersmith found in the homes of the high-self-esteem children.[8]

Parental Modeling. Martin was also very impressed with the consistent findings from studies about the impact of parents as models. *Observed parental behavior, whether directed toward children, spouses, or other adults, was shown to be very influential in how children behaved and* *developed.* Strong and nurturing parental models were most often imitated and followed, but so were aggressive and threatening parental models. Thus, Martin's review of numerous studies showed that the overall behavioral and psychological models provided by parents, and their overall pattern of childrearing practices and attitudes, were highly important in the development of a wide range of child characteristics and achievements.[9]

Responsiveness, Involvement, and Maturity Demands. A few years after Martin's review was published, Doctors Eleanor F. Maccoby and John A. Martin of Stanford University reviewed an additional 300 studies of parent–child relationships for their chapter in the *Handbook of Child Psychology*.[10] They uncovered additional parenting dimensions and patterns that were valuable in understanding how parents influence or shape the behavior and futures of their children. These included the previously described *Feeling* and *Control* dimensions and added new phenomena from the additional studies. Specifically, those studies highlighted how important it was for parents to be sensitive and responsive to cues from infants, while also continuing to be responsive and sensitive to the behavior of older children and teenagers. The additional studies were also uncovering the power of positive parental involvement versus the destructiveness of noninvolvement. Here, parents who were regularly engaged in their children's lives, and who made their children a priority in their own lives, were shown to have children who did better overall. Finally, more studies were reflecting the value of parents' making age-appropriate demands on their children for mature behavior, demands that were consistent with a child's current capabilities. For example, expecting 10-year-olds not to have temper tantrums where they fall on the floor and kick and scream is an age-appropriate demand or expectation. Expecting a toddler to express frustration without having a temper tantrum is not an age-geared demand, as a child that young has very few other means of expressing intense feelings. The parents whose maturity expectations were consistent with children's developing capabilities were more likely to have healthy children.

The Productive Parenting Pattern. Taken together, the results of these studies, which included the studies of noted researcher and parenting authority Dr. Diana Baumrind of the University of California, contribute to what deserves to be termed *the Productive Parenting*

Pattern (see Figure 3.2). It deserves such a title because research has consistently shown that parents whose overall approach to their children consists of providing a great deal of warmth and acceptance, being firm and restrictive in controlling their children's behaviors and making age-appropriate demands for maturity, and being very responsive and making children a priority in their lives, have children who get along very well in their homes, schools, and communities.

Study after study has demonstrated that this particular pattern of parenting is associated with and contributes to children becoming:

- Independent
- Highly competent in social and academic pursuits
- Socially responsible

FIGURE 3.2. The Productive Parenting Pattern

High Parental Acceptance and Warmth

- Seeks out and enjoys the company of the child
- Is satisfied with child, and the child's characteristics and abilities
- Is sensitive to child's needs and viewpoints
- Provides much positive reinforcement

Moderate to High Restrictiveness

- Engages in firm enforcement of rules and standards
- Uses commands and sanctions when necessary
- Firmly and consistently enforces rules
- Does not give in to child's coercive demands

Insistence on Mature Behavior

- Expects age-appropriate behavior
- Provides standards for age-appropriate behavior

High Responsiveness

- Is responsive to children's signals, states, and needs
- Is responsive to children's behavior
- Provides frequent and regular feedback

High Positive Involvement

- Engages children in frequent interactions
- Makes child a central part of personal and family life

- Able to control aggression
- Self-confident
- Popular with peers and others
- High in self-esteem[11]

In addition, studies that have followed these children into adulthood show that they are more likely to have successful careers and healthy marriages.

Clearly, these research findings, which come from numerous studies with parents and children from a variety of backgrounds and walks of life, show that there is an excellent overall approach to raising children and that some parents are already raising their children in these ways. In addition, because patterns of parenting are made up of learned attitudes, skills, and behaviors, the Productive Parenting Pattern can be learned and used by any parent who is willing and committed to putting in the time and effort.

All of the guidelines in this book, and all of the parenting programs that are mentioned, teach skills and ideas that are in harmony with and reinforce this Productive Parenting Pattern.

PARENTAL INFLUENCE PROCESSES

The studies just reviewed speak to how parents influence their children's behaviors, characteristics, and capabilities. As has been mentioned, there are certain processes of influence, such as parental modeling.

Here we will look more closely at the various kinds of modeling influences, as well as at other, more direct forms of influence, such as the use of consequences. Knowing how these processes of influence work allows for a more educated appreciation of how to be the best parent possible.

The Influences of Modeling

The research and theory of Dr. Albert Bandura of Stanford University is most instructive.[12] His conception of psychological modeling or observational learning is powerful and multidimensional. Drawing on his own research with children, like Martin in the previous study, Dr. Bandura has come to conclude that most human behavior is learned by observation through modeling. By observing others, one forms rules of behavior, and on future occasions this coded information serves as a guide for action. Because people can learn approximately what to do through modeling before they perform any behavior, they are spared the costs of faulty effort. The capacity to learn by observation enables people to expand their knowledge and skills on the basis of information exhibited and authored by others. Much social learning is fostered by observing the actual performances of others and the consequences for them.[13]

Bandura has noted that for observational learning to occur, the individual must attend to the behavior of a model, be able to retain the information that is observed, and be able both to reproduce the observed behavior and be motivated to do so. Thus, modeling involves attentional, retentional, reproductive, and motivational dimensions.

In his classic modeling studies with children, Bandura and his co-workers demonstrated that children whose attention was riveted on adult models who engaged in very aggressive behavior, which the children themselves were quite capable of doing (hitting a large doll with a mallet, for example), clearly learned or retained the aggressive behavior simply by observing it. How much of the aggressive behavior they actually engaged in themselves at a later time depended on what subsequently happened to the model and on what was in it for the children if they engaged in the behavior.

By showing that different factors were involved in acquiring and engaging in modeled behavior, Bandura was able to demonstrate the difference between *learning* and *performing* modeled behavior. This important distinction should serve to alert parents to the likelihood that their children will repeat the behaviors they model if the parents themselves seem to get something out of it (such as enjoyment, relief, or satisfaction) and that the behavior may be repeated far in the future. This type of knowledge can help parents realize the power of the examples they set, as well as the power of other models in their children's environment (siblings, peers, teachers, etc.) to influence children's behavior and functioning.

Bandura further discovered that there are five types of effects that models can have on children. These effects showed that what can be learned from models not only includes new patterns of behavior, but also standards against which children can judge themselves and their abilities, their competencies in problem solving and conceptualization, and their internal rules for creating behaviors. The five effects of models are:

1. *Models Teach New Behavior.* This is the modeling effect where children learn entirely new patterns of behaviors that were not previously part of their repertoire, such as learning how to dress themselves or how to ask questions in a polite manner, how to say unusual words like *Supercalifragilisticexpialidocious,* or how to hit a baseball.

2. *Models Strengthen or Weaken the Use of Prohibited Behaviors.* Here the actions of models serve to weaken or strengthen those behaviors that children already possess and which they have learned are prohibited. For example, when a model's use of swearing does not result in any adverse effects to the model, the child's inhibition to swear is weakened. Another instance would be when a model is punished for some action, like speaking when they were supposed to be quiet. This increases the child's own reluctance to engage in the same or similar actions. Another example would be a child observing an older sibling taking some money from the purse of their mother and thereby being less inhibited to do so himself.

3. *Models Encourage the Use of Already Learned Behaviors.* Here the actions of the model serve as social prompts for previously learned behaviors that have not been inhibited but haven't been used because of insufficient inducements. This prompting effect of models can facilitate children in behaving altruistically, volunteering their services, delaying or seeking gratification, showing affection, selecting certain foods and apparel, conversing on particular topics, being inquisitive or passive, thinking creatively or conventionally, or engaging in other acceptable forms of action.

4. *Models Change How Objects and Situations Are Used and Appreciated.* In this type of influence, the behavior of models serves to direct the child's attention to particular objects or settings that the model favors. Examples would include instances such as where the aggressive model in the previously mentioned study drew the child's attention to using a mallet to strike dolls, or when children observe parents eating in bed and begin eating in their own beds.

5. *Models Arouse Similar Feelings.* This type of modeling effect takes place where the modeling of some action involves a display or expression of emotion and the child reacts in similar emotional ways. An example would be seeing a parent cry when being spoken to harshly by someone else, such as another parent, and the child feeling sad and humiliated herself.

Another example would be a child observing another child
feeling elated over receiving a gift, and feeling uplifted also.

In terms of what determines whether or not a child follows the example of a model, Bandura found that one of the most important de-
terminants was what happens to the model as a result of engaging in
the behavior. If the consequence to the model is positive, the example
of the behavior is more likely to be followed. If the consequence to
the model is negative, then the example of behavior is less likely to
be emulated. Similarly, regardless of whether the consequence to the
child for engaging in the behavior learned from the model is positive
or negative, the consequence would influence whether the behavior is
actually followed.[14]

Another major determinant is the importance and status of the
model in the eyes of the child. The more important the model is to the
child, the more likely the child is to copy and be influenced by the actions of the model.[15] This, of course, helps to explain why parents are
such powerful models.

The Influences of Consequences

Whether or not children have learned how to behave through modeling, their learning is greatly influenced by the consequences of their
own actions. And, as we have just reviewed, if those consequences
are positive, or understood by the child as being positive, the child is
much more likely to continue to engage in those behaviors.

This happens in two ways. A positive consequence follows some
behavior, or the behavior averts an anticipated negative consequence.
For example, when a child helps to clean up his room, two scenarios
can occur: In the first, he or she is praised or otherwise acknowledged
and rewarded. In the second, the child avoids the negative consequence of disappointing a parent he loves and respects by being tidy.
In either instance, the child is more likely to continue cleaning up in
the future.

Children also learn through receiving consequences they consider
to be negative, and from having positive consequences withdrawn.
They learn, for example, not to touch a hot stove because it will burn
them or not to speak to a parent when the parent is drunk or in a lousy
mood because they will get sarcasm or nastiness in return. They may
also learn not to help around the house because they have parents who

are never satisfied with what they do and therefore always say they should be doing more.

Knowing how modeling has its many effects and how consequences do their work provides parents with an educated framework for appreciating the impact they have on their children. And, as we have seen over and over again, that impact can be very positive. It also can be quite destructive. Let's spend a little time reviewing what the research has to say about these dark sides of parenting.

BAD PARENTING

There is research that looks at how parents contribute to their children becoming delinquents and drug abusers, as well as research that shows that certain parental practices carry with them a variety of risks for orienting children to becoming violent and to decreasing their chances of reaching their full potential.

Parenting, Substance Abuse, and Delinquency

The research that has been done to find what causes or contributes to children becoming abusers of alcohol and other drugs indicates that there are several family or parent and child facets operating, including a very different pattern of parenting. As is probably obvious, a parent's dependency on alcohol and other drugs, and a family history of such dependency, have been found to be major contributors to children abusing substances. So have parental psychological and social dysfunction and high levels of family conflict. In addition, having infants and children with special needs is a contributor, as is a family holding antisocial attitudes and being socially isolated.[16]

In addition, non-nurturing and ineffective parenting has been found to contribute to children using alcohol and other drugs at earlier ages and to escalating the use to more potent and destructive substances. Here the research has shown that parents who are not very warm and accepting and who would fall on the hostile/rejecting end of the previously mentioned Feeling Dimension of parenting, are the most likely to have substance-abusing children. This is even more likely if they are poor, inconsistent, and/or coercive rule-enforcers.

It is probably also not surprising that this pattern of parenting has been found in the backgrounds of many children who also become delinquents and gang members. So, just as we have seen that there are patterns of parenting that predispose children to healthy existences, there are other patterns that point children in unhealthy and harmful directions. It is critical that all parents keep in mind that they have it within their power to either increase or decrease the chances of their children leading happy, healthy, and successful lives.

Spanking, Other Forms of Corporal Punishment, and Verbal Aggression

In reviewing the research on parenting thus far, we have found that overall patterns of parenting seem to be the most crucial in influencing how children behave and turn out. There has also been research on specific parenting practices that points to their being influential in and of themselves, regardless of whether they are part of an overall pattern of parenting attitudes and practices. These include various types of corporal punishment and verbally aggressive practices. The research shows that such practices can and do have serious consequences.[17]

Corporal punishment practices are intended to cause physical pain or discomfort. They range from pinching, slapping, punching, and kicking children, to spanking, hitting, and beating children with or without objects such as swithches, brushes, belts, and cords. Each of these practices can be mild or severe, depending on their force or duration. When they leave bruises and other notable physical injuries, they are considered in the United States to be illegal and instances of child physical abuse. Verbally aggressive practices directed at children include such practices as putting children down, insulting them, swearing at them, and saying and doing things to spite them. Here again, when they are severe and continuous, they are considered a form of legally reportable child maltreatment, emotional abuse.

Verbal Aggression. An analysis of data from a nationally representative sample of 3,346 American parents with a child under age 18 living at home found that 63% of the parents reported one or more instances of verbal aggression directed at their children.[18] This research further showed that the more frequent the use of verbal aggression, the higher the chances of the children

- Becoming physically aggressive with others,
- Experiencing a variety of interpersonal problems, and
- Becoming juvenile delinquents.[19]

This study also indicated that children who were exposed to both verbal aggression and severe corporal punishment exhibited the highest rates of aggression, delinquency, and interpersonal problems.

Corporal Punishment. In terms of corporal punishment itself, a major national survey focused on the use of milder forms of corporal punishment ("ordinary corporal punishment"), including 1. spanking on the bottom with a bare hand; 2. slapping on the hand, arm, or leg; 3. pinching; 4. shaking (on children age 3 or older); 5. hitting on the bottom with a belt, brush, stick, or other hard object; and 6. slapping on the face, head, or ears. The survey was conducted in 1995 and the results were reported in a 1999 article in the professional journal *Clinical Child and Family Psychology Review.*[20] The results showed that *the greater the use of corporal punishment by parents, the higher the chances were of their children*

- Becoming depressed,
- Having suicidal thoughts,
- Striking siblings and peers,
- Performing poorly in school,
- Becoming delinquents and committing crimes,
- Having career problems, and
- Abusing their own children and spouses, when they become adults.

In 2002, a study of 62 years of research on the effects of corporal punishment was published. It found even more extensive evidence of many of these unsettling outcomes. This study, by Dr. Elizabeth Thompson Gershoff of Columbia University, appeared in the professional journal *Psychology Bulletin* and was entitled "Corporal Punishment by Parents and Associated Child Behaviors and Experiences: A Meta-Analytic and Theoretical Review."[21]

Dr. Gershoff's study-of-studies found that parental use of corporal punishment was related to child behaviors and experiences such as:

- Greater aggression
- Poorer internalization of moral values
- Higher rates of delinquency and antisocial behavior
- Poorer quality of parent–child relationships
- Poorer child mental health
- Being a victim of child abuse
- Abusing own child and spouse[22]

Her study also found that the use of corporal punishment was associated with the short-term effect of a child more quickly complying with parental directions. It is likely that it is just this immediate effect that seduces so many parents into continuing to use corporal punishment, at least until their children become big enough to fight back.

It is important for all of us to realize that every act of corporal punishment, including spanking, constitutes violence directed toward children, because violence is an act carried out with the intention, or perceived intention, of causing physical pain or injury to another person. This has been true for centuries, and for centuries it has been ignored up to the point that corporal punishment produces physical signs and injuries.

This failure to recognize that all forms of corporal punishment and all instances of its use are acts of violence has been supported throughout history by various self-serving reasons, including religious and adult supremacy reasons. It has also been supported by the fact that the use of corporal punishment does often immediately stop children from engaging in behaviors that can be extremely upsetting to parents and other adults. But times have changed and knowledge has advanced.

We now know that many instances of physical child abuse, including some that result in child deaths, begin through the application of mild forms of corporal punishment but escalate into the more extreme forms when children do not immediately comply. And all of the research just reviewed shows that the more frequent and harsh uses of corporal punishment have destructive, long-term consequences for children and for our entire society.[23]

Indeed, we have moved away from allowing the use of corporal punishment in husband-and-wife adult relationships, where until recently it was acceptable that men could exercize their superior physical strength with wives who failed to do what they dictated. We now call this "assault" or "spousal abuse" and there are laws protecting adults from such violence. Shouldn't we extend to the youngest, smallest, and most vulnerable members of our society, our children, the same protection that is now reserved for adults?

Yes, we have child abuse laws, but they allow for the use of physical punishment up to the point where it does not exceed "ordinary, normal corporal punishment."[24] We don't allow that sort of exception when violence is directed toward adults. So we have a double standard that disrespects the dignity of our children and allows them to be legal recipients of treatment that is forbidden between adults.

We have enough violence all around us. Let's stop teaching it to our children in the privacy of our homes and within the most important relationship they will ever have. Let's also join with the honor roll of nations that have already abolished all uses of corporal punishment with children:

Austria (1998)	Germany (2000)	Latvia (1998)
Bulgaria (2000)	Greece (2006)	Norway (1987)
Croatia (1999)	Hungary (2005)	Portugal (2004)
Cyprus (1994)	Iceland (2003)	Romania (2004)
Denmark (1997)	Israel (2000)	Sweden (1979)
Finland (1983)	Italy (1996)	Ukraine (2004)[25]

Now it is time to turn to the guidelines where the research findings about what is productive in raising children are transformed in such ways as to provide you with approaches, skills, and ideas to assist you in doing the best for your children and for yourself as you carry out the job of parenting.

CHAPTER FOUR

Parenting Guidelines

Here are 16 guidelines to help you in raising healthy, happy, and successful children. These guidelines can also serve as standards against which you can evaluate your own parenting. You can use them to determine whether you are currently doing the best for your children and what else you might do.

1. Give Children Warmth, Acceptance, and Respect
2. Enjoy Your Children's Development and Be Alert to Special Needs
3. Use Firm and Fair Leadership
4. Avoid Corporal Punishment and Verbal Aggression
5. Start Early in Preparing Children for School
6. Create a Home Environment That Supports Education
7. Be an Active Partner with Your Child's School
8. Manage Your Child's Obesity and Eating-Related Problems
9. Teach Children About Their Own and Other Cultures
10. Teach Children About Substance Abuse
11. Teach Children About Sexuality
12. Teach Children to Be Financially Successful and Giving
13. Manage Your Children's Media and Technology Exposure
14. Maintain a Healthy Lifestyle
15. Nurture the Relationship in Which You Are Raising Your Children
16. Set a Good Example of Life-Long Learning

Many of the guidelines are based on what decades of research indicates is effective in raising children. Others are guidelines that address contemporary parenting realities and challenges for which there has yet to be substantial research on how best to deal with them. However, many knowledgeable organizations and professionals have provided useful approaches and I have relied upon their wisdom.

Each guideline is accompanied by concrete examples of what type of parenting is involved. Some are also accompanied by detailed descriptions of parenting skills and approaches for how best to relate to a guideline, and instruction in how to use the skills and approaches. These skills and approaches are those that are taught in modern parenting skill-building programs.

The programs from which these skills are derived are discussed in Chapter 6. Each of these programs has parent handbooks that describe the values, history, and positive parenting philosophy of the program, and homework assignments to complete as the skills are being learned. These valuable parenting handbooks, as well as nearly all of the other educational videos, CDs, and DVDs mentioned in the various guidelines, are available on the Parenting Books, Videos, and Instructor Kits section of the website of the Center for the Improvement of Child Caring (CICC), www.ciccparenting.org. For those resources that are not available through CICC, other means of obtaining them are mentioned.

Several of these guidelines also include references to where you can find additional relevant information and education.

1. Give Children Warmth, Acceptance, and Respect

Children need to know that they are loved and wanted. They need to feel accepted and to know that you think their abilities, looks, and feelings are positive and important. They need to be respected. That's how they learn to respect others, including their parents. You, the parent, need to express feelings of respect, appreciation, warmth, joy, and love on a regular basis—everyday, if you can.

- Kiss, hug, and touch your children.
- Use terms of endearment regularly.
     "I love you!"
     "You're fun to be around!"
     "I love being with you!"
     "Sweetheart, you look beautiful."
- Praise good behavior.
     "I am really happy you put your clothes in the hamper!"
- Encourage your children.
     "You can do it!"
- Send positive "I" messages.
     "When you tell me where you are, I feel relieved and I don't
       worry."
- Take time to really listen.
- Take time for casual talks about things that concern your child.
- Give children choices so they feel that they have some power in
  their lives.
- Let others know how much you love and appreciate your child—
  and make sure your child finds out what you said!

RELATED PARENTING SKILLS AND APPROACHES

The Art of Effective Praising

This is a systematic method for ensuring that your praise not only conveys warmth and appreciation, but also instructs your children about what you consider to be acceptable or appropriate behavior. When you teach your children what you consider to be acceptable behavior, you are also teaching them your family values.

Values need to be practiced if they are to become real for children. If you value cooperation and you behave in cooperative ways by helping others or helping around the house, your children will see that your value of cooperation is real.

When you praise your children, you are further helping to teach your children family values. The specific behaviors that you praise are behaviors that reflect your values. Praising children when they play or work together cooperatively, when they pick up after themselves, or when they speak in a respectful tone of voice demonstrates that you value cooperation, responsibility, and respect for others.

The use of the Effective Praising method requires that you catch your kids in the act of being good. Then you are ready to use the seven steps of Effective Praising:

1. Look at Your Child
2. Move Close to Your Child
3. Smile!
4. Say Lots of Nice Things to Your Child
5. Praise the Behavior, Not the Child
6. Be Physically Affectionate
7. Move Into Action Immediately

The first three steps have to do with the body language used while delivering Effective Praising:

1. *Look at Your Child.* Before you can praise a child effectively, you have to look at the child. This lets the child know that you are talking to him or her in particular.
2. *Move Close to Your Child.* This increases the power of praise because it is so much more personal and intimate.
3. *Smile!* Sometimes a smile alone is rewarding enough to make another person feel good. Imagine how powerful a smile can be when it's coupled with lots of praise.

Now, what do we say?

4. *Say Lots of Nice Things to Your Child.* The idea here is to make a big deal out of what your child is doing—to shower the child with attention and to say a lot of nice things, such as:
    "Thank you!"
    "That's nice!"
    "Good job!"
    "Good thinking!"

"I really like it when you speak to me in that tone of voice!"
"That really pleases me!"
5. *Praise the Behavior, Not the Child.* This is a really important step:
   Be sure to praise behavior and not the child. In other words,
   praise your child for what he *does*, not what he *is*. There's a
   world of difference, for example, between saying, "It was nice
   of you to help me do the dishes, Paul," and saying, "You are
   such a good boy, Paul." The first conveys the message that
   Paul earned praise for his cooperative behavior, washing
   the dishes. The second statement is merely an opinion or
   judgment about Paul as a person, and does not give any
   information about what he did to merit that high opinion.

The last two steps have to do with showing affection and with the best
time to deliver effective praising.

6. *Be Physically Affectionate.* A hug, a kiss, or a hand on the
   shoulder will go a long way toward making your praise
   something really warm and special to your child. Don't be
   afraid to show your affection. Get physical with your children
   when you praise them.
7. *Move Into Action Immediately.* It's important to praise your
   child right when you recognize desirable behavior. If you
   have "caught" your child helping to clean the table, praise
   him right away. Don't save it for later in the day or even five
   minutes later.

So, now you have it: all seven steps and guidance on how to carry
them out. Thousands of other parents who have learned this seven-step
Effective Praise method have reported excellent results. Their kids really like being treated this way and appreciate being acknowledged for
doing the right things. Some children even start praising their parents!

This is one of the methods taught in the *Confident Parenting* program[1]
and in the versions of that skill-building program for African and Latino American parents, the *Effective Black Parenting*[2] and *Los Niños Bien
Educados*[3] programs. When used within the latter two programs, or
with any family or culture that has developed its own unique ways
of expressing appreciation, those expressions can be used in terms of
what to say when you praise.

For example, in many homes with African American children, appreciation is expressed through the use of expressions such as, "On

the one!" or "Hey, that's too tough!" or "Go, girl/go, boy!" or "Get on down!" Using culturally or family-specific expressions adds new dimensions to your praise, reflecting that everyone is appreciative of how the child is acting.

The Encouragement Approach

This approach to conveying warmth is taught in parenting skill-building programs like *Active Parenting*[4] and *Systematic Training for Effective Parenting (STEP)*.[5] It not only conveys warmth and acceptance, but it also helps children learn from their mistakes, without dwelling on them. It helps children learn to believe in themselves and their abilities. For example, a child has missed five out of 25 words on a spelling test. Instead of dwelling on the five errors, a parent who uses and believes in encouragement would point out the 20 words that were spelled correctly. By focusing on the positive, the parent gives the child the feeling that she is okay. The child is well aware of the five errors; there is no need to point them out. Accepting the child helps her feel worthwhile as a person.

Learning the Encouragement Approach is particularly important if you have been in the habit of discouraging children. You discourage children when you have unreasonably high standards, such as when you expect them to do well in all endeavors or have every hair on their head in place or expect their rooms or personal spaces to be "as neat as a pin." You also discourage children when you promote competitions between brothers and sisters, or have double standards where you expect cleanliness from some children in the family but not others.

Using encouragement means emphasizing the positive. It means using phrases that show acceptance of a child and phrases that recognize effort and improvement, such as:

"I like the way you handled that."
"I like the way you tackle a problem."
"I'm glad you enjoy learning."
"I'm glad you are pleased with it."
"It looks as if you enjoyed that."

The Encouragement Approach also involves using communications and phrases that show confidence:

"Knowing you, I'm sure you'll do fine."
"You'll make it!"
"I have confidence in your judgment."
"That's a rough one, but I'm sure you'll work it out."
"You'll figure it out."

Encouragement also entails focusing on the contributions that children make and showing appreciation through statements such as:

"Thanks, that helped a lot."
"It was thoughtful of you to . . ."
"Thanks, I really appreciate _____ because it makes my job easier."
"I need your help on . . ."
To a family group: "I really enjoyed today. Thanks."
"You have skill in _____. Would you do that for the family?"

A very important part of using the Encouragement Approach is recognizing children's efforts and improvements through communication such as:

"It looks as if you really worked hard on that."
"It looks as if you spent a lot of time thinking it through."
"I see that you're moving along."
"Look at the progress you've made." (Be specific, tell how.)
"You're improving in . . ." (Be specific.)
"You may not feel that you've reached your goal, but look how far you've come!"

Note of Caution. These and the other encouraging communications you have been learning can be discouraging to children when they are used with an "I told you so" or arrogant attitude. Avoid giving with one hand and taking away with the other. In other words, avoid qualifying or moralizing comments.
For example, avoid communications such as:

"It looks like you really worked hard on that—so why not do that all the time?"
"It's about time!"
"See what you can do when you try?"

Remember, the main reasons for using the Encouragement Approach is to show faith in your children so that they can come to believe in themselves, accepting them as they are, pointing out the positive aspects of their behavior, recognizing effort and improvement, and showing appreciation for their contributions.

In learning the art of Effective Praising and the Encouragement Approach, you are learning skills and ideas that you can also put to work in your relationships with other adults. Most human beings appreciate being praised and encouraged, and feel kindly toward those who recognize their positive actions and efforts. You can use these skills with your spouse, other family members, friends, coworkers, and employers. Thus, you can gain other relational benefits because you have put in the time and effort to learn how to use these skills properly and frequently.

2. ENJOY YOUR CHILDREN'S
DEVELOPMENT AND BE ALERT TO SPECIAL NEEDS

The development of children is fascinating, especially in the early years. Day to day, week to week, something new is happening: They can turn in the direction of sounds. They can do baby push-ups. They can grasp something and bring it to their mouths. They can say what they hear—and on and on in a growing gathering of skills and capabilities.

Enjoy these early achievements. They are the building blocks for thinking, reading, writing, and communicating with you and others.

- Learn about the different areas and stages of child development.
- Read child development books and visit parenting websites.
- During the first 5 years of your child's life, make regular use of *The Discovery Tool*, a series of questionnaires that let you know how your child is developing compared with other children of her or his age.[6] A sample of *The Discovery Tool* questionnaires is available in the Appendix.

Some children do not develop in a normal way, and it is important to find this out as early as possible. These are the children who have needs that are greater than the average child—they are children with special needs or disabilities. Their special needs can be in any or all areas of development. They may have problems walking, hearing, seeing, learning, talking, or getting along with others. Their needs in these areas can be mild or extreme.

The earlier in their lives that these children are identified and helped, the better their chances for completing school, finding jobs, and living on their own. So be alert to the possibility that your child may have special needs. Here again, *The Discovery Tool* is useful. It lets you know whether your child may have special needs and where in your community you can turn for help.

ABOUT *THE DISCOVERY TOOL* AND RELATED RESOURCES

Let's spend a little time on *The Discovery Tool*, as its use can be so beneficial both in enjoying the development of little children and in being alert to potential problems.

The entire *Discovery Tool,* with all of its questionnaires, can be accessed over the Internet, 24 hours a day, 7 days a week at www. ciccparenting.org. It consists of several questionnaires that you complete about your child's current behavior and about the birth and medical history of your child. You complete the questionnaire that is designed for children your child's age, ranging from birth through age 4. As previously mentioned, you can find and use a sample of these questionnaires in the Appendix.

The questionnaire that you complete will let you describe your child's current behavior and skills in the following six major areas of child development:

1. *Body Development:* Motor and physical development
2. *Thinking and Learning:* Cognitive development
3. *Communication:* Expressive and receptive language development
4. *The Senses:* Vision, hearing, touch, and sensory integration
5. *Relating to Self and Other People:* Emotional and social development
6. *Self-Care:* The development of daily living skills

Most of the questions in each area will be about the skills that the average child in that age category has developed by that point in time. These are referred to as "developmental milestones." For example, in the area of body movement or motor development, by the age of 9 to 12 months, the average infant can use his or her hands to scoop or pinch to pick up a small object such as a Cheerio or raisin. This neat little achievement, which is a building block to learning how to use a pencil to write, is a milestone in this area of development.

Such "little" achievements are just as worthy of a joyous response as the child's first step or first word. Knowing that such actions are milestones expands your appreciation of your child's growth, and *The Discovery Tool* brings them to your attention.

The Discovery Tool also informs you if your child may be delayed in his or her overall development of skills. In addition, it lets you know if some of your child's current behaviors (or lack of some behaviors) can stand in the child's way of getting along with others or learning more about the world.

When taken online, *The Disocovery Tool* automatically scores your answers, and provides you with result pages that you can print. The result pages list any delayed skills and potential problem behaviors. When you use the sample version in the Appendix, you will have to score the tool yourself, and there are instructions for doing so.

If your child has yet to develop several skills and/or engages in several problematic behaviors, you are alerted to have your child seen by an appropriate health professional such as a psychologist for a developmental assessment or checkup.

In Chapter 5, Parenting Children with Special Needs, you will find more information about the areas of development that are covered in *The Discovery Tool*, as well as more complete information on developmental assessments. You will also be provided with guidance on what can and should be done if it is determined that a child has special needs.

In terms of learning about the developmental milestones of children over the age of 5, there are many relevant books, including those published by the American Academy of Pediatrics, such as *Caring for Your School-Age Child: 5 to 12* and *Caring for Your Adolescent: Ages 12 to 21*.

3. USE FAIR AND FIRM LEADERSHIP

Children do not naturally know right from wrong. You, the parent, must teach them proper behavior and basic decent human values. You must use fair, clear, and firm leadership by example.

THE COIN CONCEPTION OF FAMILY RULES

In providing such leadership, family rules are crucial. It is helpful to think that family rules are like a coin. They have a "do side" that defines acceptable behavior: "You do pick up your toys." And they have a "don't side" that defines unacceptable behavior: "You don't leave toys out for others to pick up." Spending most of your time praising "do-side" behavior helps children learn the right things to do (see Figure 4.1).

FIGURE 4.1. Family Rules: Like a Coin Concept

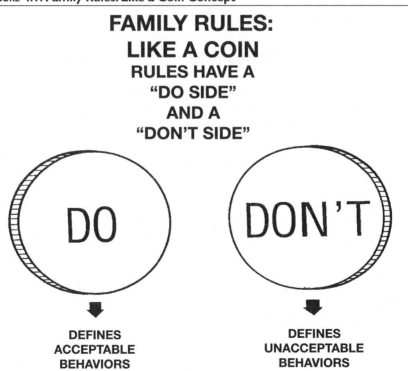

FAMILY RULES:
LIKE A COIN
RULES HAVE A
"DO SIDE"
AND A
"DON'T SIDE"

DO   DON'T

DEFINES
ACCEPTABLE
BEHAVIORS

DEFINES
UNACCEPTABLE
BEHAVIORS

- Remind children of the rules: "Remember, we put feet on the floor, not on the table."
- Hold family meetings to discuss rules so that everyone can be involved in solving problems and conflicts and making decisions together.
- Provide concrete incentives or rewards for following family rules.
- Give clear instructions in a firm voice.
- Redirect attention: "How about playing this game rather than touching these dangerous garden tools?"
- Try a "time-out" when everyone is stressed.
- Give strong "I" messages: "I get discouraged when I see my clean kitchen dirty again, and I don't want to spend all of my time cleaning it."
- Use the "First/Then" method: "First do your homework and then you can e-mail your friends."
- Whenever possible, try to find solutions that are agreeable to both you and your children.
- Withdraw privileges for major rule violations.
- Try contracting. You can make a deal to change your own behavior in exchange for your children changing theirs.

MORE ABOUT FAMILY RULES AND SPECIFIC SKILLS

These examples of fair and firm leadership and the Coin Conception of Family Rules are most effectively applied after you have gained a fuller, more detailed appreciation of what is involved. This is also true for the examples of warmth and acceptance in the first guideline. In that guideline, effective praise and encouragement were exemplified, and, afterward, the specifics of their use were shared, providing you with a broader understanding and the steps to follow in using those skills. Recall that those are skills that are taught as part of modern parenting skill-building programs. All of these firm and fair leadership examples, and the Coin Conception, are also taught in several modern parenting programs.

Here you will learn more about the importance of family rules, the Coin Conception, and the specifics of two of the skills that were mentioned above.

The Importance of Family Rules

There are many reasons for having family rules and being clear about them. First, family rules help children learn which of their behaviors are considered to be appropriate. Indeed, having family rules is probably the main way that parents teach children what is appropriate behavior. When parents are clear about family rules, children are clear about which of their behaviors are respectful in the eyes of their parents.

Another important reason for having family rules is that they help children know what is expected of them. When children know what is expected, they feel more secure. Thus, family rules can provide children with a sense of security.

A third good reason is that rules can be used to prevent problems. When children understand and are motivated to follow the rules, and when you see that your child is about to break a rule, a simple reminder of the rule can prevent conflicts and tensions. For example, reminding a child about the rule regarding standing on the couch ("Remember the rule about the couch? We sit on the couch; we do not stand or jump on it") can avoid an angry battle or prevent the need to use a stronger consequence.

Of course, your children must be motivated to follow the rules if this type of preventive reminder is to work. There are many ways to motivate children, such as praising and encouraging them when they do follow the rules, or making sure that they know the reasons for the rules. Supplying children with reasons for family rules, which I refer to as "Appealing to Their Minds and Not Their Behinds," is an often forgotten approach that is quite worthy of regular use. In this example, the reasons for not jumping on the couch that you might give your children are that jumping can break or wear out the couch and that it will make the couch look old and tattered. Everyone wants to have a house they can be proud of.

Another reason for family rules is that they help organize family life. They help let everyone in the home know what is expected of them and when to behave in certain ways. For example, when everyone knows the rules about morning time and getting ready for school, it is easier to do the things that must be done in the morning.

Another important reason for family rules is that they let children know that they are trustworthy and that they are growing up. For example, in explaining rules about taking care of family property, such as how to operate the family CD player, you are not only teaching your children what are acceptable and appropriate behaviors regarding this important family possession, but you are also showing your children that you trust them to behave appropriately toward the CD player.

Another example is when you explain a chore to your child, such as why and how to take out the trash. Here you are letting your child know that the child is old enough to take on more responsibility for the care of the home. Being able to take on more responsibility is a sign that the child is growing up and maturing.

Another very important reason for having family rules is that they foster a sense of family togetherness, cooperation, and pride. Such feelings help to keep families together.

Until children are capable of learning and appreciating the reasons behind and importance of family rules, they are very likely to break the rules on a regular basis. Indeed, you should expect a good deal of rule-breaking behavior early in every child's development. Remember, children don't come into the world knowing what is right and wrong.

How you respond when children do not follow the rules is critical, and you have already been provided with some excellent examples. Here's a little more detail on two of the methods mentioned above.

The Use of Mild Social Disapproval

This is a method for giving clear instructions in a firm voice. It is a quick and effective way to set limits on your child's behavior, and its use saves a lot of wear and tear on everyone involved. Like the art of Effective Praising, it is composed of seven basic components, each of which contributes to the overall effectiveness of your parenting:

1. Look at Your Child
2. Move Close to Your Child
3. Have a Disapproving Facial Expression
4. Deliver a Brief Verbalization or Command (fewer than three sentences)
5. Keep Your Voice at a Low Intensity
6. Make a Gesture That Is Consistent with Disapproval
7. Move Into Action Immediately

Mild social disapproval, by its very nature, must be used calmly, smoothly, and quickly in order to be maximally effective. It is intended to correct rule-breaking behaviors before they get out of hand.

Immediately upon recognizing that rule-violating behavior (misbehavior) is about to be started, use mild social disapproval to keep things under control. Misbehavior typically builds in intensity, gathering force and energy as it grows. A little mild social disapproval used early on can save everyone a lot of headaches later.

Here's an example: John and Mary, your 3-year-old twins, are playing quietly with their blocks on the living room floor. Pretty soon you notice that John is getting a little irritated with Mary because she won't share the blocks. Shortly thereafter, John starts to holler at Mary and grabs all the blocks he can lay his hands on. Mary doesn't appreciate John's attack, so she clobbers him with one of the blocks. Now the fight is on, and you've got the task of separating two screaming kids. They're all hot and bothered, and by the time you are able to straighten out the situation, chances are you will be, too.

This entire scene could have been avoided, however, simply by setting limits with some well-timed mild social disapproval just as the pot was beginning to boil.

A parent who sensed trouble as soon as the kids began to hassle each other about the blocks and quickly responded with some mild social disapproval could have saved himself, as well as his children, a lot of unnecessary misery. Walking up to Mary, looking her square in the eye, pointing a finger, and saying, "Mary, please share those blocks with John," probably would have been enough to prevent the wild scramble that ensued.

So be quick with mild social disapproval. If you can smell trouble brewing, respond immediately. It may require some practice in terms of learning to recognize trouble situations early, but as a parent, you are probably already rather knowledgeable in this regard.

Bring Back Praise Quickly

Now, once you have used mild social disapproval, you have actually done only half the job that is required to make this method as effective as possible. Mild social disapproval in and of itself only teaches what you don't want your child to do. It only deals with the "don't side" of the coin.

A skill like effective praising is a better tool for teaching a child more respectful behavior. Thus, it is imperative that you follow all instances of mild social disapproval with a heavy dose of praise *as soon as* your child begins to behave appropriately. This may be difficult at first, since most parents simply aren't in the habit of praising their children so soon after they have misbehaved. However, this is the optimal way to instruct your child in more positive behavioral alternatives. So try your best to follow the disapproval sequence with praise as soon as your child begins to behave more appropriately.

There are many other skills to employ when your children engage in rule-breaking behaviors, including skills that are designed to deal with major infractions. Several of them have already been mentioned, such as "time-out" or the withdrawal of privileges or the creation of special incentive systems where your children only receive privileges when they earn points for respectful behavior. It is beyond the scope of this chapter to include the specifics of all of these skills here. In Chapter 6, where the programs in which these skills are taught are more fully described, you will also learn where you might take a class or a seminar to learn them.

To close out this section, however, we will look more closely at one other parenting skill that is particularly helpful with older children and teenagers: contracting.

CONTRACTING

This is a method to use when there are legitimate differences of opinions having to do with matters such as the use of the car or computer, proper curfew time, who does the household chores, or the amount of weekly allowance. The subject matter of these disagreements, however, is not half as important as the manner in which they are handled. Contracting is a fair and efficient approach to family problem solving.

Contracting is unique in that nobody loses. When family members disagree, it's not uncommon for one or the other to "win" at the expense of the other. The problem with this, of course, is that hard feelings often crop up as an undesirable by-product. Contracting is a great way to avoid such hard feelings.

Let's look at an example and see how it is done. This example is from a family with a 16-year-old boy (Donald) who openly admitted that he can't stand his parents. According to him, his mother was a "witch" and his father never "got off his case."

The two parents, however, saw things a little differently. They felt their son was "bossy," "immature," and "just plain nasty." In their opinion, he was going out of his way to be, in their words, "defiant" and "impossible." He was clearly not interested in following the rules his parents wanted him to follow, and he was in no way bashful about letting them know it.[7]

Then the parents learned about and began using the contracting method, which has four major steps:

Step One: The Want List

The Want List is exactly what the name implies. It's a list of the behaviors you want from other members of your family. Notice that I am again using the word *behaviors*. Vague terms or values, such as *respect* or *generosity* are not helpful here. Instead, the Want List must be composed of specific *behaviors*. You just can't observe "respect," for example, because it is a value and an attitude. You can, however, observe and even count those behaviors that contribute to "respect," such as saying "please" and "thank you," not using profanity, listening when another person speaks, and so on. Donald and his parents made up their own Want Lists.

Donald's Want List was:

1. I want to use one of the family cars on Friday and Saturday nights, with no questions asked.
2. I want to be able to color my hair.
3. I want Dad and Mom to quit bugging me.
4. I want to be left alone in my room when I feel like being alone.
5. I want Dad not to holler at me every time I disagree with him.[8]

Donald's list was really quite specific except for item number 3. "Bugging" is a bit too vague, so he had to think more about what he really meant. As it turned out, *bugging* was simply Donald's word for "criticism." Even more specifically, he felt that his parents were overly critical of his schoolwork, his friends, and his taste in clothes and music. With this clarification, he amended item 3 to read: "I want Mom and Dad to stop criticizing my schoolwork, friends, and taste in music and clothes."

Now let's look at his parents' Want List.

1. We want no more back talk from Donald.
2. We want no more profanity from Donald in our presence.
3. We want Donald to help around the house.
4. We want Donald not to play his music so loud anymore.[9]

This, too, was a very precise and straightforward Want List, although their item 3, just as on Donald's list, was somewhat vague.

What could Donald do, in particular, that would qualify as "helping out around the house"? The parents then thought more carefully and agreed that if Donald helped with the dishes, made his bed each day, and mowed the lawn once a week, they would be satisfied, so they amended item 3 to include those specific chores.

As should be apparent in the compiling of these lists, this family's problems with rules and getting along with one another are much more manageable. And now they can move into the second phase of the family contracting method.

Step Two: The Exchange

The exchange process is simply a trading of behaviors, sort of an "If you'll do this for me, I'll do that for you" arrangement. Sometimes it can be a simple one-for-one behavior exchange; other times, it can be a two- or three-for-one. Or, family members may simply agree to abide by one another's Want Lists, making only minor modifications here and there.

That's basically what Donald and his parents decided to do. All of their items seemed reasonable; *everyone* was pleased with the exchange, and that's what is most important. Then they moved quickly on to the next step.

Step Three: Writing Up the Contract

It may seem like a silly waste of time and energy to write up a formal contract among family members, but it is really a good thing to do. First, everyone is protected when the rules are laid down in writing. A clearly written contract removes any opportunity for one or both parties to make lame excuses or dispute the terms of the agreement. It's all there in the contract, spelled out in black and white. Second, there's something about a written contract that makes it seem more binding than a simple spoken agreement. Signing one's name to a written document seems to produce a greater sense of commitment when it comes to abiding by the terms of the agreement.

At any rate, writing up a contract is easy to do, and it increases the likelihood that everyone concerned will play by the rules. So Donald wrote out the four things he was willing to do for his parents, and they wrote out the five they were ready to do for him. Then they dated and signed the family contract.

Now, such contracts are not cast in stone and can and should be modified as you try them out. As a result, there is one more phase.

Step Four: Modifying the Contract

In the case of Donald and his parents, everything went well as they began to follow the contract and they all felt better about their life together—except for one thing: the color of the hair that Donald initially wanted. He wanted green hair. This had to be renegotiated until everyone was in agreement. White, blond, and similar shading was fine with his parents. They rewrote the contract to that effect, and everyone signed on.

What eventually happened with Donald and his parents was that they kept the contract in force for 3 months and they had great success. Then they discontinued it, feeling that living up to the contract had become a habit for each of them, and as such, they no longer felt the need for the formal document.

This type of outcome—that a new and different approach becomes habitual after using it for a period of time—is usually what is reported by most parents who take the time and effort to learn this method. In short, it is usually very much worth the work!

4. AVOID CORPORAL PUNISHMENT AND VERBAL AGGRESSION

You, the parent, have many excellent ways of gaining the cooperation and respect of your children without using corporal punishment or being verbally aggressive with them. Several of these ways have just been mentioned and described. When you combine warmth and acceptance with fair and firm leadership, children usually do better in school and stay out of trouble. They also are more likely to grow into more responsible and successful adults.

The new research that was mentioned in Chapter 3 has also shown that parents who spank and use other forms of corporal punishment, and who are verbally aggressive and insulting with their children, are likely to be contributing to very different outcomes (as opposed to parents who use nonviolent methods) and are likely to be doing a good deal of harm that is not immediately apparent.

Spanking and hitting children not only sets a bad example and can lead to future problems—it is also unfair. We don't permit adults to hit one another—that's called assault. So avoid using all forms of corporal punishment and verbal aggression. Instead, follow the other guidelines and use the skills and approaches that have been suggested.

However, even the best of parents sometimes feel like hitting or insulting their children. When that happens, you can:

- Take time out when things are heated and you are about to lose control.
- Stick firmly to the rules and insist that your children follow them.
- Talk. Discussing the problem and emphasizing family rules will help make things clear.
- Phone a friend.
- Take a deep breath. And another. Remember, you are the adult.
- Pause and count to 10. Better yet, count to 20.
- Before you yell, close your eyes. Pretend you are hearing what your child is about to hear.

In addition, you will be moving in the direction of never having to use corporal punishment and verbal aggression with your children as you take the time to learn and use the skills and approaches that are discussed and presented in this book. I am not just referring to those that have already been mentioned but to the numerous additional positive parenting skills and approaches that are part of every parenting program that is mentioned throughout *The Positive Parent*.

All skills that are considered to be examples of being warm, accepting, and respectful of children, such as the art of Effective Praising and the Encouragement Approach, are skills and approaches that help you avoid ever having to use corporal punishment and verbal aggression because they lead children to engage in more cooperative and positive actions, or "do side" behaviors. The more cooperation you get from children, the less the need to use or feel like using corporal punishment.

All the skills that reflect what I have termed "firm and fair family leadership," such as mild social disapproval and contracting, are parenting methods that help you avoid spanking, hitting, and yelling because their judicious use usually gets the job done and children become more cooperative and enjoyable.

The same is true for most parents who take the time and effort to learn the other positive parenting skills that are part of the other modern skill-building programs that will be mentioned. There are also some parenting videos and DVDs that focus on the issues of avoiding corporal punishment and verbal aggression and demonstrate the skills and approaches from the modern programs. Two excellent examples are *Shaking, Hitting, Spanking: What to Do Instead* and *Yelling, Threatening, Putting Down: What to Do Instead*. These videos are often used as part of parenting skill-building programs such as the Nurturing Programs.[10]

Shaking, Hitting, Spanking shows typical situations where parents find themselves about to strike a child, and *Yelling, Threatening, Putting Down* shows scenes where parents have yelled at or threatened or put a child down. After each scene, you stop the program and think about what you have viewed. You are asked what you might have done instead of what the parents in the program did or were about to do. And then the program is turned back on and you see some excellent and nonviolent ways of handling the situations.

Here is one of the situations you would see in the spanking video and the suggested alternatives. Some suggestions have to do with preventing the situation from happening in the first place, while others show constructive methods for dealing with it once it does happen.

In a situation from the *Spanking* video, Daniel, age 2, is playing on the kitchen floor while his father reads the paper nearby. When Dad leaves the room, Daniel pulls out the cleaners from under the sink. Dad returns, gets angry, and hits Daniel. Here's what is suggested and illustrated to do instead.[11]

1. *Prevention.* The most effective alternative is to create an environment where children can enjoy playing safely without having to worry about getting into things that they shouldn't. Prevention takes a lot of energy and is a proactive view that getting children involved in safe, acceptable play is more desirable than responding to children after they have displeased you.

2. *Adopt a Non-Hitting Attitude.* Much parental behavior is dictated by how parents feel and think. An attitude is developed after years of experiences. Developing a non-hitting attitude often takes time, energy, and skills; an awareness that hitting does not promote healthy behaviors; and the emotional capacity to replace feelings of violence with feelings of caring. A non-hitting attitude is essential for using parenting techniques that are alternatives to corporal punishment.

3. *Baby-Proof the House.* Children, especially young children, love to explore. Touching, pulling, grabbing, and eating are just a few ways young children explore their environment. Since toddlers are too young to know what is safe to play with and what is potentially dangerous, you need to baby-proof your house. Baby-proofing protects children from becoming hurt, or in some instances, even killed.

   Baby-proofing the house can also enhance your positive interactions with your children. A house where dangerous objects are out of reach is a house where you aren't constantly saying "no."

   You only need to baby-proof your house once, right? Wrong! Babies grow along with their ability to reach for objects, climb on furniture, open drawers, and walk up and down stairs. You need to continually modify the house as children continue to grow. The good news is that as a child grows, he's also learning what is safe and what isn't.

4. *Verbal and Physical Redirection.* These techniques are designed especially for young preschool children and encourage them to perform desirable behaviors. Redirection is used to prevent personal injury, promote "do side" desirable behavior, reduce punishing interactions, and promote learning exploration.

   Verbal Redirection. Like mild social disapproval, verbal redirection is a means of managing a child's behavior by verbally expressing a command. It is a way to redirect your child's behavior by talking to her. Verbal redirection helps children by empowering them to perform "do side" behaviors.

Examples include: "Chairs are for sitting. No standing, please." "No standing in the tubby. Sit, please." "Oh, what a nice toy. Put it back on the shelf, please."

Inappropriate examples include: "No standing on the chair. You'll fall and break your neck." "Quit standing in the tub. What do you want, an accident?" "Yes, I see your toy. Now just don't leave it on the floor."

The appropriate use of verbal redirection helps your child know what you expect and do not expect. The inappropriate use of redirection actually doesn't redirect a child's behavior at all. Threats, statements of doom, and telling your child what *not* to do are not the correct ways to use verbal redirection.

Verbal redirection also includes directing your child's attention and behavior to appropriate activities and avoiding unnecessary confrontations. For example, David is about to run out of the bedroom when Mom is trying to finish dressing him. She calls out, "David, close the door for Mom, please." David's attention is redirected from running away and he ends up complying and feeling like a helper.

Physical Redirection. This is similar to verbal redirection with one more step. As you are verbally directing your child, you are physically redirecting him, too (as is done in mild social disapproval). In the correct use of physical redirection, you use a gentle touch to redirect your child to perform a more appropriate behavior. Gently placing a hand on the child's back or taking an object from a child's grasp are ways to use physical redirection. Redirecting a hand from a dangerous object is another way to physically redirect.

Appropriate examples include: Physically redirecting your child away from an electrical socket to a safe toy. Escorting a child from the bedroom to the living room and engaging the child in play. Taking a dangerous object away from your child and substituting it with a safer one.

Inappropriate examples include: Physically jerking a child away from an electrical socket. Spanking a child for entering the bathroom unassisted. Slapping your child's hand for touching a dangerous object.

In the appropriate examples, you are using what are called "nurturing touches" with your child. In the inappropriate examples, a harsh and abusive touch is being used. Your young, preschool child is unable to make the connection between the harsh physical touch you are administering and the danger of the object being touched. Hitting, slapping, spanking, and other forms of corporal punishment are abusive in comparison to nurturing touches. Abusive touch has no positive value in helping your child perform appropriate and "do side" behaviors.

The ideal way to redirect your child's behavior is through a combination of verbal and physical redirection. Used together, your child will quickly learn that a particular behavior is unacceptable to you.

These *What to Do Instead?* videos provide great learning and un-learning experiences, and they are very much worth viewing, by yourself, with your family, and/or with other parents in the neighborhood, at the child-care center, church, or school. They come with a discussion guide to use if you will be sharing and viewing them with others.

It is a good idea to obtain and use videos like these and to take advantage of the parenting skill-building programs that now exist. With all of these educational opportunities available to you for learning better ways to gain cooperation and respect from your children, it is no longer necessary to hit and insult children or to throw up your hands and say, "I don't know what else to do!" There's a lot else that can be done and you owe it to yourself and your children to learn these better techniques.

5. Start Early in Preparing Children for School

There's no better time to begin preparing children for school than when they are born.

- Place bright shapes, colorful mobiles, and interesting pictures in your children's environment.
- Talk to your children. Use different expressions and tones of voice. Explain what you are doing. Encourage them to speak by praising their attempts to speak and by correcting their speech. Also, listen to your children. Don't ignore babbling; it is an early attempt at communication.
- Play good listening music for children to sharpen hearing skills; sing to them and play nursery rhyme games.
- Read to your children and tell them stories.
- Take short trips as a family. Point out different sights and sounds. Show enthusiasm for learning and doing.
- Give children simple tasks or chores to do.
- Buy or borrow educational toys, games, and other things that children can handle.
- Participate in the schooling process. Show a special interest in what happens to your children at day care, nursery school, or elementary school. Ask your children to tell you what they do, who they talk to, and what they like or don't like. It is not too early to talk to schoolteachers or child-care workers about your children's progress and behavior.
- You might also want to share *The Discovery Tool* with your child's child-care teachers and directors, so they too can see how your child is developing in comparison to his or her age mates, and so they too can get to know and enjoy your child better.

There are many books, games, and other resources that you can use to help prepare young children for their formal education experiences. Right now let me alert you to a great book that is designed to provide numerous activities in which you can engage your children to prepare them for the realities and demands of kindergarten.

As you probably know, there are increasing efforts by government educational agencies to make all aspects of education more academically rigorous. Whether or not this emphasis on academics is appropriate for all very young children is subject to serious debate, given that that many young children are just not developmentally ready. But such an emphasis is taking place.

Using *The Kindergarten Survival Handbook: The Before School Checklist and Guide for Parents* by Dr. Allana Elovson is a really good idea. It indicates the wide range of basic knowledge and skills that your child should ideally possess upon entering kindergarten.

- *The Things They Need to Know to Be Ready for School,* such as their name, age, sex, phone number, and address; the names and relations of family members; the parts of their own body and where their body parts are located; the names of their clothes, some things around the house like the sink and the couch, the names of common animals and common foods; some words about how things feel and when things happen; what money buys and coins and other pieces of currency; some words for where things are and how things look, move, or do not move; places around them, such as stores, and what happens at them; which of two things is bigger or smaller; which is the largest of three different things; and words for how things compare, such as *same, different, more,* or *less.*
- *What They Need to Do and Know to Understand and Be Understood,* such as being able to speak clearly enough so that people other than their own family and friends can understand them easily; being able to understand the speech of children and adults other than their family members; understanding simple questions and giving simple answers; following simple directions such as where to sit, where to put a book, or where to throw a ball; being able to follow instructions that have two or more parts, such as, "Close the door, hang up your coat, and sit down, please;" and being able to tell someone how they are feeling, ask for what they need, and tell the events in a simple story in the right order.
- *The Self-Help and Social Skills That They Will Need,* such as being able to understand that in school, children are expected to do what their teachers ask; being comfortable away from their parent or caregiver, and with new adults and children; knowing how to wait; understanding that other people have rights and feelings, just as they do; managing, at least some of the time, to share the use of toys; sitting quietly for a while and playing with other children without having a lot of fights; knowing a few ways to try to settle fights; taking off and putting on their outer clothes themselves; taking themselves to the bathroom without help; washing and drying their hands and face without help; feeding themselves neatly using a spoon or fork; continuing to work on something, even when it starts to get hard, and finishing something before starting something else.
- *The Large Movement Skills That Will Be Needed,* such as walking with

ease; running without falling frequently; jumping, using both feet at the same time; hoping on one foot a few times without falling; balancing on one foot for a few seconds; walking up stairs one foot after the other and walking down stairs one foot after the other, and holding the banister if they are going fast or if the stairs are steep; walking backward for six or seven steps, placing toe to heel in a straight line, without turning to look behind; throwing and catching a large ball using both hands; and carrying something on top of something else, such as an apple on a plate.

- *The Small Motor Skills That Are Needed,* such as stirring something in a bowl without spilling it; picking up a palm-sized ball and rolling it across the floor or table; stacking five blocks on top of each other; knowing how to use a spoon and fork, and maybe a knife, to eat correctly; holding a pencil or crayon with the thumb and fingers; being able to open a screw-top jar and open a door by turning the knob; turning faucets on and off; lacing a shoelace through three large beads; cutting with scissors; fastening buttons on the front of their clothes; taking a pinch of salt or sugar, or anything that is finely ground; and picking up a small bean or pebble with the thumb and forefinger.

- *The Ability to Use All of Their Senses,* such as seeing (seeing differences in sizes between similar objects, and saying which is smaller and which is larger); hearing (pointing to where sounds are coming from); tasting and smelling (identifying some familiar foods by taste alone); touching (identifying objects such as pencils and spoons only by touch); and body sense, such as imitating the body posture and gestures of another person.

- *Being Able to Learn About Pictures, Words, and Letters,* through identifying drawings or photos of common objects in books, newspapers, or magazines; knowing that their names and words for everything can be written down on paper; that words are written down using letters; that all of the letters together are called the alphabet; that numbers such as three, six, and two can also be written with numerals: 3, 6, and 2; knowing how to hold a pencil or crayon correctly so that they can make marks on a paper; and knowing how to copy a simple figure, such as a squiggly line or figure.[12]

These listed items provide you with a blueprint for what any child needs to know and do to be ready for the demands and expectations of kindergarten. You can create your own checklist and figure out home activities to assist your child in learning them. Or you can obtain the *Kindergarten Survival Handbook* itself, where such lists and activities are already prepared for your and your child's use.

6. CREATE A HOME ENVIRONMENT THAT SUPPORTS EDUCATION

Creating a home that supports your child's education begins with making sure that you are meeting your child's physical health needs. If children are not physically healthy, they will not be able to reach their full potential. They are also more likely to have school problems that are misunderstood. For example, the impact of insufficient sleep or inadequate nutrition sometimes is seen as a learning disorder.

KEY COMPONENTS OF A HEALTHY ENVIRONMENT

Here are some ideas about maintaining your child's health from a parenting program called *Parents on Board* by Drs. Michael Popkin, Bettie Youngs, and Jane Healy.[13] The overall purpose of this program is to help you to be positively involved in your child's education.

Nutrition

- Avoid junk food.
- Study food package labels for caloric content.
- Balance menus from the basic food groups.
- Make breakfast, lunch, and dinner the core of your family's healthy diet.
- Don't force your child to eat.
- Make mealtimes as relaxed and pleasant as possible.

Exercise

- Put your children in charge of their own fitness.
- Be a role model by exercising yourself.
- Make exercise a family value by participating in sports and physical fitness activities together.
- Coach a sports team on which your child plays.
- Find activities that your child enjoys doing.
- Help your children focus on improving their personal best rather than winning or losing or comparing themselves to others.
- Encourage enrollment in community sports programs.
- Help your children develop and use a wall chart or other system to monitor progress.
- Limit TV, videogame, and computer time.

Sleep

Most experts recommend 8 to 10 hours of sleep a night for children. You can check out your child's sleep requirements by becoming sensitive to signs of sleep deprivation. Rethink your bedtime rules if your child:

- Has trouble concentrating on studies and other mental tasks for more than a short period of time
- Moves around and fidgets more than usual
- Becomes easily frustrated
- Is irritable
- Falls asleep on the couch, at the dinner table, or at her desk at school
- Has great difficulty waking up in the morning
- Has dark circles under her eyes

Provide Structure

A home environment that supports education also provides structure. Here are some structuring suggestions:

- Set a regular dinner time.
- Develop a bedtime routine.
- Set a weekly morning routine.
- Plan some weekend and holiday activities.
- Hold a weekly family meeting.
- Help your child organize her room.

Homework

A home environment that supports education supports children in doing their homework. You can:

- Help your child develop a work area.
- Agree on a regular time for studying.
- Provide as quiet an environment for studying as possible.

The educators and psychologists who created *Parents on Board* also turned their attention to the matter of how parents should see their overall role in supporting their children's formal education. In doing so, they raised the question of what an employer in the computerized workplace of the 21st century would want from an employee. They contend that the modern employer still wants personnel who have mastered the basic skills that are needed to communicate with others and with computers. Such skills include being able to read, write, and do math, and to reason about important ideas and practical solutions. They see learning through *rote memorization* playing a role in developing some of these basic skills, but a rather limited role.[15]

They contend that a different type of learning is needed to better prepare and relate to what today's employers see as being just as important as possessing the basic skills mentioned here. They refer to the learning that is needed to gain the additional skills as *conceptual learning,* which involves understanding, seeing relationships with other areas and forms of learning, and building on a foundation of meaning. This type of learning is more likely to lead to children's developing a broader set of abilities that modern employer's value. They contend that the 21st-century employer will want someone

- To be a highly motivated "self-starter"
- To solve new types of problems
- To come up with original ideas
- To communicate effectively—both orally and in writing
- To work well in groups
- To analyze, organize, and prioritize information
- To read, think critically, and draw conclusions from a given set of facts and opinions
- To "retool" and learn new ways of learning[16]

They further observed that traditional academic subjects can provide a foundation for these abilities and for the development of adult intelligence, rather than rote memorization, *if the subjects are taught so as to develop thinking and active curiosity about interesting ideas.*[17]

Become an Academic Coach

Based on this solid and contemporary thinking, the authors go on to talk about an approach and orientation that parents can assume at home to further this kind of valuable independent thinking: the Parent as Academic Coach. As we will see when their coaching ideas are reviewed, these psychologists and educators are major advocates of the Encouragement Approach that we learned about in the first guideline.

They also caution strongly about not turning coaching opportunities into a family battlefield. Here are seven principles for being a positive academic coach for children:[18]

Be Available

After a hard day of work, the last thing that many of us feel like doing is expending more effort—reading to a 4-year-old, going to the library, working on math facts with an elementary student, or proofreading a teenager's science report. Nevertheless, your child needs to have you around, even if it is only for moral support. What's more, your child needs your attention as well as your physical presence. No matter how exciting a TV show is, you need to interrupt it if your child needs help preparing for a quiz. Although *grown-up* time for yourself is very important, try to arrange those much-needed breaks when your child is sleeping or otherwise engaged, and make yourself available during homework time.

Offer Support, Not Criticism

If you want your child to share his learning with you, keep these goals in mind:

- Always find something positive to say before pointing out errors.
- Make your remarks honest and sincere.
- Never attack the child personally.

Focus on Effort and Improvement Instead of Grades

This rule is one of the most important to follow, but also one of the most difficult. Schools and parents have traditionally used grades as the main standard for judging children's progress, but current research shows clearly that:

- Although parents who have high expectations for their children produce better students, too much emphasis on grades alone lowers students' motivation to work.
- To be a successful leader or even an employee in a rapidly changing technological age, your child will need to feel that learning itself—not necessarily the grade he receives—is the important thing.

- School grades are very bad predictors of how successful people will be in the real world.

Although a certain emphasis on grades is necessary and inevitable for those who wish to attend a competitive college, many top colleges are now looking less at students' GPAs than at their interest and motivation to learn, their skill and involvement in nonacademic areas (e.g., music, drama, community service, debate), and their skills in working with other people. The best advice is not to ignore grades, but at the same time, to place a stronger emphasis on the child's personal qualities, effort, and improvement.

You Don't Have to Be an Expert

Parents on Board further contends that

It is the school's job to teach your child. If you find yourself constantly having to introduce or explain new learning, it's time for a conference at the school.[19]

Nevertheless, there will undoubtedly be times when you must work with concepts or skills with which you are not familiar. The important rule here is*: Don't be afraid to say, "I don't know."* It's a big mistake to blunder along, pretending you understand something and probably confusing your child even further.

Many of us are somewhat boggled by today's new and different ways of presenting math concepts, for example. In such cases, your job is to show your child that you, too, are still a learner and don't know everything. Perhaps you could find a reference source or a page in a textbook that would help you learn more about a topic, or go online with your child to find out more. If both of you are confused, however, you should probably turn that responsibility back to the student and the teacher.

Don't Expect Perfection

Regarding this pointer, the authors shared the following: A 4th-grade teacher lost patience one day with her class. "How can you be so childish?" she demanded. As the children looked innocently up at her, she confessed that she had to laugh at herself.[20]

Children need to know that you care about their achievements, but remember that they are, after all, just kids. Setting your standards too high is a sure prescription for a sullen, turned-off youngster or for one who is so nervous, anxious, and perfectionistic that she makes her life—and everyone else's—miserable. Research shows that good students tend to come from homes free from unrealistic restrictions or pressures.

It is also a mistake to expect equally expert performance in every subject or skill. Many outstanding mathematicians are terrible spellers, and some excellent readers have difficulty in gym class. Since your child probably inherited some of his talents (and liabilities) from you, try to understand and help him set realistic goals for improvement, not perfection.

Turn the Thinking Over to the Child

A common parental trap is to end up doing the work for the child, which is often easier than struggling to help her understand it herself. You can avoid this pitfall if you keep asking yourself, "Whose job/responsibility/problem is this?"

Enjoy!

The *Parents on Board* authors brought this lesson to a close by indicating:

> Our brains learn best when we are excited about what we are learning, when we feel safe and secure and when some enjoyment, humor or novelty is part of the experience. Even routine drill assignments, such as memorizing the multiplication tables, will stick better if some fun is attached (for example, you can make up silly stories, songs or drawings for number combinations). The more fun you and your child can have learning together, the better the lifetime habits you are teaching. This teaching job is perhaps a parent's most important one: Learning is fun, interesting and worth the effort it takes. If you convey these attitudes to your children, you are equipping them for success in life beyond the school doors.[21]

USE THE INTERNET

The Internet can become one of the greatest tools in the home environment for supporting education, if you know how to use it for this purpose.

Begin by using a search engine, such as google.com. Type in the topic or issue you are interested in, such as "study strategies," "report writing," "class projects," "student loans," or "student scholarships." Click and go on an educational journey through the world of already organized information, and enjoy and learn.

You could also obtain a wonderful tool that will save you the time of finding the best online resources yourself. It is a CD called *The Gateway to Academic Achievement*. It contains information about and links to more than 1,800 websites to help students, parents, and teachers. It encourages students of all ages to utilize the hundreds of available reference guides, dictionaries, maps, almanacs, encyclopedias, and other educational materials listed on the "Student Resources" pages. Links are open to various educational topics, from extensive literature, history, and math resources to an interactive chemical elements periodic table created especially for K–12 students, and much more!

The extensive college preparation area provides links to college search engines, online admissions, catalogs from more than 25,000 colleges, and detailed information on scholarships and applying for state and federal assistance. There are links to sites that explain the college application process, what high school classes to take, and how to choose a college.

Regardless of how you access the vast informational resources of the Internet, they are there for both your own and your children's immediate use all day, everyday. The modern family should take advantage of the Internet as much and as often as possible.

7. BE AN ACTIVE PARTNER WITH YOUR CHILDREN'S SCHOOL

Schools need parents' help. You, the parent, can make the difference. You have firsthand knowledge about your children's development, needs, and talents. You have a natural interest in their schooling and their future. As a parent, you can be most helpful to your children and their schools when you:

- Make sure your children get to school, on time, each day.
- Learn about the school's education program and how it works.
- Read the school newsletter and visit the school website regularly.
- Learn about the school's discipline policy and support it.
- Attend parent–teacher conferences and open houses.
- Phone or visit the school whenever you have questions.
- If you have time, join parent organizations or volunteer at school.
- Get to know your children's teachers and principal and develop positive relationships with them.
- Help schools get the respect, funding, and support they need.

When you work cooperatively with your child's school and educators, the positive impact on your children can be enormous. Developing a working relationship with your child's teachers helps you and the teachers better assess your children's readiness and ability to learn. You then have a better idea where their help is needed, and your children are more likely to feel comfortable when they sense the harmony between you and their teachers. By following a few simple steps, you can establish open lines of communication with your children's teachers. Understanding their perspective will help make your relationship productive and enjoyable.

START THE SCHOOL YEAR RIGHT

The idea here is not to wait to connect with your child's school and teacher until there are problems. If your child's school has an "open house" or "back-to-school" night, take advantage of it. These events not only provide you with information that will help you understand the school and its policies, but they can also put you in contact with your child's teachers and give you a chance to ask questions.

Here are some questions you may want to have answered by your child's teacher:

- What is the curriculum this year?
- What supplies will my child need? What is the teacher's homework policy?
- What is the teacher's policy regarding parents as school volunteers?
- How will parents be informed about additional school or classroom policies such as attendance, discipline, health, and safety?
- How will the teacher judge your child's progress?
- What is the best way to exchange information?

It is also wise to schedule personal conferences with your child's teachers. Here are some pointers to help make the parent–teacher conference a successful experience for everyone:

- Come prepared to listen.
- Come prepared to share with the teacher any relevant information about your child, such as hobbies, interests, or feelings toward school.
- Share with the teacher how you feel the year is going.
- Don't be afraid to ask questions.
- Compliment the teacher on something he is doing.
- Think carefully about how you will present the conference results to your child.

Regarding the last point, some schools may actually have you include the child in the conference. Then both you and the teacher must be tactful in sharing the purpose of the conference and any problems that are highlighted.

If the conference is held without your child, when you talk to her afterward, always start with something positive. Then explain tactfully any needs that the teacher has emphasized. Let your child express her feelings, too, and reassure her that you will try to help when possible.

As was mentioned earlier when we reviewed the many functions and responsibilities of parents, we spoke about your role as your child's advocate. Well, here's where that role becomes very important, especially if you feel your child is not getting the best education from her school or teachers. You have both a right and a responsibility to say so and to expect the school to be responsive. For example, if you feel that your child's educators are focusing too much on rote memorization as a learning method, you can inquire whether such methods are well-suited for developing the conceptual learning that we spoke about in an earlier guideline, the type of learning that best prepares children for the demands of the modern workplace. Your child's teachers may not have considered how much they are focusing on rote memorization versus conceptual learning, and they may be stimulated to place greater emphasis on the latter because of your concern and interest. Raising these types of ideas or concerns is being a good advocate for your child, and doing so in a manner that is not stridently critical is being a good partner.

8. Manage Your Child's Obesity
and Eating-Related Problems

As we learned earlier, millions of America's children are in poor health due to excess weight or obesity. For these children, the nutrition and exercise recommendations in Guideline 6 are of particular importance. However, further knowledge and commitment are necessary to help these children lose weight.

OBESITY

Here are some ideas to consider. These are based on what has been learned by one of the nation's leading weight-loss programs for children, the Shapedown Program developed by the University of California's School of Medicine in San Francisco. The parents of the 80,000 child graduates of that program have found the approaches mentioned below to be very helpful in supporting their children's weight lose.[22] Here we will review these approaches from the vantage point of a parent who has an obese child.

As such a parent, one of the first things that you need to do is take your obese child to see a physician, and to become connected with a registered dietician, exercise specialist, and a mental health professional such as a clinical social worker, clinical psychologist, or psychiatrist. As we have seen, it takes many factors to produce an obese child, and it takes a team of professionals to help that child lose weight. Gaining the assistance of such a team, which can be accomplished through a health maintenance organization (HMO) or through the referral and coordination efforts of your family physician, puts you, your child, and your entire family on the path to having everyone become healthier.

With the help of your team, here are some approaches that your family can try. These are described in much greater detail, along with specific homework assignments and helpful charts, in the book *Shapedown Parent's Guide: A Guide for Supporting Your Child*.[23]

1. *Become aware of your feelings about your child's weight.* Your feelings, such as guilt, fear, anger, sadness, frustration, and blame, are likely to have their roots in the current attitude of Western culture toward excess body fat. We are taught from the cradle that fat is ugly and lethal and that overweight

people are out of control, lazy, overindulgent, stupid, dishonest, amoral, and sinful. All of these attitudes are, of course, without basis. They do, however, influence your feelings about your child and about yourself as a parent.

Your feelings are real, and they are normal feelings to have in this situation. Managing these common feelings makes it easier for you to help your child. If these feelings persist, consult the mental health professional on your team. Don't brush them off.

2. *Understand clearly your child's weight, including its medical and psychological risks and the factors contributing to it.* Some of the causes of your child's obesity can be the cookies and ice cream that stuff your kitchen and your child, your child's overall sadness, or family chaos that's getting in the way of healthy diet and exercise habits. Some of this you will be able to change on your own; other causes will require the help of your team.

3. *Take stock of your family's current eating and exercising habits.* This involves looking closely at what you eat and categorizing your foods in terms of fat content as being "Free," "Light," "Heavy" or "Junk." This also involves noting when and how much is consumed. In addition, take account of whatever exercise is carried out by your family and be sure to reward people for exercising.

4. *Arrive at a systematic plan for changing habits in a more healthy direction, and then implement the plan.* This involves creating a light but not food-depriving environment at home, developing a general family lifestyle that is physically active, and specifically structuring an active and enriching lifestyle for your child that includes daily exercise. The nutrition and exercise recommendations at the beginning of guideline 6 are good places to start in developing your particular plan. Your plan should also include supporting each family member in openly expressing his or her feelings and needs.

5. *Be particularly vigilant to provide both abundant warmth and acceptance, and to set fair and firm limits with your obese child.* Like all children, these kids need to be effectively parented in the ways we have been reviewing and learning in the earlier guidelines.

6. *Be a good role model by improving your own weight, eating, and activity problems.* Here, too, parental modeling can be a very powerful contributor to the health of your children.

Now let's look at the reverse problem: not eating enough to stay healthy.

ANOREXIA NERVOSA AND BULIMIA

What to Look for

The classic pattern of Anorexia includes a refusal to maintain minimal body weight and an intense fear of gaining weight. In addition, some also engage in regular binge-eating and purging episodes. Obsessive exercise may accompany starving behavior and cause others, including parents, to assume that the person must be healthy.

In regard to Bulimia, binge-eating is reflected in the consumption of excessively large amounts of food within a short period of time. The food is often sweet, high in calories, and has a texture that makes it easy to eat fast.

"Inappropriate compensatory behavior" to control one's weight may include purging behavior (such as self-induced vomiting and abuse of laxatives, diuretics, or enemas) or non-purging behaviors (such as fasting or excessive exercise). For those who binge-eat, sometimes any amount of food, even a salad or half an apple, is perceived as a binge and purged.

Adolescents with Bulimia often feel a lack of control during eating binges. Their food is usually eaten secretly and gobbled down rapidly with little chewing. A binge is usually ended by stomach discomfort. When the binge is over, the adolescent with Bulimia feels guilty and purges to rid his or her body of the excessive calories.

Although occasional binge-eating is fairly common, to be considered Bulimic, a person must have had, on average, a minimum of two binge-eating episodes a week for at least 3 months.

What to Do?

The seriousness of these eating disorders is such that they require you to move into action immediately when you suspect their presence in any child. Make sure that such a child is seen right away by health and mental health professionals, preferably at an eating disorders clinic or department. Don't waste time. Have your child or adolescent checked out as soon as you see any of the signs.

Also be sure to engage all of your children in discussions about current cultural preferences and obsessions with thinness. Sharing with them some of the facts about Anorexia Nervosa and Bulimia should be eye-opening and should send a message about how destructive such obsessions can be.

Discussing your children's images of their own—and your—body can also be enlightening. What's behind poor body images? Why should any body image be considered poor?

These discussions, coupled with some of the suggested tactics for dealing with obese children, should help you and your children develop realistic, livable, and healthy habits and values.

And, once again, if you are experiencing signs of obesity, Anorexia Nervosa, or Bulimia, get yourself the professional assistance that you need. Don't wait. Be a good role model when it comes to seeking help.

9. Teach Your Children
About Their Own and Other Cultures

Your children probably attend school with other children from a rich variety of cultural backgrounds. When they graduate and get jobs, many of their coworkers and supervisors will also be people from cultures different from their own. Your children need to know how to get along with many different types of people in order to succeed. You can help them become better friends, students, and coworkers by first teaching them about their own cultural backgrounds and then by expanding their understanding of their own and other cultures.

- Tell your children about your parents, grandparents, and your people, about their achievements, their habits, and cultural characteristics, and about the hardships that they overcame.
- Expose them to dolls and toys from other cultures.
- Get books or visit the library to learn about other worlds.
- Watch and discuss news stories, films, videos, DVDs, and television shows about different cultural groups.
- Visit ethnic and history museums.
- Attend cultural festivals, parties, and reunions.
- Make friends with people of different cultures.

TEACHING TOLERANCE

There is also much you can do to teach your children about tolerance. Here are some excellent suggestions from one of America's foremost advocates for teaching tolerance, the Southern Poverty Law Center:

Talk About Tolerance. This is an ongoing process; it cannot be captured in a single moment. Establish a high "comfort level" for open dialogue about social issues. Let children know that no subject is taboo.

Identify Intolerance When Children Are Exposed to It. Point out stereotypes and cultural misinformation depicted in movies, TV shows, computer games, and other media. Challenge bias when it comes from friends and family members. Do not let the moment pass. Begin with a qualified statement: "Andrew just called people of XYZ background 'lunatics.' What do you think about that, Zoe?" Let children do most of the talking.

Challenge Intolerance When It Comes from Your Children. When a child says or does something that reflects biases or embraces stereotypes, point it out: "What makes that joke funny, Jerome?" Guide the conversation toward internalization of empathy and respect.

Support Your Children When They Are Victims of Intolerance. Respect children's troubles by acknowledging when they become targets of bias. Don't minimize the experience. Provide emotional support and then brainstorm constructive responses. Develop a set of "comebacks" for children who are victims of name-calling.

Foster a Healthy Understanding of Group Identity. For tweens and teens, group identity is critical. Remind them, however, of three things: First, pride in our own group does not mandate disrespect for others. Second, no group is entitled to special privileges. Third, we should avoid putting other groups down as a way to elevate the status of our own group.

Be Honest About Differences. Do not tell children that we are all the same; we're not. We experience the world in different ways, and those experiences matter. Help your child understand the viewpoints of others.

Model the Behavior That You Would Like to See. As parents and as children's primary role models, we must be consistent in how we treat others and in our commitment to tolerance. If we as parents treat people differently based on characteristics such as race, gender, or sexual orientation, our children are likely to do the same.

Further assistance on these important matters is easily available in the Parenting for Tolerance section of the Southern Poverty Law Center website (www.tolerance.org/parents/index.jsp). I urge you to make regular and seasonal visits to this extraordinary source. It provides insights and information about how to help you and your children become knowledgeable and sensitive members of your communities. It provides insight into the subtle and often unconscious ways that prejudice and intolerance are conveyed. Everything is age-graded so that it orients you about the best way to sensitize and educate children at different points and ages in their development.

10. Teach Children About Substance Abuse

The main reason for teaching children about substances such as tobacco, alcohol, and other drugs like marijuana and cocaine is to help them avoid becoming abusers of such substances. Helping to prevent children from becoming substance abusers is one of the most important goals you should have as a parent, given how destructive substance abuse is to the bodies, minds, and futures of our children.

As was indicated in Chapter 3, the research about how parents contribute to children becoming substance abusers indicates that there were several major parental contributors:

1.   Parents being rejecting rather than being warm and accepting in their relationships with their children.
2.   Parents being poor rule-enforcers and being harsh and unfair in their attempts to lead their families.
3.   Parents being abusers of substances themselves, i.e., poor role models.[24]

This implies that you can help prevent your children from using and abusing substances by being or becoming a warm, accepting, and respectful parent; by learning and being fair and firm in your family leadership; and by maintaining or beginning a healthy, drug-free lifestyle. These are, of course, three of the other effective parenting guidelines that are described and discussed in this book. So, by already engaging in the actions indicated in these guidelines, or starting to do so right now, you will be doing a great deal to prevent your children from becoming substance abusers.

Possibly the most difficult thing for you to do, especially if you grew up during the time when nearly everyone was using or experimenting with one illegal substance or another, is to model a drug-free lifestyle.

If you previously abused substances, and don't anymore, you can still be a good role model. Take comfort and courage in the saying, "If I tell you not to do what I am doing, I am a hypocrite. If I tell you not to do what I have done, I am a teacher."

However, if you are still using and abusing tobacco, alcohol, and other drugs, you are not in a very good role model position. You can, of course, work to change this reality. You can stop using, if possible. It is really a fine reason to stop doing something you enjoy for the purpose of helping your children lead healthier lives. If you cannot stop on your own and are addicted, get the treatment you require. Doing so is also a positive parenting action: helping children see that it is possible to change your behavior even if it is a self-destructive habit.

Regardless of your personal history and involvement with substances, there are some very concrete things you can do to help prevent your children from becoming dependent on drugs.

LEARN ABOUT ALCOHOL, TOBACCO, AND OTHER DRUGS

Here, the idea is for you to become knowledgeable about the wide range of substances that now exists, and about their effects on the body and the mind.

EDUCATE YOUR CHILDREN ABOUT
ALCOHOL, TOBACCO, AND OTHER DRUGS

You can become an educator of your children by sharing what you have learned. Most children indicate that they appreciate receiving this type of education from their parents. In addition, children who learn about the risks of substance abuse from their parents or caregivers are less likely to use drugs than those who do not. How much less likely? According to federal government health reports, children are about 36% less likely to smoke marijuana, 50% less likely to use inhalants, 56% less likely to use cocaine, and 65% less likely to use LSD.[25]

Our nation's leadership is also deeply concerned about substance abuse. Our leaders have come to understand the importance of parents in moving children toward drug-free and healthy lifestyles, a movement that I am happy to say I played a role in. As a result, there is now a federal government-sponsored program and website where parents can obtain information about various substances and how best to educate your children.

Go to the *Parents: The Anti-Drug* website (www.theantidrug.com) to obtain reliable information about:

- Alcohol
- Club drugs
- Cocaine
- Ecstasy
- GHB

- Inhalants
- Ketamine
- LSD
- Marijuana
- Methamphetamine
- Over-the-counter drugs
- Steroids
- Tobacco

This extraordinarily useful website will keep you up-to-date on trends and issues related to preventing substance use. You can also subscribe to a free Parenting Tips newsletter, which will regularly encourage you to continue to be the most important anti-drug in the lives of your children. Here's more that you can do.

HAVE CLEAR FAMILY RULES ABOUT SUBSTANCE USE

After thinking through your values about the use of alcohol, tobacco, and other drugs, you should arrive at rules that you expect your children to abide by, such as no-use rules. Then have a family rule discussion with your children to explain the rules and your reasons for the rules. Remember, rules have a "do side" and a "don't side." The "don't side" in regard to rules about substance abuse should, like all "don't sides" of family rules, have clear consequences for breaking the rules. So should the "do side"—in other words, be sure to praise, acknowledge, and reward your children for staying drug-free.

BE ALERT TO SIGNS AND SYMPTOMS
OF TEEN DRINKING AND DRUG USE

How can you tell if your child is using drugs or alcohol? It is difficult because changes in mood or attitudes, unusual temper outbursts, changes in sleeping habits, and changes in hobbies or other interests are common in teens. What should you look for?

- Changes in friends
- Negative changes in schoolwork, missing school, or declining grades
- Increased secrecy about possessions or activities

- Use of incense, room deodorant, or perfume to hide smoke or chemical odors
- Subtle changes in conversations with friends, e.g., being more secretive, using "coded" language
- Change in clothing choices: new fascination with clothes that highlight drug use
- Increase in borrowing money
- Evidence of drug paraphernalia such as pipes and rolling papers.
- Evidence of use of inhalant products (such as hairspray, nail polish, correction fluid, and other common household products); rags and paper bags are sometimes used as accessories
- Bottles of eyedrops, which may be used to mask bloodshot eyes or dilated pupils
- New use of mouthwash or breath mints to cover up the smell of alcohol
- Missing prescription drugs—especially narcotics and mood stabilizers

These types of changes and occurrences often signal that something harmful is going on—and that often involves alcohol or drugs. You may want to take your child to the doctor and ask him or her about screening your child for drugs and alcohol. This may involve the health professional asking your child a simple question, or it may involve a urine or blood drug screen. However, some of these signs also indicate there may be a deeper problem with depression, gang involvement, or suicide. Be on the watch for these signs so that you can spot trouble before it goes too far.

11. TEACH CHILDREN ABOUT SEXUALITY

It has always been a good idea for parents to discuss sex with their children, but now, because of the HIV/AIDS epidemic and the existence of so many other sexually transmitted diseases, such communication takes on a new urgency.[26] Also, because of the fact that so many children are becoming sexually active at earlier ages than before, this type of communication needs to occur earlier than the teen years.

Parents in our country have never been particularly gifted or comfortable discussing sexual issues with their children and teens. And teenagers have not felt particularly comfortable with such discussions.[27] Indeed, studies of parents and teens regarding the obstacles they perceive that stand in the way of such communication indicate some of the same concerns (e.g., potentially feeling embarrassed or possibly prying into the child's private life) and some different concerns (e.g., if I talk to my teen about sex and/or contraception, she or he is more likely to have sex; my teen won't be honest; or my mother will be suspicious if I ask any questions or say anything).

Because of these types of attitudes and concerns, many parents only share their values and attitudes indirectly through the behavior they model rather than through direct discussion. For example, whether they appear nude in front of their children, whether they engage in sexual relations outside of marriage, and how they respond to their children's siblings or friends who give birth as teenagers undoubtedly affect the values of their children. Children may or may not recognize this modeling.

Studies of teen–parent communications also show that discussing sexual matters with teens is, in and of itself, not enough to influence their behaviors in this area of life. Parental impact appears to result from a more complex set of factors that surround and predate these discussions. For example, some studies have shown that if a mother disapproves of teens having sexual relations, if communication takes place early, and if there is a close mother–daughter relationship, then formal communication about sexual matters and values may delay the daughter's initiation of sexual intercourse. This type of finding reprises some of what was learned earlier about parental influences on children's alcohol and other drug usage: The better the relationship in the early years, the greater the likelihood of having a positive influence later in the child's life.

Possibly the best approach to protecting children from HIV/AIDS and other sexually transmitted diseases is to emphasize abstaining from adult sex acts such as oral, anal, and genital sex until they are reasonably mature and in a healthy relationship with another person. Abstaining from adult sex is the only way to be totally sure of being protected, and being in a caring and mature relationship where both partners take proper precautions is the next safest approach.

For many parents, asking and expecting their children to abstain until they are in a mature relationship is a particularly daunting approach, given that so many parents did not abstain themselves. If that is true of you also, and you now want your children to abstain until they are in a mature relationship, you can gain a measure of courage by taking to heart the aphorism from the prior guideline: "If I tell you not to do what I am doing, I am a hypocrite. If I tell you not to do what I have done, I am a teacher."

Here are some suggestions on how you might approach your children to help them abstain until they are in a healthy, loving relationship.[28] A good deal of what follows is applicable even if abstinence is not one of your goals.

START TALKING EARLY

Some parents put off discussing sex until their child is a teenager. That can be too late. Three national surveys report that one out of five teens aged 14 and younger has had sex at least once.[29] So talk early and often to your preteens and teens.

Conversations about love, relationships, and sex could begin as early as age 6 and should continue through the teenage years. If your child is old enough to ask questions, he or she is old enough to receive simple, but correct, answers. By the time your child is in middle school, you need to be straightforward. You need to talk about the health benefits of making good decisions and setting goals for the future. You need to talk about waiting to have sex and why it is the healthiest choice. And you need to talk about emotions and relationships.

When your teen enters high school, you continue to reinforce what you have already talked about—dating relationships, values, self-discipline, and the consequences of sex outside of a committed, adult relationship. Always leave the door open. When it's time to talk about tough topics, you and your teen will have built a relationship that allows those conversations to sink in and have meaning.

If you have not been in the habit of talking with your children about these types of matters, it may be particularly difficult to begin when your child is a teenager. However, even though it may be difficult to start to talk to your teen about sexual issues, if your teen is like most teens, he or she wants you to. Your opinions and counsel matter. In one survey, 37% of teen boys and girls said their parents have the most influence on their sexual decisions, compared with media, friends, health teachers, and religious leaders.[30]

WHY PARENTS DON'T TALK, BUT SHOULD

As was suggested earlier, you may be concerned that you don't know what to say or how to share information about sex and relationships with your teen. Although sex is a big topic in the media and society, you may be uncomfortable discussing it. You may hesitate to talk about sex for several reasons:

- You think your teen won't listen.
- You think you don't know as much about issues like HIV and STDs as health teachers and school nurses do.
- You're overwhelmed with the responsibilities of parenting and feel like you can't do it all.
- You worry that your teen will think you're being judgmental.

As mentioned above, many teens really want you to talk to them about these matters. To make healthy life choices, all teens need to:

- Know they are important to their parent(s) and other adults in their lives, such as grandparents;
- Have a plan for a bright future and healthy relationships;
- Be involved in healthy family, school, and community activities;
- Have support from parent(s), grandparent(s), teachers, and/or other adults to promote their decision not to have sex;
- Know the facts about sex, teen pregnancy, teen parenthood, and STDs; and
- Have the skills and support systems (parents, grandparents, teachers, and/or other adults) to say "no."

TIPS FOR TALKING WITH YOUR TEEN: WISE

You want to be as wise and prepared as possible when you talk to your teen. Here are four tips that can help. They are easy to remember because they spell WISE.

"W" Is for Welcome

Your teen needs to know that you care and are eager to talk. He or she needs to feel secure talking to you. No one enjoys dinner, activities, or conversations that are tense.

Your teen is more likely to talk and listen if neither of you is angry or upset. If your teen feels calm and supported, it is a lot easier for both of you to talk about topics such as sex, peer pressure, setting goals, building relationships, preparing for marriage or establishing loving relationships with others, and being a parent.

So how do you create a supportive, safe environment so you can talk? First, you must show respect for each other. Second, your teen needs to be able to trust you. If you want your teen to make good choices, you have to be honest and reliable and expect the same. Third, you have to be available. You have to be there when your teen wants to talk—in the morning, after school, or at dinnertime. Studies show that teens who eat five or more meals together with their parents during the week make healthier choices. Take time to discuss news and television shows with sexual themes. Take opportunities to discuss peer pressure, teen pregnancy, STDs, and what's happening in your community.

"I" Is for Interest

Show your interest by asking questions in a comfortable order and style. If you ask your teen, "Do you think there is a lot of pressure to have sex at your school?" he or she is more likely to open up and talk to you than if you warn, "You'd better not be having sex!"

Adults generally introduce topics gently when they are talking to other adults. But sometimes they are not as gentle with their own children. Here are a few important guidelines to help you talk with your teen:

- Start with a general question or observation.
- Let your teen be the expert on his or her world.

- Ask about peer pressure.
- Ask how you can help. For example, ask your teen:
    "Is there someone you really like?"
    "What kinds of things do you do together?"
    "Are you ever alone together?"
    "Have you ever felt pressured or wanted to have sex?"
    "If you've felt pressured or wanted to have sex, how did you
        handle that?"

"S" Is for Supporting Good Goals

If your teen has hope for the future, he or she is more likely to make better choices. Do you know if your teen has goals? Do you know what they are? Ask your teen about his or her goals for marriage, family, and a career. Ask him or her about goals for jobs now and in the future, and what his or her plans are to prepare for them. Then listen and offer support.

Share your own hopes and values. Goals, values, and beliefs are important to teens. They are some of the most powerful reasons for the sexual choices teens make. You can guide your teen to develop the values of honesty, responsibility, and caring. Remember, values about education, relationships, marriage, and trust are more easily "caught" than "taught." You and your behavior are the most valuable "values" educator!

Another part of goals and values for many families is their religious or spiritual base. If your family is involved with a church, mosque, synagogue, or other faith organization, encourage your teen to participate. Teens who are actively involved in a religious organization, who study faith, and who pray or worship are less likely to begin early sexual activity. Share your family's values with your teen and encourage service to others and the community.

"E" Is for Encouraging, Educating, and Empowering

Educate and encourage your teen to make healthy decisions. When topics come up about sex, do not think that you need to know all the answers. Be honest when you do not know, and offer to help find the facts.

If you made poor sexual decisions when you were young, that should not keep you from guiding your teen to healthier decisions.

Many of today's parents were teens when they began having sex. Now we know more about STDs and the consequences of sex at an early age.

RULES

As has been emphasized throughout these guidelines, it is important to have family rules that everyone is aware of and that help organize family life. These matters of sexuality and relationships also need to be governed by clear rules. Even though most teens may not admit it, they like to have rules that are enforced. Rules give structure to their lives and help them feel cared for and secure.

Here are some rules you might want to consider regarding these matters:

- Encourage supervised group activities. Know and support the groups in which your teen participates.
- Set an age for dating. Be clear that there will be no dating before this age.
- Make it clear that your teen will not be allowed to date anyone more than 2 years older or younger than he or she is.
- Make sure that your teen is not spending a lot of time in unsupervised situations. Sports, tutoring, and even after-school jobs are positive ways to ensure that your teen is safe and productive during the after-school hours.
- Tell your teen that it is against the rules to entertain a boyfriend or girlfriend in personal spaces such as bedrooms. "First sex" often happens at home in an unsupervised area of the house.
- Set clear guidelines for your teen's outings. Ask: Where will you be? What will you be doing? Who will you be with? When will you be home? How can I reach you?
- No alcohol. No drugs. No tobacco.
- Be available to pick up your teen if he or she calls in an uncomfortable or threatening environment or situation.
- Set rules for what your teen son or daughter can listen to, read, and watch. Consider keeping the TV and computer in a public area of the home so you will know what your teen is viewing.
- Be available to talk with your teen daily. Good communication supports good decisions.

TALK ABOUT GROWING UP

Body changes during puberty can happen early or late, fast or slow. Educate your child about changes that are or will be happening. Reassure teens through those self-conscious stages and talk to your healthcare provider about concerns that you or your teen may have.

TALK ABOUT WAITING

Your teen needs to know why you do not want him or her to have sex now. Tell them that abstinence is the healthiest choice. They will not have to worry about getting pregnant or getting someone pregnant. They will not have to worry about STDs, including HIV/AIDS. Nor will they have to worry that the person they are dating is only interested in them because of sex.

Waiting for sex shows self-respect. Let your teen know that even though they are capable of having sex, it will not make them an adult—making good choices will.

TALK ABOUT HOW YOUR TEEN MIGHT FEEL

"If you think it is hard to say 'no,' just wait until you say 'yes.'" Many teens have found this out the hard way. In fact, two out of three teens who have had sex say they wish they had waited.[31] If teens have sex, not only can they get diseases, get pregnant, or get someone pregnant, but they can also get a broken heart or a bad reputation.

WHAT IF YOUR TEEN HAS ALREADY HAD SEX?

If you find out that your son or daughter has already had sex, it is important for you not to be punishing in your reactions. Take your teen to a health-care professional to be screened for pregnancy and STDs. Be sure to tell your teen that having multiple partners can be one of the biggest threats to their physical and emotional health. Tell them it is not too late to stop having sex, and that it is never too late to make healthy choices. Let them know they are worth it!

WHAT DO TEENS THINK ABOUT TEEN SEX?

When teens were asked in a survey what they thought about sex, more than half said sexual activity for high school–aged teens was not acceptable. Three out of four teens did not think it was embarrassing to admit that they were a virgin. And 9 out of 10 teens thought it was important that society sends a strong message that teens should abstain from sex until they are at least out of high school.[22]

If this is the message you want to send to your teens and other children, following some of the above advice will make you a pretty good messenger. Even if you are not committed to an abstinence message, the advice is worth serious consideration.

If you approve and support your teens engaging in sex, be sure they are well-informed about how to protect themselves from getting STDs.

ADDITIONAL PERSPECTIVES

The matter of teaching children about sexuality is more than a matter of helping them make healthy choices. There is also the issue of what constitutes a healthy relationship, what is abusive, and what is exploitative. If your relationship with your partner is a healthy one and if your relationship with your children is of high quality, you are way ahead of the game in being able to teach about and model healthy relationships. Even so, you need to be clear with your children that there are many people who can be and are abusive and exploitative in relationships. Your children need to know that you will be there to help extricate them from such relationships and that you will not explode when you hear that they have gotten into a bad relationship. Your children also need to know that they, too, could be the perpetrators of such relationships if they are disrespectful of the needs and values of others. Here again, you need to be open to hearing about what your teen may be doing without getting angry and making matters worse.

There is also the issue of your children's own gender and sexual identity. Most young people have tender and sexual feelings and thoughts about members of their own sex. Does this make them gay, lesbian, or bisexual? Not necessarily, although for about 10% of all children, these feelings are the first signs of these sexual orientations. Because these orientations are still often looked upon negatively or

misunderstood by so many people, children need particularly compassionate parents to help them sort out this important aspect of their
development.

Such compassion is difficult, of course, if parents happen to view
these sexual orientations negatively or are uninformed about them.
This difficultly also exists for many of the gay, lesbian, and bisexual
adults who are themselves raising children. They know all too well
the indignities, hatred, and challenges that exclusively heterosexual
and homophobic people can visit on gay, lesbian, and bisexual people.
Sharing these possibilities and realities is often just as difficult for them
as it is for exclusively heterosexual parents who have children with
different orientations.

Fortunately, there are excellent resources that can be utilized. One
such resource is Parents, Families and Friends of Lesbians and Gays
(PFLAG), which is devoted to promoting the health and well-being
of gay, lesbian, and bisexual persons and their families and friends.
PFLAG accomplishes these humanitarian goals through support,
education, and advocacy. They can be reached through their website,
www.pflag.org, or at

PFLAG
1726 M Street NW, Suite 400
Washington, DC 20036
(202) 467–8180

12. Teach Children to Be
Financially Successful and Giving

When you model and teach wise money management, your children have a better chance of becoming financially successful. When you also share with them the fact that you give money to charities, causes, and disaster relief, you show them that money can be used for humanitarian as well as personal purposes.

Here are some specific things you can do:

- Begin early in teaching your children the value of money.
- Use four piggy banks in which your children can keep their money—one bank for money they will spend for themselves, one for saving, one for investing, and one for the money they will give to charities, causes, disaster relief, and civic, political, and lobbying efforts.
- Teach them about saving and interest.
- Teach them about investments.
- Teach them about charities and causes they can support and about other ways they can use their money for humanitarian purposes.
- Teach them that contributions can be made to political and advocacy organizations as a way of promoting a person's values and beliefs through supporting and electing like-minded politicians, citizen action, and lobbying.
- Have your children earn their allowance.
- Teach them how to generate other sources of money.
- Discuss the purchases your children want to make with their money and help them make wise decisions.
- Give and read books on financial literacy to children.
- Give and play games with your children about financial literacy.
- Orient them to financial literacy websites for children.
- Draw their attention to your own budgeting, checking, and credit card, savings, investing, and giving activities.
- Involve your children as your assistants in managing household finances, saving, investing, and giving.

THE 10/10/10/70 CONCEPT

It is very important to give children some guidance about how they might use whatever money they earn now and in the future. An idea that those in the new field of financial literacy for children have suggested for helping children build wealth and control over their financial destinies is this: For every dollar they are given or earn, have children:

Give: 10% to a charity or cause of their choice
Invest: 10% to build their fortunes
Save: 10% for the future, and
Spend: 70% for everyday expenses.

This basic concept can begin to be taught to your children very early in life by getting them separate piggy banks for each purpose, as mentioned above. With whatever dollars they earn or are given, distribute the coins into different banks as the 10/10/10/70 ratio indicates.

LORI MACKEY'S PRODUCTS

If you don't want to get or create four separate banks, you can obtain the *Mommie (Money Mama the Smarter Piggy Bank) Piggy Bank* that has been created for this purpose by a parent who has made a business out of her concern for her children's financial futures, Lori Mackey (see Figure 4.2). The piggy bank that Lori has created is handmade and constructed in such a way that there are four coin slots over different-sized parts of the bank. Each part has its own compartment, which helps make the 10/10/10/70 ratio vividly apparent and easier to grasp.

Related to this unique bank is a beautifully illustrated book that can also be used in teaching young children the importance of saving, investing, giving, and making wise decisions about spending money. It is called *Money Mama and the Three Little Pigs*. The book is accompanied by a read-along CD narrated by Lori's two children, Briana and Devin. Briana reads the book so little kids can follow it, and Devin makes a little cash register "cha-ching" sound to let listeners know when it is time to turn the page. This engaging book and the child-narrated CD present basic financial literacy ideas in ways that even children as young as 4 can begin to grasp.[33]

FIGURE 4.2. The Money Mama Piggy Bank

EARNING AN ALLOWANCE

In regard to how you can set things up so that your children earn their allowances, let me suggest an approach that is akin to the Special Incentive System taught in parenting skill-building programs such as *Confident Parenting, Effective Black Parenting,* and *Los Niños Bien Educados.* This approach involves children earning a portion of their allowance each day for completing helpful household chores and tasks. The money that is earned is then used according to the 10/10/10/70 ratio.

This approach is symbolized and facilitated by the use of an allowance chart that should be placed in a prominent location in the home. Such a chart has been created by money-wise parent Lori Mackey (see Figure 4.3). Her attractive allowance chart comes with instructions on how to determine the daily allowance amount and examples of daily chores. The chores can be affixed to the chart and so can dollar signs and happy faces to show success. It all comes together in a package called *It's Only a Dollar Until You Add to It!*[34]

FIGURE 4.3. The Allowance Chart Kit

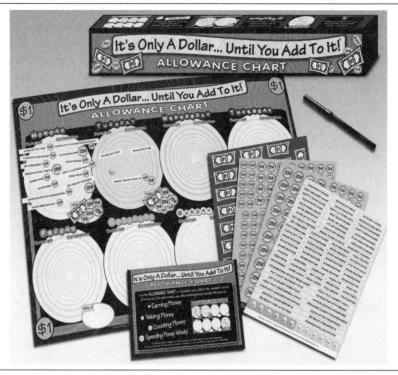

Other knowledgeable people from the financial literacy for children field have suggested a variety of other ways that parents can take the lead. Here are a few more that you can use with children of different ages:

- To teach children about investing, set up a hypothetical portfolio of several stocks and track it online. Have your children choose stocks they like by exploring the things in their lives that they enjoy. For example, they may like the breakfast cereal Cheerios. They will learn that Cheerios is a brand and that General Mills is the corporation that issues the stock. Have them invest the 10% of their "investing" monies (or a portion of such monies) in that stock and track it over time.
- Create a lesson out of bill paying. Have children, for example, look at the family utility bills and see what it costs to have services that are often taken for granted, such as the Internet, cable television, and a cell phone.

- Use grocery shopping as an opportunity to teach children about bargain shopping, discounts, coupons, and best values.
- To teach budgeting and tracking expenses, have your child help track expenses for budgeting. If you have a home computer, she can enter monthly expenses and note variances. She can graph the results on the computer or on paper. The positive side of this experience is that your child will learn about how households are run, complete with graphs and historical analysis. The downside is that you may have your child judging your spending habits.
- Engage in financial games with your children that involve dining out. For example, you can ask each child to pay attention to what is ordered. Their assignment is to come as close as possible to the total bill for the meal before taxes. Make it a competition with an incentive. In the case of a tie, the child who comes up with the closest total after tax wins.
- If each child has his or her own room, have them redecorate their rooms. If they share rooms, have them engage in the redecoration project as a group. Give them a specific budget and ask them the ways they would decorate their room. What colors would they use for the wall? What kind of furniture? What labor would be involved? How long would it take? Does the budget allow for paying professionals to do the redecorating? If so, how would they find these professionals?

A topflight resource for teaching children about money is the Jump Start Coalition for Personal Financial Literacy (Financial Smarts for Students), whose website can be accessed at www.jumpstart.org. Included there is a wide range of games that can be purchased and/or played to learn about various financial issues and challenges, such as the Stock Market Game.

Your personal financial literacy, which is, of course, the foundation of your being a fine financial mentor for your children, is also addressed at the end of guideline 16 about life-long learning.

13. Manage Your Children's
Media and Technology Exposure

By the time most children graduate from high school, they will have spent the equivalent of 3 years watching television.[35] This means that they will have seen many enjoyable and interesting sights and programs. They will also have seen thousands of murders, beatings, and other acts of violence. Children who watch a steady diet of violent programs increase their chances of becoming:

- Too aggressive with other children and adults
- Less willing to cooperate and share with others
- More afraid of the outside world[36]

You, as a parent, must become actively involved in your children's use of television. You should:

- Limit how much they watch.
- Limit what they watch.
- Watch by the show and not by the clock. Select shows from the *TV Guide* or local newspaper. When the chosen show is over, turn the television off.
- Watch television with your children. Plan special viewing times together.
- Discuss what you watch. Let your children know your opinions and feelings about what you see. Talk about the values and consequences of actions. Explain conflicts between desire and responsibility, and the importance of solving conflicts without resorting to violence.

Be as in charge as possible in regard to your child's exposure to films, music, and the Internet:

- Use film ratings to decide what your children are allowed to see.
- Listen to the lyrics of the songs they hear. Orient them away from violent and sexual content.
- Use parental Internet access controls to block unsuitable websites.

The Internet has become increasingly more interactive. Millions of young people are now using it for personal communication and socializing purposes. E-mailing and text messaging of friends is becoming a daily and even hourly practice. Many youth now have their own websites and weblogs (blogs). Millions are members of friendship sites such as *Myspace, Friendster,* or *Xanga,* where they not only can post messages but can also have pictures and video footage of themselves that they create with webcams. They are also using the Internet for school and class-related projects, homework assistance, and researching purposes. And, as we have seen, they are often doing all of this at the same time through multitasking.

One of the concerns about multitasking that we discussed is that it may be negatively affecting the important ability to concentrate and give full attention to complex issues and academic assignments. It is probably wise to talk to your children about sequencing their use of all this technology and media, and orienting them to confine themselves to specific activities for specific time periods. For example, you can create rules about only using the Internet for study purposes between 6:00 and 8:00 in the evening, taking a socialization and communication break from 8:00 to 8:30, then going back to using the Internet for study from 8:30 to 9:30, with a break for viewing a saved television program right after that, and so forth. This approach provides structure to children's uses of technology and media, allowing them to use what they want to use, but only in sequence and with no overlap. For this to work, you need to be able to observe on occasion to ensure that your children are playing by the rules. Having the computer in a public place would help greatly.

These latest uses of the Internet have brought with them an array of other issues and dangers to which parents must attend. For example, sexual predators have become clever at using the Internet to entice gullible children and teenagers into illegal and dangerous activities. To protect your children from these types of dangers, you can use the Internet itself to learn about how to protect your children. There are now several excellent websites that can provide you with the facts about such dangers and how best to cope.

One of the best sites for these purposes is *I Safe America* (www.isafe. org). The I Safe website not only provides authoritative information about many types of Internet dangers (sexual predators, cyberbullying, cyber security and identity theft), but it also shows how parents in a particular neighborhood can band together and join with local schools to protect their children from Internet dangers. In addition, I

Safe provides youth themselves with ways to become leaders in educating their peers about Internet safety. Other very helpful websites for these safety purposes include www.wiredkids.com, webwisekids.org, and www.netsmartz.org.

In terms of getting a grasp on the types of films, television shows, and videogames that are good and bad for your children, the CommonSense Media organization and website is probably the best place to turn. You can become a member and receive a regular newsletter that keeps you up-to-date and extremely well-informed. You can become connected at commonsensemedia.org.

CommonSense Media also contains a terrific *Internet Safety Survival Guide for Parents*, which you can download. The guide includes a good deal of the wisdom and information that can also be accessed by the previously mentioned Internet safety organizations and websites. The CommonSense guide includes sections on communicating, web surfing, online gaming, and social networking. Here's an example of the types of tips and guidance you can receive in the section on your children's use of the Internet for communicating by e-mail, instant messaging (IM), chat rooms, and blogs:

1. *Never reveal personal information.* No real names, birth dates, phone numbers, addresses, or anything identifiable should be used in profiles or blogs. Screen names should be gender neutral. Explain the dangers: one out of every five kids gets sexually solicited online.[37]
2. *Never meet a stranger.* Ever. No talking, no meeting, no way. Make sure your kids know that if someone contacts them, attempts to meet them, or tries to turn them against you or their teachers, these are alerts, and they should tell you right away.
3. *Establish codes of conduct.* If your kids wouldn't say something to someone's face, then they shouldn't put it in an IM or e-mail. That means no cyberbullying. E-mailing an embarrassing picture of someone is a form of cyberbullying!
4. *Be careful with passwords.* This means no password sharing. Sharing a password with a friend is like sharing a germ—it doesn't spread anything good. Ask your kids for their passwords. Older children may not want to give their passwords to you, citing privacy. (It's up to you whether to accept that.) But for middle schoolers and younger children,

it's fine for you to be able to check their correspondence for inappropriate or dangerous communications.

5. *Set limits on time and use.* For younger kids, keep the computer in a central place. Draw clear boundaries: Whether it's no IM during homework or no e-mail behind closed doors, make rules, preferably before the computer is turned on.

You can also learn about what you can do about the hate your children will be exposed to on the Internet by using the resources provided by the Southern Poverty Law Center in the section of its website entitled Parenting for Tolerance (www.tolerance.org/parents). For example, the center suggests an activity that you can engage in with children over age 13 that includes your reviewing real-life hate sites with them. Here are the steps that are provided:

1. *Prepare your children.* Say something like, "I know that you go online by yourself a lot. We've talked before about the 'bad stuff' that's on the Web. I want you to be prepared, however, in case you ever come across a hate site by accident."
2. *Peruse hate on the Internet with your children.* (The sites to be perused or toured are available on the above website, and they include white supremacy sites.)
3. *Ask your children:* "What symbols or terminology did you see that might serve as warning signs in the future? What might you look for to avoid these kinds of sites in the future?"
4. If your children see information on the hate sites included in the tour that disparages them, your family, or friends, remember to *reassure them*: "Your father and I are not 'errors.' And neither are you. We are a good family, and we are good citizens."[38]

You are further encouraged to bookmark equity and diversity websites on your home computer, and to only have your children use vetted search engines for any online research. In addition, the people from Parenting for Tolerance ask you to ponder the following question: Some organizations that are concerned about hatred advocate banning hate sites, or lobby for the use of filters to keep such information out of the hands of both children and adults.[39] Did you hesitate to take your children on the hate site tour? Why?

TECHNOLOGY, MEDIA, AND FAMILY BONDING

An overriding issue for parents and children regarding computers and the Internet is how these technological advances are influencing the quality of family life. Many are finding themselves so engrossed in cyberspace that they are in virtual cyber-cocoons for hours at a time, are oblivious to what is going on around them, and do not want to be disturbed.

This is, or should be, a concern for everyone involved. It is not just a matter of what is being focused upon while engrossed in such cyber-cocoons, but what such engrossment is doing to the relationships between family members. For many families, it is taking each other away from the opportunity and enjoyment of bonding with each other. Bonding is one of the most critical and important aspects of family life and the basis for becoming a sensitive and compassionate human being.

There is much that you as a parent can do to prevent this from happening in your household. One protective action involves placing computers in public places in the house, rather than having them in your children's rooms. Another set of actions that would be helpful is for you to use computers and the Internet for joint learning and enjoyment purposes with your children.

You and your children can challenge each other to find different types of information and websites quickly. You can play games together on the Internet. You can also teach your children how they can use the Internet to find health information, or community service opportunities or employment, as well as help them to use the Internet for educational purposes, as was mentioned earlier in using the CD *Gateway to Academic Achievement* with your children.

Engaging your children personally in the use of computers and the Internet is one of the best ways to use these marvelous technologies to promote rather than detract from family bonding.

14. Maintain a Healthy Lifestyle

You can't be truly helpful to your children unless you are as healthy as possible. When your body is healthy, when your mind is clear, when your relationships with other people are positive and rewarding, you are able to be as effective a parent as possible. You are also setting a wonderful example for your children by maintaining a healthy lifestyle:

- Eat a balanced and sufficient diet.
- Get enough rest, relaxation, and exercise.
- Have regular medical checkups.
- Take breaks or vacations.
- Get counseling or therapy for personal, marital, or family problems.
- Take prescription medication as directed.
- Find time for yourself.
- Avoid the use of tobacco, alcohol, and other drugs. As has been mentioned so many times already, parental use of any of these substances makes it harder to convince children not to try them. Parental use of recreational mood-changing drugs makes it nearly impossible to give children the type of attention that is needed to keep them safe.

15. NURTURE THE RELATIONSHIP
IN WHICH YOU ARE RAISING YOUR CHILDREN

As we saw in Chapter 2 about the many benefits to children and adults that accompany healthy relationships, it is wise to do everything possible to nurture the relationships in which you are raising your children. This is true whether yours is currently a marriage or a relationship between adults who are not married. It is also true for single-parent families, because single parents often have an intimate relationship with another person who is helping to raise the children.

Regardless of the type of relationship, the goal of nurturing it should be as high as possible on your priority list. Yes, it is often very difficult to give these significant relationships the time and energy they deserve, given the childrearing, work, and other demands that most parents face. But such nurturing must be part of your life, for your own sake and for the sake of your children. High divorce and relationship breakup rates and the damage that is involved truly make it a necessity to nurture these relationships.

Here are a few ideas and suggestions about how to give these relationships the nurturing they deserve.

KEEP ROMANCE ALIVE

One of the most important and difficult things to do with our relationships is to keep the romance alive, especially when children first arrive and are so demanding and tiring. Here are some ideas about how to keep romance as part of your relationship.

> *Flirting and cyberflirting:* Be creative. For example, bet on the outcomes of sporting events, with the winner getting "special favors." Send each other sexy e-mails.
> *Shower power:* Jump in the shower together for shower sex, hugging, or just talking.
> *At-home dating:* Cook together and create a meal you would otherwise go out for, and have a date dinner after the kids go to bed. Put blankets in front of the fireplace, turn out the lights, have some wine and cheese, and get to know yourselves again.
> *Frisky pictures:* Take and e-mail each other suggestive and fun pictures, using your knowledge of what turns on your partner.

Playing hooky for nooky: Take a vacation day during the week and get together while the kids are in child care or school.

Little things count: Go to bed at the same time. Write love notes and poems, and leave them around. Give each other massages.

Organize cultivating your relationship into your schedule: Take date nights twice a month or occasional weekends away, have sex during nap times, and so forth.

MARRIAGE AND RELATIONSHIP ENHANCEMENT CLASSES AND EDUCATION

If it is possible for you to take a vacation without your children, you might want to take one that includes classes and activities in marriage and relationship enrichment. These include mountain and desert retreat vacations and cruises where you can take workshops in the best relationship education programs. These workshops teach emotional reeducation skills to prevent, explore, problem solve, and heal relationship problems, or reawaken relationships that have gone stale. Some focus on helping you become unconditionally present for your partner, and on identifying and dissolving fears about intimacy.

Of course, these types of relationship enhancement workshops can be taken in your own community. To find more about these workshops and vacations, contact:

Coalition for Marriage, Family and Couples Education
5310 Belt Road NW
Washington, DC 20015–1961
(202) 362–3332
cmfce@smartmarriages.com

National Healthy Marriage Resource Center

This extraordinary website, which is a collaborative undertaking of the University of Minnesota, Syracuse University, Texas Tech University, Brigham Young University, Norfolk State University, and the Child Trend research center, came into existence in early 2006. It provides the most extensive array of helpful information for couples who are interested in marriage education services and for those who have chosen marriage for themselves. The educational information contained is, of course, also applicable to gay and lesbian parents who are raising anywhere from 4 to 14 million of America's 85 million children, even though most are currently unable to marry. The information and education is also relevant and helpful for those who are single parents, as they usually are in some form of relationship with other adults that affects their children's development.

The Resource Center website is www.healthymarriageinfo.org. It places a good deal of stress on education for healthy marriages, just as this book stresses education for being an effective parent. By visiting this resource, you will learn how to pick a marriage education program, how to have a healthy marriage, and how to discover the keys to a healthy marriage.

Here are some tips for a healthy marriage, all of which apply to any relationship in which children are being raised:

- Be careful about criticizing your in-laws or your partner's family; most partners will defend their own family even if they agree with the criticism.
- When you have a problem with your partner, look in the mirror first! Look for how you might be contributing to things going poorly.
- It's always easier to change your attitude or behavior than it is to change your partner.
- Try calling "time-out" when an argument starts to get out of control. Take a break and pick up again when you both have had time to calm down.
- Most people crave more appreciation than they receive from their partners. Tell your partner what you like and admire about her or him; these words will go a long way.
- Don't "mind read." When listening to your partner, don't assume that you know the thoughts or feelings behind the words; let him or her tell you.
- Don't try to solve a problem before you understand one another. These premature solutions rarely work.
- Listen to what your partner is saying, even if the way it is said bothers you.
- How you begin a conversation usually determines how it ends. If you need to have a difficult conversation with your partner, start off the conversation by saying something positive.
- Remember that all couples will have problems; it's how you handle them that determines your happiness in your relationship.

- Find 15 minutes a day to give your partner your full attention—turn off the TV, put away the newspaper, and make sure your kids are occupied elsewhere.
- Every couple has a few problems that never go away. Healthy couples learn to accept this fact.
- Learn to see the difference between normal relational problems and truly unacceptable ones, such as violence and abuse.
- Make a big deal of your wedding or relationship anniversary. Treat it like the birthday of your marriage or partnership.

16. Set a Good Example of Life-Long Learning

So much of what you can do for your children depends on the kind of example you set for them. If we want our children to value education, each of us needs to show them in our behavior that we value education, too. Show them that education never stops!

The most obvious place for parents to show a life-long commitment to this value is to seek out and receive education about being the best parents you can be, as has been mentioned throughout this book.

- Take parenting skill-building classes and seminars.
- Join a parent support group.
- Read books and pamphlets about parenting and child development.
- Watch and listen to television and radio programs on child development and parenting.
- Visit parenting and child development websites.

Involving yourselves in this kind of education not only sets a good example, but it also shows your children that they are important enough for you to spend your free time learning how best to raise them.

BUDGET EACH YEAR FOR YOUR CONTINUING EDUCATION FOR PARENTHOOD

Just as you budget for anything else that is valuable to you and your family, you should get in the habit of budgeting for the classes, seminars, and materials that you will be using to learn how to be the best parent possible. I suggest that you put aside at least $150 to $350 a year for these purposes, and that you plan to attend at least one parenting class or seminar each year.

There are numerous parenting programs and materials available to you, the 21st-century parent. Indeed, there have never been so many educational options to help in raising healthy, happy, and successful children. Many more will be shared in subsequent chapters. Do yourself, your children, and your family a great favor, continue to take advantage!

BECOME AS FINANCIALLY LITERATE AS POSSIBLE

It is a great practical idea for your life-long learning to also become as financially literate as possible. The high direct and indirect costs of raising children speak to the need for you to learn as much as possible about how to budget and spend efficiently, as well as how to save and invest wisely. If you don't have basic financial literacy, it will not only be difficult to plan for your children's college education and for your own retirement, it will also be hard for you to be seen by your children as a good financial model and mentor. Indeed, all of the strategies that were recommended under the prior guideline on teaching to be financially successful and giving are best carried out when you have a solid financial education yourself.

You can learn a great deal about nearly every facet of money management from using the books, bulletins, and fact sheets that are available from the Cooperative Research and Extension Program at Rutgers University, the State University of New Jersey (www.rcre.rutgers.edu).

Titles include: *How Much Am I Worth, Twenty-Five Ways to Live on Less, Programming My Dollars: Where Does the Money Go?, Twenty Ways to Save Money, Planning Ahead for the Cost of College, Kinds of Credit, Be Credit Wise, Give Yourself Credit: Twenty-Five Tips for Smarter Borrowing, Where Can I Get Credit?, Retirement Myths and Realities,* and *How Much Do I Need to Save for Retirement?*

Here are some examples of the "Ways to Live on Less" that you will learn through this excellent resource.

- Don't buy insurance you don't need. If you have an adequate emergency fund (3 to 6 months of income), consider increasing deductibles. Also be sure to take advantage of special prices for nonsmokers, good students, and multicar households.
- Get a handle on your spending habits—list all current income and expenses and decide where cuts can be made the least painfully.
- Make and follow a shopping list with prices itemized in advance. Avoid "impulse buying." Don't go to the supermarket unless it is absolutely necessary. Avoid shopping at convenience stores that charge a big markup on products.
- Contact your local utility companies to arrange installation of energy conservation measures. Some companies will send a contractor to your home and you'll be charged only for materials used. Details of each company's program vary. Zero-interest loans may also be available for larger projects.

- Invest in no- or low-cost energy-saving activities, such as an annual tune-up and cleaning of an oil heater (furnace or boiler), an insulation wrap on the water heater, and a cleaning of the outside coils of a refrigerator once or twice a year.
- Cut your children's hair and cut or trim an adult's hair between professional cuttings.
- Consider carefully answers to the questions "What do I really need?" and "What can I do without?"—e.g., new clothes, CDs, book clubs, cable TV, health club memberships.
- Break costly habits such as smoking or buying a lunch or snack out every day. Pack lunches. Use free or low-cost recreation instead of going bowling or to the movies.
- Share a ride with others or take turns carpooling to work, school, and to civic organization meetings and community activities, where possible.
- Pay off high-interest credit card bills and consumer debt and switch to credit cards with lower interest rates and annual fees.

This brings us to the close of these guidelines and their related resources. These are, as has been said, pertinent to any parent in any life situation. Now let's turn to some suggestions, perspectives, and ideas about the parenting of children with special needs. All of us need to become knowledgeable and sensitive. As we discovered earlier, all of us need to be alert to the possibility that our children may have such needs. In addition, all of us and our children will be interacting with children with special needs or with adults who were children with special needs. And many of us have such vulnerable children in our families.

CHAPTER FIVE

Parenting Children with Special Needs

What is a special need? The answer to this question is far from simple, and not far from controversy. Indeed, how children with special needs are defined can evoke very strong feelings and determine who gets help from whom, and has many other practical consequences for the children themselves, their families, and our entire society.[1]

The initial definition to be provided is the one that was mentioned in the guideline in Chapter 4 about enjoying child development and being alert to special needs. Here, that general definition will be amplified, and related information about child development and the causes of special needs will be shared. Then we will move to consider the more specific definitions employed by the health-care professionals who are responsible for assisting children with special needs and their families.

We will move forward to consider various types of children with special needs, why it is important to identify them as early in life as possible, and how to identify and help them. We will also address the matter of managing the behavior of these vulnerable young people.

In our explorations of children with special needs, it is worthwhile to keep in mind that children with special needs are among the most likely to be maltreated by their parents and other caregivers. This is because their behavior is often much more difficult to manage and, therefore, creates special stresses and challenges for their caregivers. In addition, as we have already seen, child maltreatment in its various forms can and often does produce children with special needs and other disabilities. Recall that maltreated children are more likely to become substance abusers and engage in other risky, unhealthy, and costly actions.

As we go about exploring the definitions, issues, facts, and management resources about and for children with special needs, we will find ourselves once again in an area where preventive actions (including early identification and early intervention) can be used to reduce a wide range of human suffering and expense.

WHAT IS A SPECIAL NEED?

All children have an array of needs, especially when they are very young. They all need love, nurturance, and guidance from caring parents and other adults. They need food, drink, shelter, clothing, and protection from a variety of possible harms. They also need stimulation and opportunities to exercise and refine their skills and abilities.

In the most general sense, a child with "special needs" is:

> a child who, because of his or her unique medical, family, birth or developmental difficulties, and/or because of traumatic environmental experiences, has needs in addition to those of his or her peers.[2]

These additional needs are expressed and exemplified as problems, delays, and regressions in the growth and development of their skills and abilities. These skill problems, delays, and regressions can be in one or two or all areas of their development. The six basic areas of child development are herein described, reflecting what types of skills are involved, as well as the relative importance of each area. The descriptions focus on the earliest years of child development.

1. *Body Movement: Physical Development and Motor Skills.* When a child turns over, or pulls him- or herself to a standing position for the first time, we see physical and motor development in action. This area of maturity involves the growth and development of the body and brain and how they interact with one another. Milestones such as reaching, sitting, crawling, walking, running, and jumping are part of a child's mastered skills.
2. *Thinking and Learning: Cognitive Development Skills.* Cognitive development involves the mental and intellectual growth of the child. As with other areas of development, cognitive development occurs in stages. From the very early sensorimotor stage when a baby learns about his or her environment through the senses, to the capacity for abstract thinking found in the formal operational stage of adolescence

and adulthood, children progress through these stages
depending on level of maturity, experience, and other factors
such as interaction with caregivers. Mastery in various tasks
of learning, memory, reasoning, and problem solving are
evidence that a child's cognitive development may be on
target.

3. *Communication: Language Development Skills.* Language
is the means by which we communicate our thoughts,
feelings, needs, and wants with one another. It is our most
human characteristic, essential to all human relationships.
There are many different ways that people use language to
communicate. Speech, gesturing, sign language, and writing
are a few. Technically, language is the code made up of a set of
rules that include what gestures, utterances, or words mean
and how to combine these to express thoughts or desires. The
ability to communicate begins early in a newborn's life and,
like other areas of development, follows predictable patterns.
From early cries to indicate needs, to the development
of babbling, then single words, and ultimately complex
sentences, human beings are designed to communicate with
others.

4. *The Senses: Vision, Hearing, Taste, Touch, and Smell (Including
Sensory Integration).* Infants and young children first learn
about the external and internal world through their senses of
sight, sound, touch, taste, and smell, as sensory information
is transmitted to the brain. Sensory integration involves the
ability to take in the information gathered through the senses
from the internal and external world and put it together in a
meaningful way. The complex interplay between the various
senses is necessary as the child learns about, acts, and responds
to the environment in appropriate ways. For example, a
baby's sense of sight will help him reach out for a rattle on
the table. A sense of touch will enable him to feel for and grab
the rattle and to determine how much pressure to exert to
hold and shake the rattle. A sense of hearing will allow him
to distinguish the sound made by the shaking rattle. As all of
this sensory information is processed, the child learns how to
interpret and respond to various environmental cues.

5. *Relating to Self and Others: Social Development Skills and
Emotional Development Skills.* Human beings need relationships
in order to survive and grow. A baby's first relationship is
with his or her primary caregiver, most often the mother. It

is in the context of this environment that an infant's social and emotional development occurs. In a good relationship, the primary caregiver and the baby learn to respond to one another. The infant coos. The mother coos back. The baby smiles. The mother smiles and talks to her child in response. The baby giggles in delight. They hold each other's gaze in a playful exchange of mutual pleasure. As the child matures, the exchanges become more sophisticated. The child imitates the mother as she talks on the phone and offers hugs of affection. With the help of the mother's focused response, the young child begins to put her emotions to words. A tightness in the tummy is understood as feeling scared. Laughter becomes associated with feeling happy. What were once only known and felt as bodily sensations, now become understandable as feelings. This is the development of *affect*.

6.   *Self-Care and Daily Living Skills: Adaptive Development.* Adaptive development refers to the ability of a developing child to care for him- or herself in age-appropriate ways. Mastered skills progress in the area of feeding, for example, from feeding oneself by scooping up food, to using two fingers pinched together, and later to using a spoon or a fork. Later the child acquires more sophisticated self-care skills, such as teeth-brushing or being able to prepare simple snacks.

Within each of these areas, the average child develops her or his basic skills—that is, achieves developmental milestones—at about the same general time (or within the same general time range). For example, research on developmental milestones indicate that around the end of the 7th month, an infant should be able to roll from front to back and from back to front (motor development), use sounds to show pleasure and displeasure (language development), find an object that is partially hidden (cognitive development), and enjoy social play (social and emotional development).[3] Achieving milestones at generally the same time as peers is what is considered to be normative development.

Normative development is also characterized by skills developing in sequences or stages. In normative development, simple skills or components of skills usually develop before more complex ones; for example, a child usually crawls before walking. Also, it is not unusual for many children's skills to be more advanced in one area of development than in another. In addition, some skills develop in growth spurts, with little progress happening for a while, followed by quick substantial progress. It is also fairly normative that skills may be demonstrated inconsistently while a child is still mastering them. Thus, arriving at the time or time span when the average child should achieve mastery of various skills is a very complex and difficult undertaking.

With these variations in mind, a child may be considered to possess a special need when several of his or her skills in a particular area of development or across areas are considerably delayed. A child may also be considered to have special needs when the child regresses back to using skills or skill components from an earlier time, such as when a child stops expressing her feelings in words and only communicates with gestures and facial expressions. A child could also be considered to have special needs when there is a problem in exercising a particular skill, like only hearing the last part of a word or reversing the sounds of a word. A special need is also likely to exist when a child continuously uses skills in a manner that is not appropriate for the child's age, such as when a 10-year-old continually expresses frustration and anger through falling on the floor, kicking, stamping, and having a major tantrum. Such demonstrations would be more age-appropriate expression for a 2-year-old, but not for a child of 10. A child lacking a basic skill would also be considered to have a special need, like not being able to hear or see.

As these examples indicate, these delays, regressions, and problems can range from mild to moderate to severe. The severe types are usually very obvious, while the mild ones are often not obvious and are thus difficult to detect. Also some are available and detectable at birth, whereas others emerge later in the lives of young children. And some special needs are life-long, while some are temporary.

These variations often have to do with the causes of a child's special needs. As the general definition reflected, there are a variety of causes. Some children are born with special needs due to a genetic inheritance or birth complications. Others develop special needs because of what they are fed or not fed, or how they are treated or not treated by their parents and other caregivers.

The following is a list of those child and environmental factors that are used to determine whether a young child is eligible for certain kinds of early intervention programs, for children who either have special needs or who are at high risk for developing special needs. In reviewing this list, the varied nature of what causes, contributes to, and characterizes children with special needs will become more evident.

> Was born significantly premature (born more than 8 weeks early)
> Had a very low birth weight (weight at birth less than 3 pounds, or 1500 grams)
> Used a breathing tube for more than 2 days within the first month of life
> Had or has failure to thrive (severe weight loss or significant lack of weight gain and growth)
> Has been previously admitted to a Neonatal Intensive Care Unit
> Has had seizures (not due to a fever)
> Has had a brain injury, anomaly, or infection
> Has had a serious injury, accident, or illness which may affect development
> Has a genetic disorder or syndrome (such as Down Syndrome)
> Has a severe hearing, visual, or orthopedic problem
> Has been diagnosed with an ongoing and serious medical condition (such as a heart valve disorder)
> Had prenatal exposure to drugs, alcohol, medications, or toxic chemicals known to affect an unborn baby
> Is unusually stiff or unusually floppy (like a rag doll)
> Was previously, or is currently being, served by a program for children with special needs
> Has a parent who is developmentally disabled
> Has been the victim of child abuse and/or neglect[4]

Other conditions that are known to increase the chances of a child having or developing special needs include: major life changes, natural or man-made disasters, violent neighborhoods, poverty, home language environment, and culture.

Major Life Changes

Even the healthiest and most advanced children can develop temporary special needs when there are major changes in their lives. These major changes can include the death of a parent, sibling, other family member, or even an adored pet; the serious illness of a loved one; violence between parents or between a parent and a boyfriend or girlfriend; or the separation or divorce of parents or those serving in the parent role.

Children who experience these major life changes can regress and behave as much younger children. They can develop new behaviors or emotional difficulties in trying to cope with these traumatic experiences.

Natural or Man-Made Disasters

Earthquakes, floods, tornados, hurricanes, and terrorist attacks can also cause children to develop temporary special needs and special coping mechanisms.

Violent Neighborhoods

Some children grow up in neighborhoods where violence is rampant and where they fear for their lives on a daily basis. These conditions can also cause regressions and can produce behavioral and emotional difficulties.

Poverty

Growing up in poverty often means being deprived of many basic life necessities, like adequate food, clothing and shelter, adequate health care, and physical surroundings that are safe to explore and enjoy. Growing up poor is also often associated with being exposed to more violence and more frequent major life changes.

All of these environmental deficiencies and hazards serve to place poor children as a group at greater risk for all sorts of problems, and for not developing their skills as fully or as quickly as their more advantaged peers.

Home Language Environment

The development of language skills requires having a stimulating language environment at home. Without regular opportunities to hear and speak, a child's receptive and expressive language skills may not develop as quickly or as fully as they do in a home where parents and children converse regularly. In these enriched language environments, parents and other caregivers expand on what children say, thereby stimulating their children to learn a larger vocabulary and to gain a fuller appreciation of the value of language usage.

Many children grow up in homes where more than one language is spoken. These can be very rich language environments and can lead to children mastering many useful and beautiful languages. In the early years, however, the need to master more than one language can result in lags or delays in learning a specific language. This becomes particularly evident when the primary language spoken at home is different than the language spoken in the neighborhood or in the child-care center, preschool, or kindergarten. Children from these circumstances are more likely to be seen as "delayed" in the development of the language that is spoken outside of the home.

Culture

Closely related to considerations about language are those about culture, as many cultural groups speak languages other than English. Culture-influenced parenting values and behavior can affect how quickly children develop their skills in various areas of development. For example, a value about the importance of nurturing and keeping young children close to their mothers can result in such parenting behaviors as feeding and dressing a child well into his or her earlier years, well beyond the time that other groups foster such dependency. A child being brought up this way is not likely to develop certain self-help skills as quickly as children who are brought up in homes where early independence is stressed. This means that cultural practices, values, and attitudes are important considerations regarding when children from different cultural groups master certain skills.

PROFESSIONAL DEFINITIONS

Professionals such as medical doctors and psychologists who are responsible for helping children with special needs and their families tend to use two kinds of definitions of children with special needs. One is the functional development definition, which is based primarily on the current status of a child's skills in all areas of development, compared with the norms for a child of that age. The other definition is based on categorizing the child's overall pattern of behavior and skills as a specific clinical diagnostic category or diagnosis. The use of these approaches and definitions often has different practical consequences, and their use tends to generate certain controversies because of their social implications.

Functional Development Definition

The advantage of using a functional developmental approach to defining children with special needs, and to evaluating and treating them, is that it is consistent with the reality that every child is a unique individual with specific strengths and weaknesses. No two children are alike, even children with specific known disorders. For example, Adam and Katherine, both 4 years old, have been diagnosed with an Autistic Spectrum Disorder. Adam has now developed age-appropriate verbal skills, but he has trouble holding a crayon and copying shapes. He falls often when he plays. Katherine is mostly nonverbal, yet she has no trouble running around the playground and she loves to draw pictures. She can copy almost any design with apparent ease.

Defining these children on the basis of exactly what they currently can and cannot do and basing intervention on their functional development would take their individual differences into consideration, rather than simply providing the same generic treatments for both of these children with an Autistic Spectrum Disorder. The team of professionals who are assigned to help Katherine would create an individualized treatment plan for her that emphasizes the development of language. Adam's treatment, on the other hand, would focus more on his fine and gross motor skills. Each child's areas of strengths can be enhanced and each child's unique difficulties and challenges can be addressed with specific treatments and services.

Another advantage of defining and evaluating children with special needs in this manner is that it leaves room for improvement in all areas of functional development. A diagnosis is often viewed as a permanent condition with little change expected. Yet children grow and change, even children with special needs. With the appropriate individualized services, Katherine can improve her language skills and learn to communicate more effectively with the world. Adam can strengthen his motor skills so he can learn to write legibly and move about freely on the playground, thus enhancing his success in school.

Seeing the unique functioning of each child helps parents and professionals tailor a program to help get the child's development back on track. In doing so, each child has the opportunity to reach his or her full potential through a specially tailored program. In many cases, a child may even outgrow the condition or problem that led to his or her being identified as a special needs child.

Stephanie's story describes a child with special needs who was helped by professionals using this functional developmental approach.

Stephanie is a beautiful, 2½-year-old child with wide brown eyes and rich chestnut hair that brushes her shoulders with gentle curls. The friends and family who know her think she should be a child model because she naturally embodies that irresistible charm and innocence that makes people break into a spontaneous smile of delight and want to pick her up and hold her. Despite her natural beauty, however, Stephanie is a child with special needs.

Stephanie was slower than average to achieve various developmental milestones, such as turning over, crawling, and walking. She still walks with an awkward gait and falls often. She has a difficult time holding a crayon and frequently drops things. Stephanie began speaking later than most children her age. Because of the difficulty she had expressing herself, she had frequent and intense temper tantrums and fits of rage. And when all attempts at communication failed, she retreated into a world of her own. Now, at the age of 2½, she has a vocabulary of 50–100 words but she still doesn't speak in three-word sentences, as is typical for children her age. Her father, a lawyer, and her mother, a schoolteacher, are both very concerned about some of the unusual behaviors they notice in her, but they have reassured themselves by saying that each child develops at a different pace. They want the best for their daughter, and they have tried to accept Stephanie's unique way of being in the world.

Stephanie's introduction to preschool was a challenge because of the requirements to interact with peers, follow instructions, and focus in a group setting. She was fortunate to have a teacher who accepted her and recognized her need to be tested. Although Stephanie was never given a specific diagnosis, a local psychologist determined that she had developmental delays in language and motor development. She was given an Individual Family Service Plan (IFSP) by the early intervention program in her community, complete with services to help her reach her potential. She improved rapidly and was able to enter school with only minor special assistance.[5]

Clinical Diagnostic Definitions

Another way to determine whether a child has a special need is to see if the child may be identified by a specific diagnosis. Although this is no longer the primary way that professionals define children with special needs, providing a diagnosis is often helpful. To paraphrase the Webster dictionary definition, a diagnosis is the art or act of identifying a condition, disorder, or disease from its signs and symptoms. When a qualified professional diagnoses a child, he or she looks at the signs or symptoms that the child displays, such as various behaviors, ways of communicating, or thoughts that a child may have.

Each child is a unique individual; therefore, no two children will have the exact same signs or symptoms. However, according to various diagnostic criteria, such as the DSM-IV-TR (*Diagnostic and Statistical Manual of Mental Disorders*) or the ICD-9 (*International Classification of Diseases*, 9th edition), certain symptoms may be grouped together in a cluster.[6] When a child has a certain number of these symptoms, he or she can be considered to have a particular diagnosis.

For some parents who have worked for months and even years to understand their child's unique difficulties, a diagnosis may come as a welcome relief. Finally, the pieces fit together and make sense. Their child isn't bad or defiant. He or she is a child with unique medical, behavioral, or neurobiological difficulties. For other parents, a label may create feelings of fear of a permanently disabling condition from which their child will never emerge. It is important to remember that diagnoses are useful because they serve to describe a group of symptoms or behaviors, yet every individual is unique and won't fit perfectly in a box, nor should we attempt to make them fit. Individuals grow and change, including children who have been given a specific diagnosis. A diagnosis doesn't define the ultimate potential of any given child.

Why Diagnose, Then?

There are understandable reasons why a parent or caregiver may be hesitant to have a child receive a diagnosis, and these reasons can make the use of the clinical diagnostic definition controversial. One reason is that a diagnosis can label children. If those who love and work with the child see the diagnosis as a restriction resulting in the child's not growing to his or her full potential, the diagnosis may be a disservice. In addition, if the child and those in his or her world see the diagnosis as a problem with little or no opportunity for growth or change, this can hurt the child's self-esteem. Nobody wants to be seen as a problem; we all want to be seen as human beings and individuals who have potential.

Yet there are many benefits that a diagnosis can provide. It can be helpful to make sense of previously unexplainable behavior. For example, Miguel is concerned about his son Antonio's lack of verbal language and the problems it is creating in his studies at school. Through the help of a psychologist who specializes in communication, Miguel recently was informed that his son had been diagnosed with Expressive Language Disorder. Miguel finds this diagnosis a relief. He knows that his son has had communication problems, and now he knows what he is dealing with and can move more effectively to get Antonio the help he needs.[7]

A diagnosis can also give parents, medical personnel, and others a common language to understand a child's particular difficulties. In addition, most diagnosable conditions have been studied extensively, and everyone has access to records of the different ways people have been treated for the particular condition. As a result, everyone can draw from what has worked and stay away from what hasn't.

Perhaps most importantly, a diagnosis may be essential for obtaining the services needed for the child. Some agencies and programs will not admit a child for treatment unless the child has a specific diagnosis. However, it is important to be aware that in many circumstances, it is not required that a child have a specific diagnosis in order to receive services. A delay in one or more areas of functional development, and not a diagnosis, may be all that is needed to obtain services.

There are various ways by which a child can receive a diagnosis. Only a trained and qualified professional can make a formal diagnosis. These professionals often consult books and references that are standard to the medical and mental health fields, such as the classification manuals mentioned previously. Miran's story provides a description of a child who was helped by professionals using the clinical diagnostic approach.

Miran is an energetic toddler with an infectious smile and skin the color of the shell of a coconut. He was a much-wanted baby, the fourth child and only son of a couple who immigrated to America to start a new life with their young family. Miran's father, Saresh, a solidly built man, suddenly softens when he talks about his son. He tells the story as if it happened yesterday.

"We were all in the delivery room so excited about Miran's birth. Everyone was congratulating my wife and me. We were so happy to finally have a son. Suddenly, my wife's doctor and the nurses became really quiet and the doctor told us that she thought that there might be a problem with Miran. She said that he might have a genetic condition called Down Syndrome. She showed us some of the features on his face and hands that children with Down Syndrome usually have. They called in another doctor to look at him and they ran some tests. Waiting for the results of the test felt like forever.

"Later the doctor told us that the tests showed that Miran did have Down Syndrome and that kids who have it usually have mental retardation. After he told us that, we really did not hear the rest he had to say that day. We were shocked. We didn't think it was possible because we have three other healthy children. We had lots of questions and didn't know what we would do with a child like him." He smiled at Miran and rubbed his son's hair with his hand. "Now we think he is the greatest."[8]

Because of Miran's specific diagnosis, he was referred to a local center for children with developmental difficulties to receive services. Miran's parents learned that even though Down Syndrome can't be cured, getting help as early as possible for Miran could help him to be the best he can be. Today, Miran is a happy toddler surrounded by his doting sisters and parents and is enrolled in an early intervention program that will help him reach his full potential.

There is a broader issue regarding the use of the clinical diagnostic definition of children with special needs that deserves some discussion before we move on. By using or requiring a diagnosis, a child is clearly labeled as having a disability. Being so labeled puts that child and others like him or her in the category of people for whom health and special education laws can be written that enable them to receive government-supported or tax-based services. It is easier to justify the use of tax funds for people with disabilities than for people with special needs. Indeed, there are advantages to referring to special needs children as children with disabilities. Some groups and states have now begun to use both terms to designate these children, referring to them as "children with disabilities and other special needs." Such a dual designation preserves both the legislative advantages of the disability term, and the more humanistic benefits of special needs terminology.

TYPES OF CHILDHOOD DISABILITIES
AND OTHER SPECIAL NEEDS

There are 14 types of childhood disorders and other special needs that are recognized in the Individuals with Disabilities Act (IDEA).[9] Here each type is briefly defined, and the areas of a child's development that are most affected are noted.

Autistic Spectrum Disorder (language and social and emotional development). Autism is a neurologically based disorder that is usually evident by age 3 and varies from low to high functioning. It affects a child's ability to communicate, understand language, play, and relate to others.

AD/HD (multiple areas of development). AD/HD is a neurobiological disorder that causes developmentally inappropriate levels of inattention, hyperactivity, and impulsivity.

Blindness and Visual Impairments (sensory development). This category includes partially sighted, low vision, legally blind, and totally blind children.

Cerebral Palsy (motor development). The condition is caused by injury to the parts of the brain that control the ability to use muscles. *Cerebral* means "having to do with the brain". *Palsy* means "weakness" or problems with using muscles.

Deafness and Hearing Loss (sensory development). Hearing loss is an impairment in hearing, whether it is permanent or fluctuating. Deafness is a condition that prevents a child from receiving sound in all or most of its forms.

Down Syndrome (multiple areas of development). Down Syndrome is the most common and readily identifiable chromosomal and genetic condition associated with mental retardation. A Down Syndrome child usually experiences developmental delays and often has concurrent conditions, including mental retardation, a small mouth, and short height.

Emotional Disturbance (social and emotional development). The term *emotional disturbance* is used to describe children with emotional, behavioral, or mental disorders, such as depression and unsocialized aggression problems.

Epilepsy (multiple areas of development). Epilepsy is a physical condition that occurs when there is a sudden, brief change in how the brain works that affects a person's consciousness, movement, or actions. These physical changes are called "epileptic seizures."

Learning Disability (cognitive and language development). This general term describes specific kinds of learning problems. The skills most often affected are reading, writing, listening, speaking, reasoning, and math.

Mental Retardation (multiple areas of development). This term is used when a child has limitations in mental functioning and in skills such as communicating, taking care of him- or herself, and social skills.

Speech and Language Impairment (language and social and emotional development). Speech and language disorders are problems in communication and related areas, such as oral motor function. Communication problems that have to do with speech disorders include not speaking at all, speaking at a later time in life than peers, substituting sounds, or having difficulties with the coordination of the tongue, lips, and mouth to perform certain sounds.

Spina Bifida (motor development). Spina Bifida means "cleft spine," which is an incomplete closure in the spinal column that causes muscle weakness or paralysis.

Traumatic Brain Injury (multiple areas of development). A traumatic brain injury is an injury to the brain that affects how the child acts, moves, thinks, and learns.

Severe and/or Multiple Disabilities (multiple areas of development). Children with severe disabilities are those who traditionally have profound mental retardation as well as additional disabilities, including movement difficulties, sensory losses, and behavior problems.

AUTISTIC SPECTRUM DISORDERS (ASDs)

As the name "Autistic Spectrum Disorder" suggests, ASDs cover a wide range of behaviors and abilities. Children who have ASDs differ greatly in the way they act and what they can do, as we learned in the stories about Adam and Katherine. No two children with ASDs will have the same symptoms. A symptom might be mild in one child and severe in another. Some examples of the types of problems and behaviors that characterize children with an ASD follow.

Social Skills

Children with ASDs might not interact with others the way most children do, or they might not be interested in other people at all. A child with an ASD might not make eye contact and might just want to be alone. The child might have trouble understanding other people's feelings or talking about his own feelings. Children with ASDs might not like to be held or cuddled, or they might cuddle only when they want to. Some children with ASDs might not seem to notice when other people try to talk to them. Others might be very interested in people, but may not know how to talk, play, or relate to others.

Speech, Language, and Communication

About 40% of children with ASDs do not talk at all.[10] Others have echolalia, which is when they repeat back something that was said to them. The repeated words might be said right away or at a later time. For example, if you ask a child with echolalia, "Do you want some juice?" he or she will repeat, "Do you want some juice?" instead of answering your question. Or the child might repeat a television ad that he heard sometime in the past. Children with ASDs might not understand gestures such as waving good-bye. They might say "I" when they mean "you," or vice versa. Their voices might sound flat and it may seem like they cannot control how loudly or softly they talk. Children with ASDs might stand too close to the people they are talking to, or they might stick with one topic of conversation for too long. Some children with ASDs can speak well and know a lot of words, but have a hard time listening to what other people say. They might talk a lot about something they really like, rather than have a back-and-forth conversation with someone.

Repeated Behaviors and Routines

Children with ASDs might repeat actions over and over again. They might want to have routines where things stay the same so they know what to expect. They might have trouble if family routines change. For example, if a child is used to washing his or her face before dressing for bed, he or she might become very upset if asked to change the order and dress first and then wash.

Children with ASDs develop differently from other children. Children without ASDs develop at about the same rate in areas of development such as motor, language, cognitive, and social skills. Children with ASDs develop at very different rates in different areas of growth. They might have large delays in language, social, and cognitive skills, while their motor skills might be about the same as those of other children their age. They might be very good at things such as putting puzzles together or solving computer problems, but not very good at some things that most people think are easy, such as talking or making friends. Children with ASDs might also learn a hard skill before they learn an easy one. For example, a child might be able to read long words, but not be able to tell you what sound the letter "b" makes. A child might also learn a skill and then lose it. For example, a child may be able to say many words, but later stop talking altogether.

The causes of autism are unknown. Currently, researchers are investigating areas such as brain development and structure, genetic factors, and biochemical imbalance in the brain as possible causes. It is generally believed that these disorders are not caused by psychological factors. According to the Centers for Disease Control and Prevention (CDC), as many as 500,000 American children are diagnosed as having ASDs.[11]

ATTENTION-DEFICIT/HYPERACTIVITY DISORDERS (AD/HD)

AD/HD is a condition that can make it hard for a child to sit still, control behavior, and pay attention. These difficulties usually begin before the child is 7 years old.[12] However, these behaviors may not be noticed until the child is older.

Doctors do not know just what causes AD/HD. However, researchers who study the brain are coming closer to understanding what may cause the disorder. They believe that some children with AD/HD do not have enough of certain chemicals (called "neurotransmitters") in their brain. These chemicals help the brain control behavior. Parents do not cause AD/HD.

As many as 5 out of every 100 children in school may have AD/HD. Boys are three times more likely than girls to have AD/HD. There are three main signs, or symptoms, of AD/HD.[13] These are:

- problems with paying attention
- being very active (called "hyperactivity")
- acting before thinking (called "impulsivity")[14]

More information about these symptoms is listed in the *Diagnostic and Statistical Manual of Mental Disorders* (DSM) of the American Psychiatric Association. Based on these symptoms, three types of AD/HD have been found:

- Inattentive type, where the child can't seem to get focused or stay focused on a task or activity
- Hyperactive-impulsive type, where the child is very active and often acts without thinking
- Combined type, where the child is inattentive, impulsive, and too active[15]

Inattentive Type

Many children with AD/HD have problems paying attention. Children with the inattentive type of AD/HD often display the following signs:

- They do not pay close attention to details.
- They can't stay focused on play or school work.
- They don't follow through on instructions or finish school work or chores.
- They can't seem to organize tasks and activities.
- They get distracted easily.
- They lose things, such as toys, school work, and books.[16]

Hyperactive-Impulsive Type

Being too active is probably the most visible sign of AD/HD. The hyperactive child is "always on the go." (As he or she gets older, the level of activity may go down.) These children also act before thinking (called "impulsivity"). For example, they may run across the road without looking or climb to the top of very tall trees. They may be surprised to find themselves in a dangerous situation. They may have no idea of how to get out of the situation.

Hyperactivity and impulsivity tend to go together. Children with the hyperactive-impulsive type of AD/HD often may:

- fidget and squirm
- get out of their chairs when they're not supposed to
- run around or climb constantly
- have trouble playing quietly
- talk too much
- blurt out answers before questions have been completed
- have trouble waiting their turn
- interrupt others when they're talking
- butt in on the games others are playing[17]

Combined Type

Children with the combined type of AD/HD have symptoms of both of the types described above. They have problems with paying attention, with hyperactivity, and with controlling their impulses.

Of course, from time to time, all children are inattentive, impulsive, and too active. With children who have AD/HD, these behaviors are the rule, not the exception.

These behaviors can cause a child to have real problems at home, at school, and with friends. As a result, many children with AD/HD will feel anxious, unsure of themselves, and depressed. These feelings are not symptoms of AD/HD. They come from having problems again and again at home and in school.

LEARNING DISABILITIES

Learning Disability (LD) is a general term that describes specific kinds of learning problems. A learning disability can cause a person to have trouble learning and using certain skills. As previously indicated, the skills most often affected are reading, writing, listening, speaking, reasoning, and doing math.

Learning disabilities vary from child to child. For example, one child with LD may have trouble with reading and writing, while another with LD may have problems with understanding math. Still another may have trouble in each of these areas, and also with understanding what people are saying.

Researchers think that learning disabilities are caused by differences in how a person's brain works and how it processes information.[18] Children with learning disabilities are not "dumb" or "lazy." In fact, they usually have average or above-average intelligence. Their brains just process information differently.

The definition of "learning disability" from the Individuals with Disabilities Education Act (IDEA) is

> a disorder in one or more of the basic psychological processes involved in understanding or in using language, spoken or written, that may manifest itself in an imperfect ability to listen, think, speak, read, write, spell, or do mathematical calculations, including conditions such as perceptual disabilities, brain injury, minimal brain dysfunction, dyslexia, and developmental aphasia.

However, learning disabilities do not include, "learning problems that are primarily the result of visual, hearing, or motor disabilities, of mental retardation, of emotional disturbance, or of environmental, cultural, or economic disadvantage."[19]

There is no one sign that indicates a child has a learning disability. Experts look for a noticeable difference between how well a child does in school and how well he or she could do, given his or her intelligence or ability. There are also certain clues that may mean a child has a learning disability. Several are listed below. Most relate to elementary school tasks, because learning disabilities tend to be identified in elementary school. A child probably won't show all of these signs, or even most of them. However, if a child shows a number of these problems, then parents should consider the possibility that the child has a learning disability.

When a child has a learning disability, he or she:

- may have trouble learning the alphabet, rhyming words, or connecting letters to their sounds
- may make many mistakes when reading aloud, and repeat and pause often
- may not understand what he or she reads
- may have real trouble with spelling
- may have very messy handwriting or hold a pencil awkwardly
- may struggle to express ideas in writing
- may learn language late and have a limited vocabulary
- may have trouble remembering the sounds that letters make or hearing slight differences between words
- may have trouble understanding jokes, comic strips, and sarcasm
- may have trouble following directions
- may mispronounce words or use a wrong word that sounds similar

- may have trouble organizing what he or she wants to say or not be able to think of the word he or she needs for writing or conversation
- may not follow the social rules of conversation, such as taking turns, and may stand too close to the listener
- may confuse math symbols and misread numbers
- may not be able to retell a story in order (what happened first, second, third)
- may not know where to begin a task or how to go on from there

As many as one out of every five people in the United States has a learning disability. Almost 3 million children (ages 6 through 21) have some form of a learning disability.[20] There is no "cure" for learning disabilities. They are life-long problems. However, children with LD can be high achievers and can be taught ways to work around their learning disability. With the right help, children with LD can and do learn successfully.

IMPORTANCE OF
EARLY IDENTIFICATION AND EARLY INTERVENTION

There is abundant evidence that when vulnerable children are found and helped through high-quality early intervention programs that provide them and their families with the needed remedial and educational services, they are much more likely to lead healthier and more productive lives. When helped in these ways, children with LD have a greater chance at graduating from high school, holding jobs, and living independently. They are also less likely to become teenage parents or to cause teen pregnancies, and are less likely to engage in delinquent acts or commit crimes.

When economists study the cost-benefit prospects of providing early intervention programs to children with special needs and their families, they find an enormous long-term advantage. First, they calculate the cost or expense of providing a high-quality early intervention program with its multiple services. This program expense is subsequently subtracted from the money that can reasonably be estimated to be saved by not having to provide as many remedial education, mental health, and legal services throughout the remainder of the children's childhoods; and from the money that can reasonably be estimated to be saved by not having to provide these children with housing or institutional care as adults because they will be able to work and live independently. After determining how much money would be saved, the economists then estimate how much that now-independent working adult is likely to pay in income taxes. Then they add up the savings to be gained and the taxes to be paid, and subtract from that figure the expense of the early intervention program. The result of these analyses and calculations has been to show an estimated overall savings that ranges from $30,000 to $100,000 per child with special needs.[21]

Now, for a child with special needs to be helped through early intervention, that child must first be identified early in life. Unfortunately, only about 30% of children with special needs under age 5 are currently being identified before they enter school.[22] There are many reasons for this under-detection, including the fact that it is very hard to detect certain kinds of special needs early in life, and that some types of special needs do not become evident until after the preschool years. Also, parents have not been educated to be vigilant in helping to identify special needs children, and, until the advent of online methods such as *The Discovery Tool*, it has not been easy for parents to participate in this detection process.

If, however, all parents and all other child-caring persons were involved, and if all such vulnerable children were found and helped before entering school, we could estimate what the overall monetary savings would be to our society. This can be done by multiplying the number of special needs children under age 5 who are not being detected before entering school by the savings per child if they were found and helped. If we use the low end of the estimate of the number of children under 5 who have special needs (the 12% estimate, which turns out to be 2.3 million children) and multiply that by the low estimate of the cost savings per child ($30,000), we learn that we could be saving $48.3 billion!

That's quite a benefit. And that monetary benefit does not even speak to the reduction in suffering and heartbreak that occurs when special needs children and their families are creatively assisted. Without these types of early and effective responses, these children are much more likely to remain problems for everyone concerned and to feel like they are major burdens. Parents are likely to be stretched to the brink of abuse and feel inadequate and guilty. More marriages are likely to end in separation and divorce. But with these early and creative responses, these types of suffering are considerably lessened.

Together with the monetary benefits, we truly have an achievement of which we can all be proud.

Let's strive toward that achievement. Here again, as with our child maltreatment problem, we can do better. And we can be better off for doing so.

The challenge is to first to find those children under 5 years of age who are most likely to have special needs, or who already do have such needs. This is a matter of developmental screening. Then they must have a comprehensive developmental assessment, where a team of professionals checks out all areas of their development to determine whether they do indeed have special needs that require professional assistance, and, if so, what is the best type of assistance for that child and family.

Developmental Screening

During the second half of the 20th century, whatever screening that was done of young children for special needs usually involved bringing a child to a clinic, hospital, or doctor's office. There, a nurse or other health professional met with the parents and child before the child saw the doctor, who, in many instances, was a pediatrician. The nurse interviewed the parents and the child, and asked the parents about the child's abilities in different areas of growth. Often, the nurse used a screening questionnaire that indicated which abilities most children of a certain age have mastered and which therefore allowed for a comparison of the child's current abilities with those of the norms for his age group. The nurse then scored the questionnaire, noting whether the child had delays or problems in any areas, and then relayed the findings and her or his observations about the child and the family to the doctor. Based on what was relayed, the doctor was thereby alerted to examine the child more carefully in certain areas.

Toward the end of the 20th century, methods were created where parents themselves could complete a screening questionnaire about a child's background and capabilities before seeing the doctor. The nurse would score the questionnaire and relay the results to the doctor. Then, if the questionnaire indicated the possibility of any type of special need, it could be used to justify the beginning of a developmental assessment. Also at that time in history, government and community Child Find agencies and organizations were coming into existence. (The main purpose of these groups is to provide guidelines and direct assistance in finding or identifying these children early in life.) Their mission included the screening of children for special needs.

Today, many clinics, hospitals, and doctors that are supported by government health-care funding are required to conduct developmental screenings on the children under their care, which they can do by having nurses or parents complete screening questionnaires. However, fiscal pressures and time constraints often make it such that these screenings are not conducted even though they are mandated. For private health centers and hospitals and private doctors, the developmental screening of children is considered a best practice but is not legally required. The result is that only some children in some facilities with some doctors are screened routinely for special needs.

However, it is now possible for parents to play a more proactive role in the screening stage of the early identification process, and to do so without having to leave their homes. This is now possible because of such online methodologies as *The Discovery Tool*.[23] As you know from our earlier discussions of this Tool, and from the sample in the Appendix of this book, the Tool consists of age-geared questionnaires about a child's skills and behaviors in various areas of development, and a questionnaire about the child's background. Parents answer the questions online and then the Tool is automatically scored. The results are provided in the form of a report that can be printed out and that lists any potential skill delays, behavior problems, and risk factor experiences.

The report alerts a parent to whether the number of delays, problems, and risk experiences mentioned are numerous enough to suggest that the child may have special needs. If there are enough signs to indicate this possibility, the report urges the parent to seek out pediatricians, psychologists, or other appropriate professionals to have the child assessed developmentally. The online report is accompanied by information about how to find such professionals (Professionals, Agencies and Websites That Can Help).

The Discovery Tool also mentions the possibility that special needs may not be apparent right now but could emerge in the near future, thereby suggesting that the parent also use the Tool more than just one time. The use of the online *Discovery Tool*, which covers the first 5 years of a child's development, costs $7.95 to take one time for a particular child, and $14.95 to use an unlimited number of times for one year for the same child.[24]

Another online methodology allows for the screening of children up to 8 years of age for developmental and behavior problems (www.

forepath.org). It is called Parents' Evaluation of Developmental Status (PEDS), and it works by having parents type in the concerns they may have about their child in the different areas of development. The PEDS then automatically considers whether such concerns could be suggestive of a child with special needs. It also provides a report that can be printed out and that tells parents how to use this information with health professionals. PEDS costs $9.95 to take one time for a particular child.[25]

It is very important that parents take advantage of these self-administered screening opportunities, because, as has been mentioned, just taking a child to a doctor, clinic, or hospital does not guarantee that the child will be screened for developmental and behavioral problems. When parents arrive with the results of *The Discovery Tool* or PEDS in hand, it alerts the health-care personnel that there is good reason to check this child for special needs. It also alerts them that they are dealing with parents who have already begun the early identification work themselves. This thoughtful and educated act on the part of parents is an excellent example of being an advocate for your children.

Developmental Assessment

It may require some assertive advocacy by parents to have the second stage of the early identification process carried out, the actual developmental assessment of a child by appropriate professionals. This includes learning about what a comprehensive developmental assessment consists of, as well as learning what your options are.

A developmental assessment is a comprehensive examination of a child's skills, behaviors, and family situation, conducted by a highly trained professional such as a licensed psychologist. This in-person examination usually includes testing the child using a variety of professional instruments such as language, intelligence, and social adaptation tests, and careful interviewing of the child's family members. The best types of developmental assessments also include observations of children in natural settings like the home, school, and the playground, as well as examinations conducted by a team of experts, including psychologists, pediatricians, and neurologists. These comprehensive developmental assessments should conclude with detailed treatment plans on how best to help the child and family, with clear objectives and time lines for accomplishing the needed help. These are often referred to as Individual Family Service Plans (IFSPs).

Any parent who suspects that his or her infant or child has special needs can seek out qualified psychologists in the area to conduct a developmental assessment. Such psychologists can be found through contacting the American Psychological Association Information Service at (800) 964–2000, or by directly contacting your state psychological association. Explain that you are looking for a qualified psychologist to do a developmental assessment on your child, and indicate your child's age and why you want the assessment to be done.

If your child is under 3 years of age and eligible for services from your area's government-supported early intervention program for children with special needs, a developmental assessment can be done by that program. The eligibility criteria for those programs are the criteria listed earlier in this chapter, including having a child born significantly premature or low birth weight, and so forth. You can find the infant/toddler early intervention program closest to your home by contacting your state coordinator (Part C Coordinator) at http://nectac.org/search/confinder.asp. Different states have different names for these early intervention programs. For example, in California they are called Early Start Programs, while in Wisconsin they are referred to as Birth to Three Programs. The other types of services that these programs offer will be mentioned below.

Another type of government-supported early intervention program through which you may be able to obtain a developmental assessment are the Head Start programs for children under 5 years of age: the basic Head Start program for children 3 to 5 years of age, the Early Head Start program for children birth to 3 years of age, the Migrant Head Start programs for children birth to 5 of migrant or seasonal worker families, and the American Indian Alaskan Native Head Start program for children birth to 5 years of age from these populations. Eligibility for these programs is primarily based on being at the low end of the family income scale, but these early intervention programs can have a percentage of children from other income backgrounds, and they are also required to serve at least 10% of children who have special needs.[26] You can search for the Head Start program closest to where you live at http://www.acf.hhs.gov/programs/hsb/hsweb/index.jsp.

So, there are several ways that you can obtain a developmental assessment for a child you suspect may have special needs. One of the main purposes of such assessments is to connect you to early intervention programs if it is determined that your young child does have special needs.[27] Let's now look at the full spectrum of services that can be obtained through these types of programs, which are designed for children with special needs and their families.

Early Intervention Programs

The Early Start and other similar programs in all states provide a wide range of services, including:

Medical services: For diagnostic or evaluation purposes.

Psychological services: For diagnostic and psychological testing purposes, as well as counseling, psychotherapy, and parent and family training services to support and educate parents and family members.

Speech and language therapy: Professionally conducted treatment services to address speech and language impairments or deficits.

Assistive technology: Devices, equipment, or services used to help assist a child with special needs. For example, a computer language program may be used for a child who has difficulty with fine motor skills and handwriting.

Occupational therapy: Professionally conducted health-care treatment to improve self-help skills and adaptive behavior for children with development delays, illnesses, or injuries that impede their ability to function independently. New skills are taught and children receive assistance in the areas of motor and sensory development.

Physical therapy: Professionally conducted treatment or therapy designed to help a child who has difficulty with physical movement. The physical therapist uses heat, exercise, water, and other treatments to help improve muscle strength, range of motion, and motor skills.

Respite care: A supportive service that involves a short period of rest or relief for parents where someone else temporarily cares for the child. This enables the parent(s) to take care of other needs away from the child, such as their own needs or those of other children in the family.

Social work services: Professionally conducted services to support the family and better connect them to other helpful therapeutic and educational services in the community.

Vision services: Professionally delivered services to ensure that the child is seeing properly.

Age-appropriate special education services: Group or individual
    services to help a child learn and improve the academic and
    social skills that are expected for children entering school.

The Part C Coordinator in your state can tell you which organization closest to your home has been designated to provide these types
of government-supported services. The Coordinator may also know
of other agencies that provide such services, including child guidance
and child mental health centers.

It is also possible for you to obtain information about agencies
and professionals that can provide one or more of these services on
their own and not as part of a comprehensive early intervention program. These can be found by contacting an Information and Referral Service in your community. It is now possible in the majority of
communities in the United States to find your local information and
referral service simply by dialing 2-1-1. If you find that your area is
not covered by calling 2-1-1, go to your local phone book or call information and ask for the Information and Referral Service for your
city or county.

Head Start Programs

Head Start programs are primarily early childhood education programs that provide children with a variety of preschool educational
experiences to better prepare them for the demands of kindergarten
and regular schooling. These programs often provide parent education
services, and are able to provide developmental assessments for children who are suspected of having special needs. Like the government-
supported early intervention programs described above, Head Start
programs and services are provided free of charge to eligible children
and their families.

Other Programs for Children with Special Needs

Many school districts provide unique education service programs
for children with special needs 3 to 5 years of age, including children
with developmental delays. These programs are similar to the early
intervention programs mentioned above for children from birth to age
3 in that they can provide a wide spectrum of services. Calling your

local school district or going to their website can put you in contact with their preschool program for special needs children. If your district does not have a 3 to 5 program, the special education department at the district should be able to help you find such a program in the community.

All school districts in the United States are required to provide special education services for all school-age students with disabilities and other special needs. These services include creating an Individual Education Plan (IEP) for such children and then providing or facilitating providing the types of services that the plan recommends. The purpose of the plan and the recommended services is to maximize the child's educational growth.

It is wise to learn what your and your child's rights are under the law that governs these services, the IDEA Law. Current information for parents is available at the Wrightslaw website (www.wrightslaw.com).

MANAGING A CHILD WITH SPECIAL NEEDS

As should be apparent from what we have learned thus far, the parental management of these vulnerable children requires a good deal of assertiveness and advocacy to obtain what the child and your family need in order to help your child achieve his or her full potential. There are numerous agencies and professionals that may be contacted and whom you will need to integrate into your and your family's life. These groups and agencies can be lifelines for you and your family but they do require extra time and extra endurance.

Although all of this begins formally with developmental screening and developmental assessment, it begins informally and personally with coming to emotional grips with the possibility that a child of yours has something wrong with him or her. Accepting this possibility is not easy, as every parent dreams of having normal, healthy children. Thus, it is not uncommon for parents to need time, support, and assistance in accepting this possibility. During this initial personal acceptance state, strong emotions such as anger, denial, and guilt are likely to emerge, and must be addressed. Indeed, if these common and very justified feelings are not addressed and understood, they can stand in the way of getting the help that you and your child deserve and need. Having a child with special needs is one of the most emotionally demanding challenges that any parent can face and you should not berate yourself for experiencing any or all of these emotions.

The professionals you will meet in helping your child can be excellent allies in helping you cope with these feelings. Those professionals—particularly the psychologists, social workers, counselors, and educators who have been trained to provide parent training services—can also be extremely helpful in preparing you how best to deal with the daily challenges of raising a child with special needs.

In addition, you will find that there are many groups or organizations composed of the parents of children with special needs. These peer groups provide emotional support, education, and a base from which to advocate for your children. These groups, and the professionals who work with children with special needs, are most responsible for seeing to it that our nation now has laws that mandate the availability and delivery of services for children with special needs. By joining and supporting the organizations that best relate to your particular child and situation, you will not only gain support and education, but will also be able to advocate for improved services for your child and family. Here are some of the groups you may want to consider contacting:

American Society for Deaf Children
3820 Hartsdale Drive
Camp Hill, PA 17011
(717) 703–0073
Hotline: (800) 942–2732
www.deafchildren.org

American Speech-Language-Hearing Association
10801 Rockville Pike
Rockville, MD 20852
(800) 638–8255
www.asha.org

Autism Society of America
7910 Woodmont Avenue, Suite 300
Bethesda, MD 20814–3067
(800) 328–8476
www.autism-society.org

Children and Adults with Attention-Deficit/Hyperactivity
    Disorder
8181 Professional Place, Suite 150
Landover, MD 20785
(310) 306–7070
www.chadd.org

Epilepsy Foundation
8301 Professional Place
Landover, MD 20785–7223
(800) 332–1000
www.epilepsyfoundation.org

Junior Blind of America
5300 Angelas Vista Boulevard
Los Angeles, CA 90043
(800) 352–2290
www.juniorblind.org

Learning Disabilities Association of America
4156 Liberty Road
Pittsburg, PA 15234–1349
(412) 341–1515
www.ldanatl.org

Mental Health America
2000 N. Beauregard Street, 6th Floor
Alexandria, VI 22311
(800) 433–5959
www.nmha.org

United Cerebral Palsy
1660 L Street, NW, Suite 700
Washington, DC 20036
www.ucp.org

Another major source to use in becoming more educated in the
day-to-day management of a child with special needs is the previously mentioned National Dissemination Center for Children with
Disabilities (NICHEY). The NICHEY website (www.nichey.org)

contains extensive information and referrals about managing your child at home. In addition, the NICHEY website has sections on managing your child's behavior at school and dealing with the bullying that children with special needs are likely to encounter. NICHEY deserves to be a regularly used resource as it will keep you up to date on nearly everything you need to know about raising a child with special needs. You can now receive a regular electronic newsletter from NICHEY, NICHEY's eNews, by signing up for the newsletter on their website. That newsletter can be tailored to your particular needs.

Another major resource for your education and child management purposes are the excellent books, videos, DVDs, and CDs that are now available to the parents of children with special needs. A wide range of such resources can be obtained from the bookstore on the website of the Center for the Improvement of Child Caring (CICC; www. ciccparenting.org). The bookstore contains an entire section for parents of children with all types of special needs, with books on how best to relate to schools regarding your child's special education. The CICC website also contains information about many parenting skill-building programs, including programs that have been developed specifically for parents of children with special needs, such as the *Steps to Independence Program* and the programs for parents of AD/HD children and for parents of defiant children and teens. These programs are highly recommended.

Before moving on, it is worth reminding ourselves that any program that teaches good parenting skills is also recommended for the parents of children with special needs. Remember that children with special needs are children first, and have the same basic needs that all children possess, such as the need to b`e nurtured, loved, respected, and accepted. Any parenting program that teaches strategies for being warm and accepting is appropriate.

CHAPTER SIX

Skill-Building
Programs and Services

Now let's become more informed about the resources that are most relevant to your day-to-day relations with your children, the resources that teach, refine, and reinforce effective parenting skills. These reside mainly within skill-building programs such as *Confident Parenting, Effective Black Parenting, Los Niños Bien Educados, Active Parenting,* and *Systematic Training for Effective Parenting.*

We have already learned some of the skills from these programs in Chapter 3 on parenting guidelines. Recall that under the guideline about the importance of providing children with warmth, acceptance, and respect, we learned the art of Effective Praising and the Encouragement Approach. In the guideline about using fair and firm family leadership, we learned mild social disapproval and contracting skills. All of these techniques came from modern skill-building programs.

Smart parents who take the time and energy to learn these skills and to participate in these programs find that the skills are also helpful and enriching to their other relationships, such as those with their partners, friends, other family members, and even with coworkers and employers. Thus, what is learned can help you with all relations in your life.

So we will begin by gaining an overview of these skill-enhancing programs, learn where to find them and how best to relate to them, and how to advocate for having the full spectrum of such programs available in your community.

PARENTING AND FAMILY SKILL-BUILDING PROGRAMS

Let's start with a little history.[1] The importance of educating parents to be as effective as possible in raising children has been recognized in the United States since at least 1815, when the first parent group meetings were reported. These and other early efforts allowed groups of parents to gain emotional and social support from each other and to learn about child development.

In the late 1960s, a new approach to educating and training parents emerged—the creation and use of carefully constructed parenting and family skill-building programs. The first program of this nature that became widely known was the *Parent Effectiveness Training (P.E.T.)* program created by psychologist Dr. Thomas Gordon.[2]

P.E.T. and the many other skill-building programs that have been created since the late 1960s are designed to improve parental effectiveness by providing a clear parenting philosophy and a series of positive parenting skills and strategies that can be used immediately to address a variety of childrearing challenges and problems. The programs give you ideas and skills to better manage and cope with a wide range of childrearing challenges.

What these excellent programs teach and promote is consistent with the pattern of parenting (the Productive Parenting Pattern) that decades of research has shown to be so helpful in raising healthy, happy, and successful young people. It is no wonder, then, that studies that evaluate the impact of these programs on children, parents, and families consistently find that these programs:

- Increase parental confidence
- Reduce parental stress and anxiety
- Improve parenting skills
- Reduce or eliminate spanking and hitting
- Improve parent–child relations
- Reduce child behavioral problems
- Improve child cooperation
- Improve child self-esteem
- Improve child adjustment
- Improve child academic performance
- Strengthen families

These programs bring people together in groups. Most are designed for groups of parents, although some also include children and are best understood as family skill-building programs because the children are also trained and educated to use new skills and ideas about how best to relate to their parents.

Types of Programs

In general, these programs fall into five major categories:

General Parenting Skill-Building Programs. These are programs that have been designed for any parent, regardless of the age of his or her children and regardless of cultural or religious background. Examples are the *P.E.T.* program, a version of Family Effectiveness Training, and the *Confident Parenting Program.*

Age-Related Parenting Skill-Building Programs. These are designed for parents of children of different ages. Included here are *Active Parenting,* with its versions for parents of young children (*1, 2, 3, 4 Parents!*), its program for parents of elementary school children (*Active Parenting Now*), and its program for parents of teenagers (*Active Parenting of Teens*). *Systematic Training for Effective Parenting (STEP)* also has age-related versions such as *Early Childhood STEP, STEP,* and *STEP Teen. The Incredible Years* is designed for parents of children in the 4 to 8 age range.

Population-Specific Parenting Skill-Building Programs. These include such culturally specific, general skill-building programs such as *Effective Black Parenting* for parents of African American children and *Los Niños Bien Educados* for parents of Latino American children. There are also supplemental materials and translated versions of other programs, such as the *Nurturing* programs and the *Strengthening Families* programs, that are sensitive to the unique parenting challenges of different cultural groups. Also included here are parenting programs or versions of programs that have been created for different religious denominations, such as the versions of *Active Parenting* for Christian and Jewish denominations, and the version of *STEP* for Christian settings. In addition, there are the *Nurturing Program for Teenage Parents and Their Families* and the *Steps for Independence* program for parents of children with special needs.

Topic-Centered Skill-Building Programs. These focus on one major childrearing issue and provide in-depth approaches and assistance. Good examples are the *Siblings Without Rivalry* program that provides numerous ways of understanding and productively dealing with this common and challenging phenomenon, and the *Stop and Think* program that helps teach children basic social skills to use in their relationships with

others, including their relationships with teachers. Another
example of a topic-specific program is one we have already
heard about, the *Parents on Board* program that helps you be a
good coach of your children regarding their formal education.
Family Skill-Building Programs. These are programs that include
your children in the training. Groups of families participate at
the same time, usually in sessions where they are all together,
and in sessions where there is training for just parents
and for just children. A good example is the *Strengthening
Families* program. Another example would be the previously
mentioned *Nurturing* programs, because those population-
specific programs are designed to be taught to both parents
and children.

These programs are taught by professional instructors who have received specialized training in how best to teach or facilitate them. These
instructors include social workers, educators, psychologists, child and
family counselors, nurses, parent involvement coordinators, and prevention specialists. These are your neighbors who have committed
themselves to a helping profession and have taken it upon themselves
to receive additional education and training to be knowledgeable and
skillful in helping you be more effective with your children.

Where the Programs Can Be Found

These knowledgeable neighbors mainly teach the programs
through the agencies, schools, and organizations that employ them,
such as child guidance centers, schools, Head Start agencies, mental health and drug abuse treatment agencies, hospitals, and child
welfare agencies (see Figure 6.1). Indeed, nearly every public and
private organization that serves children and families in your community has determined that their missions can best be accomplished
when parents are skillful and humane in raising children. So, by hir-
ing and/or training personnel who can deliver parenting and family
skill-building programs, they will have the capacity to carry out their
mandated missions.

Trained instructors also find themselves offering these programs
through the religious organizations of which they are a part or with
which they consult. Some also offer the programs through their private practices or through employee assistance and wellness programs
or health maintenance organizations.

Figure 6.1. Where Parenting Programs, Classes, Seminars, and Workshops Are Taught

Schools—Adult education divisions, parent education departments, PTA/PTO-sponsored

Early Start and Head Start agencies

Churches, synagogues, and mosques

Child guidance and mental health centers

Child welfare departments

Social and family service organizations

Civic and cultural organizations

Drug abuse treatment agencies and departments

Preschools and child-care centers

Hospitals and HMOs

Employee assistance and wellness programs

Colleges and universities—Extension divisions and community services

Program Formats

Skill-building programs are taught in different settings through different formats. Sometimes they are taught as multisession parenting classes, all-day seminars or one-session meetings.

Multiple-Session Parenting Classes. These classes meet once or twice a week for anywhere from 6 to 20 weeks. Here, all of the program's parenting skills, strategies, and concepts are presented and discussed, and a variety of methods, such as role-playing, instructor demonstration, and lecturing, are used to educate you about how best to use the skills and ideas with your children. These classes are for small numbers of parents (10 to 25) and are akin to a college practicum or small group seminar. Parents receive homework assignments where they actually use the skills with their children and then they report back to the group and receive further technical assistance and support from both the instructor and from the other parents.

One-Day Seminars. Here, only some of the program skills and concepts are taught, because there is not enough time to present the entire program. These seminars are for large numbers of parents (50 to 200).

One-Session Meetings. These include *Lunch-and-Learn* meetings in work settings, where one or two program skills are taught, or where a specific topic from the program is covered.

The longer, more intense teaching formats—the multiple-session classes—are generally the most effective because you have more time to learn and practice the skills and to integrate the parenting ideas and values into your overall approach to parenting. These more intense and intimate training formats also allow for a good deal of mutual support and understanding among parents, and often lead parents to exchange phone numbers and continue to meet and help each other. This bonding and support is even more likely to happen when the program is for particular groups of parents, such as parents of the same age children, parents from the same cultural or religious group, or parents who all have children with special needs.

The briefer formats—the one-day seminars and one-session meetings—are helpful because they give you at least one or two good ideas and some skill training that can be used immediately with your children. They can also motivate you to want to take and learn the entire program once you have realized how much you and your family can gain from this type of education.

Making the Most of Programs

The first thing you need to do is find a program that relates to your current parenting needs. This requires that you have some knowledge of what the programs actually teach. In the next chapter, you will be able to gain a good deal of relevant knowledge.

As part of the programs you select, you will receive a handbook that covers what is taught and that will have homework assignments in it. Read each section as it is assigned. Having the handbook available after you have completed the program allows you to refresh your knowledge when you keep it around the house for frequent reference.

Other things you can do include having a good attitude about participating. You are the most knowledgeable person about your children and your home situation, so you are *the* authority on parenting your children. But don't let that reality stand in the way of learning additional ideas about parenting and new skills, or finding out that you have not been doing as good a job as possible. Have an open mind. Try out the ideas and use the skills, do the homework assignments, and don't fight this learning opportunity.

It is also wise to attend every class session of the multisession programs, as these programs are carefully organized so that a parenting skill or concept that you learn in one session provides a foundation and justification for what you will be learning in subsequent sessions. If you miss a session, try to take it over, talk to the instructor, or talk to your fellow parents to bring yourself up to speed.

One of the things that all of these programs teach is to be very positive with your children and to appreciate and acknowledge effort and appropriate behavior. Your instructor and the agency or organization that hosts or sponsors your class, seminar, or workshop also deserve similar treatment. Let them know how grateful you are for this opportunity. Like your children, they are then more likely to continue to make your life easier when you treat them well. Also share what you are learning with other family members, friends, and coworkers. Word of mouth from someone who has experienced the benefits of becoming an educated parent is the most powerful advertising and endorsement possible (see Figure 6.2 for a summary of how to get the most out of parenting sessions).

Advocating for the Programs You Want

All of the places that have been mentioned are the places where you should look for parenting skill-building programs. If you find that they are not offering any such programs, ask why not and advocate for them to do so. You and your children are the reason these organizations exist, and you, as a consumer, have the power to shape what services are being made available. Use that power. Ask and advocate.

FIGURE 6.2. How to Get the Most Out of Parenting Programs

Select a program that meets your current parenting needs

Have a good attitude

Do the homework—Read the handbook, do the assignments

Attend regularly

Make up missed classes

Acknowledge instructors and sponsoring organization

Share what you have learned with others

Spread the word

And if, for some reason, the agency or school or church leader you speak with does not seem to be knowledgeable about parenting and family skill-building programs, share this book with them. If they ask you how they might bring such programs to their organizations, you can let them know that there are three ways:

1. They can obtain the instructor kit for a particular program and have a parenting instructor from their organization use the instructor manual and teaching aides to run the program through their organization.
2. They can send a qualified staff member, volunteer, or consultant to take an instructor training workshop to learn to deliver the program and to obtain the instructor kit.
3. They can contract with a qualified instructor or with an effective parenting organization to have them deliver the program for the parents and families that they serve.

A good group that organizations can look to for help in this regard is the Center for the Improvement of Child Caring (CICC). It distributes the instructor kits of many fine programs, regularly conducts instructor training workshops, and can facilitate contracting for programs (www.ciccparenting.org). Another place where information about many skill-building programs can be obtained is NEPI, the National Effective Parenting Initiative (www.effectiveparentingusa.org).

Other Group Parenting Education Experiences

In addition to classes and seminars in these carefully organized parenting skill-building programs, there are a variety of other parenting education experiences that often are provided by community organizations. For example, religious and other community organizations frequently sponsor *Mommy and Me* and *Daddy and Me* classes where parents bring their young children to learn how best to relate to and enjoy each other. Many schools offer other types of parenting classes through their adult or parent education departments.

INDIVIDUALIZED PARENTING EDUCATION AND SUPPORT

Some communities now are in the habit of providing parenting education on a one-to-one basis.

Home Visiting

Home visiting involves having a trained service provider visit the parents of newborns and young children in their homes to educate and support them in being effective and humane in raising their babies and youngsters. The home visitor supplies emotional support and authoritative child development information, teaches parenting skills, and facilitates a family's connection to other community services that they may need. Home visiting is an extraordinarily friendly and personal service.

Several home visiting efforts emerged out of the health fields and were initially developed for the purpose of providing families who are at high risk for abusing their babies with special support and education. Possibly the most widely used and known of these types of home visiting is the *Nurse Home Visiting* program created by Dr. David Olds, a professor of pediatrics, psychiatry, and preventive medicine at the University of Colorado. Since 1977, Dr. Olds has been developing and testing his approach to home visiting, called the "Olds Model," and it has proven to be extremely successful in educating high-risk, low-income mothers to be very effective with their children.[3]

Dr. Olds's exemplary work has blossomed into the Nurse-Family Partnership, a nonprofit organization serving more than 20,000 mothers in 20 states across the nation.[4] From the organization's website (www.nursefamilypartnership.org), you will be able to learn more about the overall program and find the groups closest to your home that are providing home visiting services. The program's emphasis is on working with first-time parents.

Another national home visiting effort that originated to prevent child maltreatment is *Healthy Families America.* It is designed to help expectant and new parents give their children a healthy start. This home visiting effort was launched in 1992 by Prevent Child Abuse America (formerly known as the National Committee to Prevent Child Abuse). Families participate voluntarily in the program, and *Healthy Families America* programs now exist in 430 communities in the United States and Canada.[5] You can learn more about this highly effective effort and locate the closest *Healthy Families America* organization by visiting the program's website, www.healthyfamiliesamerica.org.

Another nationally prominent home visiting effort emerged out of the education fields and is directed more at providing parents with information, skills, and supports to help guide their young children's educational growth. The best-known of this variety of home visiting is *Parents as Teachers*. It originated in Missouri and now has a national reach through the training of thousands of *Parents as Teachers* parent educators to deliver its home visiting services.[6]

The mission of *Parents as Teachers* is to provide the information, support, and encouragement that parents need to help their children develop optimally during the crucial early years of life. Its goals include: increasing parent knowledge of early childhood development and improving parenting practices, providing early detection of developmental delays and health issues, preventing child abuse and neglect, and increasing children's school readiness and school success.

Information about the excellent work of *Parents as Teachers*, and the location of the program nearest to you, can be obtained from the website of the Parents as Teachers National Center, www.parentsasteachers.org.

Parenting Coaching

This is also a one-on-one method for learning how to be a more effective parent. It is often done over the Internet and/or the telephone. Parenting coaching over the Internet involves being linked to a trained coach, who is usually a professional from the field of clinical social work, counseling, education, or psychology. The coach relates to you through e-mailing, text messaging, and live chats. This service focuses on your particular parenting needs at this particular time in your and your family's life. In addition to the individual coaching they provide, these coaches can also inform you about valuable books, videos, DVDs, and community services. Because of the backgrounds and training of the individuals who become parenting coaches, their services are generally considered to be a combination of family education and family counseling.

One of the most comprehensive and well-developed online Parenting Coaching services is called *About My Kids* (www.aboutmykids. com). You receive the services by becoming an *About My Kids* member. The services include:

> *Your own personal Parent Coach who gets to know you and your family.* Your personal Parent Coach is a highly trained and degreed parenting professional who will be your coach as long as you are a member. You can work with your coach on any issue, any topic, or any need.

Your own parenting resource center designed just for you. Using a personal library, parenting plans, and educational resources, you and your coach work toward your parenting goals. Along the way, your coach will personally select and create educational materials and activities that meet your family's needs. All of these resources are kept conveniently in your password-protected member page so that you have access to them whenever and wherever you wish. It's like having your own personal, online parenting center.

Your own Personal Assistant to make your life easier and save you time. A personal assistant service is included with your membership in *About My Kids.* Your Personal Assistant will do everything for you, from planning birthday parties and vacations to ordering dinner and buying movie tickets. Your Personal Assistant is ready, willing, and able to help make your life easier.

Family Health Resource Center. The Family Health Resource Center helps you stay informed and get the latest information on important health issues for you and your family. The center includes access to the highest-quality, discount fitness club program in the country. It also offers sophisticated online exercise planning and motivational tools. These tools will help you get fit and stay fit to keep your energy high. The Family Health Resource Center puts the world of health at your fingertips.

Other places where you will be able to find online and telephone parenting coaches include some of the organizations that train coaches, such as the Parent Coaching Institute (www.parentcoaching institute.com) and the Academy for Coaching Parents International (www.academyforcoachingparents.com).

Now let's learn more about what you can expect when you enroll in some of the parenting and family skill-building programs that have been mentioned.

CHAPTER SEVEN

Program Descriptions

Here is a sampling of some of the best parenting and family skill-building programs that are available to help parents be as effective as possible and actualize the Productive Parenting Pattern. Let's begin with the program that began the modern skill-building approach to parenting education.

PARENT EFFECTIVENESS TRAINING (P.E.T.)

Program Philosophy

Dr. Thomas Gordon's *P.E.T.* program imparts a philosophy of human relationships and a set of childrearing skills that are intended to assist parents in building warm, close, and enjoyable relationships with their children and in fostering a family environment that is supportive of the needs and growth of each family member.[1] It is based on the philosophy that maximum growth occurs within relationships that are characterized by high degrees of acceptance and genuineness. Acceptance entails being nonjudgmental, and genuineness entails being honestly self-disclosing. Being genuine or real also means revealing when you are feeling judgmental and unaccepting.

P.E.T. translates these ideas into a philosophy of parenthood that defines "genuine" or "real" parents as those who do not hide their true feelings, who feel both accepting and unaccepting toward their children, who feel different degrees of acceptance toward different children, who have different attitudes toward the same behaviors of their children at different times, and who accept that their partners are real persons with similarly varied feelings toward their children.[2]

P.E.T. believes that the use of physical and psychological power in parent–child relationships contributes to dehumanization and alienation. These values get translated into an injunction against the use of parental power, which means being very careful and judicious in using rewards and punishments in managing the behaviors of children.

P.E.T. also considers that children possess civil rights. This means that children have rights to hold and express feelings and viewpoints, and are entitled to their own values, beliefs, preferences, style, and philosophy of life. P.E.T. cautions against intruding into those spheres of children's lives that do not have tangible or concrete effects on parents.[3]

Based on these assumptions and values, an effective parent, according to P.E.T., would be genuine, self-disclosing, fallible, accepting, and respectful of the feelings, ideas, and values of spouses and children. The effective parent would also be fair, using influence or persuasion rather than power (rewards and punishments) to get their personal needs met. The fairness value implies the involvement of all family members, including children, in decisions that influence them, and therefore involves a democratic framework for decision making. Not using punishment also implies that an effective parent is nonviolent and does not use corporal punishment.

Parenting Strategies and Skills

The P.E.T. program begins by teaching parents to understand their children's behavior as being either acceptable or unacceptable based on the changing moods and needs of the parent and the child, and based upon the changing characteristics of the environment. It teaches a method of *Problem Ownership* that shows parents how to identify when 1) their child's behaviors are acceptable to the parents but the child indicates that he or she is experiencing a problem in living; 2) their child's behaviors evoke feelings of unacceptance in the parents, which indicates that the parents have a problem; and 3) the child's behaviors are acceptable and no one has a problem.[4]

Active Listening. P.E.T. teaches therapeutic listening skills to use when the child is experiencing a problem—a "language of acceptance," or active listening.

In order to listen actively, parents need to be sensitive and articulate about their child's feeling state, and P.E.T. also teaches parents how to identify what their children are feeling. Parents need to empathize with their children's problems as they actively listen. An example would be when a child remarks about not being allowed to play ("I never get a chance to get the ball when the bigger kids start playing catch.").

The parent actively listens and responds by saying, "You want to play, too, and you feel it is not fair for them to leave you out." This usually stimulates a longer conversation in which the actively listening parent frequently uses this communication technique to help the child find a solution to the problem.[5] There are many subtleties and nuances in how and when to listen actively, and the *P.E.T.* program presents a variety of options, examples, and pitfalls.

Confrontive I Messages. *P.E.T.* teaches confrontive communication skills to use when the child's behavior is creating a problem for the parent—Confrontive I Messages. In delivering these messages, parents:

1. Describe the unacceptable behavior without blaming
2. Disclose their feelings about the child's behavior
3. Indicate the tangible effect that the child's behavior is having on them

These are highly individualized messages that alert the child to attend to and consider the parent's needs. Examples of Confrontive I Messages include:

> "I'm feeling frustrated and angry because I cannot rest when
>   someone is crawling on my lap."
> "I sure get discouraged when I see my clean kitchen dirty again,
>   and I don't want to spend more of my time cleaning it."
> To a 6-year-old who hit the baby on the head: "Bryant, I get scared
>   to death when the baby is hit on the head! I would sure hate to
>   see him hurt badly. And I get really mad when I see someone
>   big hurting someone a lot smaller. I was so afraid that his little
>   head was going to bleed."

There are also many varieties of I Messages and subtleties of usage. There are interrelationships between I Messages and active listening. For example, after a parent has delivered an I Message, the child may be resisting or feeling guilty, so the parent may need to shift gears to listen actively to the child's new feelings.

Positive I Messages. *P.E.T.* also teaches parents to use I Messages when they are spontaneously expressing positive feelings to the child. Examples of these Positive I Messages include: a child phones to say he has stopped at a friend's house after school and the parent says, "When you let me know where you are, I feel relieved because then I don't worry about you." Or a child may surprise a parent by cleaning up the kitchen after a snack and the parent says, "When the kitchen was cleaned up as I started to fix dinner tonight, I appreciated it because I didn't have to spend time cleaning it myself."

Environmental Modification. The program also teaches parents a set of Environmental Modification and childproofing strategies to reduce the likelihood that a child's behavior will create problems. These strategies are called adding, removing, changing the environment, and planning ahead.

When the child's behavior is unacceptable to the parent and an accurate application of Confrontive I Messages or Environmental Modification doesn't work to change the child's behavior, the *relationship* between the child and the parent now has a problem. Relationship problems are conflicts. These conflicts are seen as inevitable aspects of family life and can either strengthen or destroy a family, depending upon how they are resolved.

Two types of conflicts are identified: conflicts of needs, where the child's needs have tangible and concrete effects on the parent; and conflicts of values, where the child's needs do not have such effects, or where the child doesn't "buy" the effects that the parent says he or she is experiencing.[6] Parents are taught to distinguish between the two types of conflicts and to utilize different methods in dealing with them.

The No-Lose Conflict Resolution Method. When conflicts of needs exist, parents are taught systematic and democratic negotiation skills for resolving them without having to resort to parental power—the No-Lose Conflict Resolution method. Examples of conflicts of needs are:

> when the child doesn't help with the dishes and instead starts reading a book in preparation for an upcoming school exam;
> the child leaves the parents' tools on the front sidewalk and the parent is afraid they will be stolen;
> the child continues to play baseball in a next-door lot even though he has been told that the family has to go somewhere in an hour;
> a child continues to stop and gaze in store windows after the parent has indicated that there is reason to rush.

The program indicates that most parents deal with these conflicts in a win-lose fashion. Either the parent gives in and loses, and the child wins (a permissive parent), or the parent uses power and wins, and the child loses (an authoritarian parent).

The No-Lose Conflict Resolution method is an alternative to this win-lose approach. This method enlists the ideas and viewpoints of the child in arriving at mutually agreeable solutions. It is clearly more time-consuming than the win-lose approach, and it consists of six interrelated processes:

1. Identifying and defining the conflicting needs
2. Generating possible alternative solutions
3. Evaluating the alternative solutions
4. Deciding on the best acceptable solution
5. Working out ways of implementing the solution
6. Following up to evaluate how well it worked[7]

This method interrelates with the other *P.E.T.* methods. For example, during a conflict resolution sequence, the parent often has to shift gears and employ I Messages and active listening in order to facilitate arriving at an acceptable solution. Parents are also taught to use this method to help others resolve conflicts, such as helping two children resolve conflicts by using this method in a facilitator or consultant capacity.

Conflicts of values exist when parents feel unaccepting toward a child's behavior and the child doesn't believe that the behavior tangibly affects the parents or that the behavior is bad for him or her. Examples of values conflicts include: when children swear and the parents find this unacceptable; when children choose friends, clothing, or hairstyles that parents find unacceptable; when children stop wanting to go to church, and so forth. At such junctions, the program orients parents to own the problem and either model, consult, or modify themselves.

Within the *P.E.T.* program, *modeling* refers to engaging in behaviors that are consistent with the values you would like to see in your child (e.g., not swearing). *Consulting* refers to giving information or offering opinions, but not preaching or demanding that the child change. *Modifying self* includes a close examination of one's values with the possibility of the parent accepting the child's values.[8]

This classic and pioneering skill-building program is usually taught in eight 3-hour sessions by a highly trained instructor whose roles include being a facilitator of learning, a skill model, and a course manager, rather than a therapist.

There is also a self-study or self-taught version available that enables parents to learn *P.E.T.* skills at home on their own, or with a spouse or other partner. It is called *Family Effectiveness Training*. The program is led by Dr. Gordon. It provides 18–20 hours of study and practice, using video and audiotapes and study and resource guides.

Further information about *P.E.T.* can be obtained from Gordon Training International (www.gordontraining.com).

CICC's TRIO OF PARENTING PROGRAMS

Here you will learn more about the three parenting skill-building programs created by the Center for the Improvement of Child Caring: *Confident Parenting, Effective Black Parenting,* and *Los Niños Bien Educados*. These programs are designed for use with all parents, regardless of the age of the child and regardless of whether the children do or do not have special needs. The programs teach a positive parenting philosophy (the Social Learning Philosophy) and a series of very practical parenting skills to enhance the quality of family life and to decrease child behavior problems. The Social Learning Philosophy is reflected in the basic assumption that all parenting practices are learned and, therefore, new practices can not only be learned at any time, but old ones can be unlearned.

The *Effective Black Parenting* and *Los Niños Bien Educados* programs are culturally adapted versions of the *Confident Parenting* program. These are the first culturally adapted parenting skill-building programs in the nation. They teach a similar positive philosophy, and also teach all of the skills that are taught in *Confident Parenting*. In addition, they teach the skills in a culturally sensitive manner, they frame the teaching of the skills within the values and histories of each of the cultural groups, and they contain additional content, skills, and topics that address parenting challenges that are unique to each cultural group.

Confident Parenting: Survival Skill Training

Parents often feel controlled by their children's misbehavior because they do not know how to set limits effectively. They may pay so much attention when their children misbehave that they forget to notice the cooperative and peaceful times.

The *Confident Parenting* program teaches parents how to pay attention to and increase the times when their children's behavior is good.[9] It also teaches effective limit-setting skills so that parents will not feel victimized by their children's misbehavior. The *Confident Parenting* program is usually taught as a 10-session class that meets once a week for 2 hours. There is also a briefer version of the program that is taught through a one-day seminar format.

The program provides parents effective skills to manage child behaviors such as:

Disruptiveness
Fears
Shyness
Tantrums
Bedwetting
Restlessness
Disobedience
Laziness
Aggressiveness[10]

Parents are taught skills and strategies to increase their children's self-esteem and cooperation, and to nonviolently manage the above behaviors. These strategies include:

Learning How to Pinpoint and Chart Child Behaviors
Effective Praise
Mild Social Disapproval
Systematic Ignoring
Time-Out from Social Attention
Special Incentives
Contracting
Family Rule Guidelines[11]

The 10-session version of the program begins by teaching parents that behavior is shaped by its consequences. Here, a good deal of emphasis is placed on helping parents transform their usually global descriptions of their children's functioning ("he's selfish," for example) into specific behavioral descriptions ("he doesn't share his toys with his brother").

They are then taught exactly how to pinpoint the specific behaviors that they would like to see their children engage in more frequently and those they would like to see less of. This pinpointing involves not only being specific about observable behaviors, but also indicating where and when the parent would like to see more or less of the behavior (at bedtime, in the morning, at the dinner table, and so on).

Parents are then advised about various procedures for counting and charting specific behaviors so they have a record of what is taking place. This record serves as a standard against which the effectiveness of the parenting skills or methods that are taught in the *Confident Parenting* program can be judged, as the methods are designed to increase or decrease specific behaviors. Thus, the charting of behaviors can be used to see whether or not a method is actually working.

Through a combination of instructor presentations and demonstrations, and parental role-playing and home assignments, parents are taught exactly how to use the program's various skills to bring out more of their children's positive and appropriate behaviors and to decrease their negative or inappropriate actions.

Parenting Skills

We have already been exposed to the *Confident Parenting* program skills of Effective Praising, mild social disapproval, and contracting. Here are descriptions of some of the other skills that are taught in this program.

Time-Out. This skill is a form of punishment that is used when all else fails and the child's behavior has exceeded reasonable limits. It refers to time-out from social interaction and attention. Time-out is explained to the child as going to a "cooling off" place for a short period of time when her/his behavior has gone too far.

Parents are instructed to make a rule about how time-out is to be used. For example, the parents may articulate a family rule about how disagreements are to be handled (We "do" tell each other what our opinions and feelings are. We "don't" hit each other.). The child is informed that when he or she breaks this family rule, time-out will be used. Then, when the child breaks the rule, the parents begin and follow through on the time-out sequence: 1) remain calm, 2) state the rule and its consequence, 3) ignore the child's extraneous verbalizations and excuses, and 4) follow through quickly by initiating the time-out procedure.[12] Soon after the child is removed from time-out, and when he/she is behaving appropriately again, parents are instructed to praise the child to show that they still love him or her and that they do not hold grudges.

Systematic Ignoring. This method is also a way of decreasing child misbehavior. It involves ignoring or withdrawing attention. The essence of this skill is that it must be used consistently in response to the behaviors that it seeks to reduce. It is best used the first time a child engages in a new inappropriate behavior, such as swearing, and with annoying behaviors, such as persistently asking for cookies or interrupting while the parent is on the phone or talking with someone else. It consists of five behavioral components: 1) looking away from the child, 2) moving away from the child, 3) neutral facial expression, 4) ignoring the child's verbalizations, and 5) ignoring immediately upon noticing the problematic behavior.[13]

Special Incentive System. This *Confident Parenting* method consists of teaching parents how to design and implement a Special Incentive System. In this system, the child earns points, stars, or tokens for engaging in specified desirable behaviors (the "do sides" of various family rules). The child turns these points in for various tangible rewards and/or special privileges. The rewards or privileges are chosen from a reward menu that is negotiated cooperatively by the parent and the child.

The components of a Special Incentive System are: 1) defining desirable behavior, 2) counting the target behavior(s), 3) creating the reward menu, 4) establishing the exchange ratio, i.e., how many points earn which rewards, 5) charting behaviors, 6) praise for positive behavioral changes, 7) program adjustments, and 8) phasing out the program.[14]

In the 10-session class version, parents carry out homework projects where they apply the various skills. They receive feedback on their use of the skills from the instructor and the other parents as they report the outcome of these projects to the entire class.

Effective Black Parenting

Raising African American children in the United States is an extremely challenging task. Although all children progress through similar stages of development, and all children need nurturance and sensitive guidance, African American children and their parents face special problems as a result of our country's history of racism and discrimination. These problems often make it harder to raise proud and capable African American children.

Until CICC created the *Effective Black Parenting* program (*EBPP*) in the late 1970s, there were no skill-building programs that addressed these problems head-on. There were also no programs that taught parenting skills in a manner that was respectful of African American patterns of communication and that recognized the African roots of the extended black family. Thus, the program occupies a very special place in the history of parenting education in the United States.[15]

EBPP provides an excellent learning and relearning context to help parents of African American children do the best job possible. Its basic ideas are derived from the writings of African American parenting scholars, from research with African American parents, and from adaptations of *Confident Parenting* skills that have been found to be helpful in raising children of all ethnic and socioeconomic backgrounds.

The research that was conducted to help inform what would be taught in the program was done with low- to middle-income African American parents from urban settings. That research showed that 1) the parents had very high expectations for their children's achievement, 2) most of the parents used harsh disciplinary practices that originated historically as survival adjustments to slavery, and 3) less than half of the parents shared positive aspects of their culture with their children and many made disparaging comments about their culture and heritage.[16]

These findings were used as a basis for creating new instructional units about cultural issues that could be taught along with the skills from the *Confident Parenting* program, and were also used as the basis for creating additional parenting skills and strategies. The new instructional units included an achievement strategy for raising African American children, the Path to the Pyramid of Success for Black Children, which linked the life goals that parents have for their children with the characteristics the children need to develop in order to achieve those life goals, and explained what parents had to do to help this happen. Thus, the program itself was presented as a pathway for parents to follow in building a pyramid of success for their children. (See Figure 7.1 for an illustration of the Path to the Pyramid of Success for Black Children.)

Figure 7.1. The Path to the Pyramid of Success for Black Children

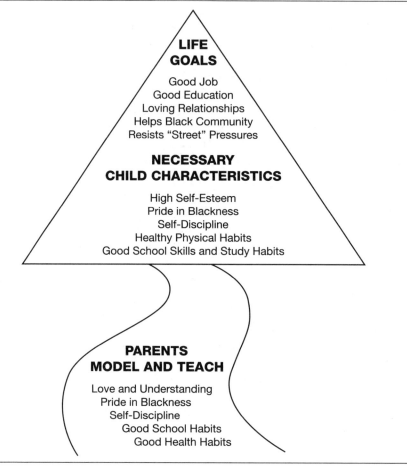

**LIFE
GOALS**

Good Job
Good Education
Loving Relationships
Helps Black Community
Resists "Street" Pressures

**NECESSARY
CHILD CHARACTERISTICS**

High Self-Esteem
Pride in Blackness
Self-Discipline
Healthy Physical Habits
Good School Skills and Study Habits

**PARENTS
MODEL AND TEACH**

Love and Understanding
Pride in Blackness
Self-Discipline
Good School Habits
Good Health Habits

Parenting Strategies, Skills, and Topics. The parenting skills that are taught in the program are:

Describing and Counting Behaviors
Effective Praise
Mild Social Disapproval
Systematic Ignoring
Time-Out from Social Attention
The Point System Method
Chit Chat Time[17]

Three culturally specific parenting strategies are also taught: the Path to the Pyramid of Success for Black Children, Traditional Black Discipline versus Modern Black Self-Discipline, and Pride in Blackness.

Other parenting strategies and topics are also taught and covered, including:

Family Rule Guidelines
The Thinking Parent's Approach
Children's Developing Abilities
Drugs and Our Children
Single Parenting[18]

Each of the parenting strategies and skills in *EBPP* is taught by making reference to African proverbs such as "Children are the reward of life" and "A shepherd does not strike his sheep." The systematic use of these proverbs helps to ground the teachings of the program in the wisdom and skillfulness of the African ancestors, and is an example of one of the many ways that the program promotes cultural pride.

The complete program is taught in 15 3-hour class sessions, with the last session also serving as a graduation celebration. This program also has a briefer version that is taught through a one-day seminar structure.

Here are some examples of how the program is taught and the culturally specific parenting strategies it uses:

Session One and the Pyramid of Success for Black Children. The instructor begins with a self-introduction and indicates that he has received special training to learn how to deliver the program, using the proverb, "He who learns, teaches." He indicates the main reasons for having such a program, mentioning that "children are the reward of life," and then engages the parents in a loosening-up exercise where parents share information about themselves and their families.

Then the instructor begins a series of exercises and presentations that evolve around the concept of Building a Pyramid of Success for Black Children. The concept contains the core values of the program and is taught in such a way as to serve as a motivational tool, stimulating the parents to try out the ideas and skills that the program provides. The concept is reinforced during each session through regular "Pyramid Peptalks" where the parents take the lead in reviewing what the Pyramid and the program is about.

Teaching the concept begins by looking at the goals that the parents have for their children. This is accomplished through the use of a call-and-response teaching method that is similar to the way many Black clergy address their congregations. The instructor uses this method to elicit five life goals that most Black parents have for their children: 1) achieving good educations, 2) getting good jobs, 3) forming loving relationships, 4) helping the Black community, and 5) resisting pressures to engage in illegal and unhealthy lifestyles (resisting "street" pressures).

Then the instructor indicates and defines the types of characteristics that children need to develop in order to have a good chance at achieving these goals, including characteristics such as having high self-esteem, pride in Blackness or cultural heritage, self-discipline, good study and school skills, and healthy physical habits.

The life goals constitute the top half of the Pyramid of Success, and the necessary child characteristics form the foundation from which the goals can be achieved.

The parents are then alerted to the fact that there is much that they can do to help their children develop the necessary qualities and thereby provide their children with a better chance of reaching their life goals. They are informed that they can teach and model five qualities, and each quality is explained. The five parenting qualities are love and understanding, pride in Blackness, self-discipline, good study habits, and good health habits. When they are modeling and teaching these qualities, parents are told that they are on the Path to the Pyramid of Success for Black Children. They are informed that what the program is all about is supplying them with additional parenting ideas and skills to help them stay on the path with their children. They are also told that a pyramid is used as the primary program symbol because the best-known pyramids originated in Egypt which is part of Africa, the continent of their origins.

The parents are then given their class handbooks and assigned their first homework, which is to review and reflect upon the interrelationships of the life goals, child characteristics, and what they can do.[19]

Session Four: Traditional Black Discipline Versus Modern Black Self-Discipline. Sessions two and three covered learning how to chart children's behavior, the teaching and use of the Effective Praise method, and the involvement of extended family members in learning about the program and its goals. Session four focuses on conveying and considering the meaning and significance of the traditional and modern approaches to discipline. The parents are given an exercise to explore their meanings of disciplining children. They are shown the responses of other African American parents that reflect an appreciation for discipline that consists of the use of harsh consequences such as whipping, hitting, spanking, and verbal chastisement as the primary methods for gaining child obedience.

The instructor then provides some historical perspective on this "Traditional Black Discipline" orientation. Quoting from African American scholars on parenting and using descriptions from the classic television show *Roots,* the instructor conveys that this approach was developed in response to the demands of slavery and more recent periods of racial discrimination. It responds to the need for survival in a hostile world where opportunities for advancement are limited and where the consequences of violating social role expectations are severe (e.g., imprisonment, brutal physical assault, death). The primary goal of this approach is to ensure the child's survival and reduce the risks of the undesirable social consequences by raising respectful Black children who do not question authority.

The instructor contrasts this approach with "Modern Black Self-Discipline," which is based on positive, self-directed, achievement-oriented approaches to discipline that are designed to enhance self-esteem, self-confidence, and feelings of personal and collective competence. This approach to Black parenting evolved during the civil rights and Black Power movements.

The parents are then informed that in the modern approach, positive consequence methods such as Effective Praise are considered to be disciplinary methods. They are further advised that the use of clear family rules and reasons for rules, along with the frequent use of positive consequences, reduces the need for corrective consequences such as punishment, spanking, and whipping. The full spectrum of parenting methods that the program teaches is introduced, and parents see that they are consistent with the more modern approach. They are also introduced to the proverb "A shepherd does not strike his sheep," and to the idea of "Appealing to their minds and not their behinds" in considering how to discipline their children.

EBPP has become the program of choice for hundreds of institutions nationwide that serve African Americans. These institutions have different missions. Some are institutions whose missions are substance abuse prevention, child abuse prevention, delinquency prevention, and school reform. Thus, nearly every type of health and human service, educational, and faith group has found *EBPP* worthwhile.[20]

Los Niños Bien Educados

Developed especially for Spanish-speaking and Latino-origin parents, the *Los Niños Bien Educados* program (*LNBE*) is respectful of the unique traditions and customs of families of Latino descent and is sensitive to the variety of adjustments that are made as such families acculturate to life in the United States.[21]

The program is built around the traditional Latino family value of raising children to be *bien educados,* i.e., well-behaved in a social and personal sense and well-educated in an academic sense. This includes, in general, knowing one's place in the family and being respectful of adults and elders . However, because of the variety of countries from which parents of Latino descent come, and because some are newly emigrated while others have been part of the United States for generations, the program does not assume that all parents of Latino descent have the same definition of *bien educados.* Thus, the program begins by exploring parental definitions of the term *bien educados.*

These definitions are usually of a very general nature, such as saying that it means being well-mannered, well-behaved, respectful, and so forth. The parents are then asked to provide specific examples of the behaviors that they consider to be reflective of a child who is well-mannered (*bien educado*). They also explore their definitions of a child who is behaving in a *mal educados* fashion. The program mentions that all children sometimes behave in such a fashion.

From these basic cultural groundings and definitions, *LNBE* looks at how these definitions are expressed in the traditional family, gender role, and age expectations of children. Then it teaches parents a wide variety of strategies and skills for promoting and maintaining those child behaviors that they define as constituting *bien educados* and for reducing those that they see as reflecting *mal educados.*

As part of the program, parents are oriented to consider the potential causes of *mal educados.* Parents are taught basic child development to assist them in arriving at age-appropriate expectations. Information about child abuse and child abuse laws helps broaden understandings of what is considered proper and improper parental behavior in the United States.

This program also addresses important cultural issues having to do with the different types of adjustments that families of Latino descent make to the United States, and the impact of traditional family and gender roles on the expectations that parents have for their children. All skills are taught with the use of *dichos,* or Spanish sayings, to help nest them in a culturally and linguistically familiar context. Amusing drawings of family life also enliven the teaching of skills and concepts, and all sessions end with a *platica* where parents take leadership roles in solving common problems.

Here is a listing of the parenting strategies, skills, and topics covered in the complete program:

Culturally Specific Parenting Strategies

Defining *Bien* and *Mal Educados*
Traditional Family and Gender Roles
Adjusting and Acculturating to the United States

General Parenting Strategies

Social Learning Ideas and Pinpointing and Counting Behavior
Parental Functions and Responsibilities
Family Expectations Are Like a Coin, and Family Expectation
    Guidelines
The Causes of Child Behavior and Considering the Causes Before
    and After You Act

Basic Parenting Skills Taught in a Culturally Sensitive Manner, Using Latino American Language Expressions and Dichos

Effective Praise
Mild Social Disapproval
Systematic Ignoring
Time-Out from Attention
The Point System (Special Incentives)
First/Then (First You Work, Then You Play)
Show and Tell (Modeling and Demonstrating *Bien Educados*
    Behaviors)
Family Chat, or *Platica* (e.g., regarding family changes in
    schedules)

Special Topical Coverage

Child Abuse Laws and Proper Parenting[22]

The program is designed to be taught in Spanish or English and consists of 12 3-hour training sessions, the last of which includes a graduation ceremony. Like all of the CICC programs, this one also is taught as a one-day seminar version.

POSITIVE INDIAN PARENTING

This unique parenting program was developed by the National Indian Child Welfare Institute. Its subtitle, "Honoring Our Children by Honoring Our Traditions," highlights the fact that it draws on traditional American Indian childrearing to help contemporary Indian parents approach their children in a very positive and culturally knowledgeable way. The developers relied heavily on consultation with tribal elders, Indian professionals, and parents in evolving this eight-session program.

The developers note the tremendous tribal and regional diversity of the American Indian population, with more than 500 federally recognized tribes or bands.[23] Each of these groups has its own childrearing patterns, value systems, communication patterns, and behavior.

Despite this rich diversity, the program developers believe that there are at least three major traditions that are common to most, if not all, American Indians: the oral tradition, or storytelling; the spiritual nature of childrearing; and the role of the extended family.[24]

As for the oral tradition, they explain that "through the telling of stories and legends, children learned about proper relationships with other people and the environment. They were taught to be good observers and to understand the meaning of non-verbal communication."[25]

The spiritual nature of childrearing was evident in the belief held by some tribes that children were special gifts from the Creator. The tribal elders used praise and reassurance to encourage positive and loving relationships between parents and their children. Prophecies were often made about the worth of the child and his or her future. The whole community recognized a child's growth and development through rites-of-passage ceremonies. These ceremonies were important for the children, too. The naming ceremony, for example, helped a child establish his or her identity in the tribe.

The extended family was the major socializer of children.

Individuals lived in small communities where they relied on each other for survival, and children learned quickly how important it was to cooperate, share, and show respect for elders. The consequences of breaking the community's rules or limits were clearly understood and accepted. Discipline was carefully tailored to make the child understand a specific rule or limit.

Nurturing was an important part of traditional childrearing. The use of cradleboards, for example, meant that infants were rarely separated from their mothers. However, no one person carried the whole burden of raising a child. Grandparents, aunts and uncles, and cousins were always nearby to help when parents had other responsibilities. Sometimes extended family members had specific roles to play—e.g., grandfather the storyteller, uncle the disciplinarian.[26]

These are the "old ways"—ways that existed prior to White influence. The program developers assert that the White influence, through such institutions as boarding schools, not only stripped away cultural traditions but instilled a "spare the rod and spoil the child" philosophy that runs against the traditional American Indian nurturing approach to children. It is out of a dual desire to reclaim traditional modes of childrearing and to abandon the "spare the rod" approach that this program was created.

The topics covered in the eight sessions are Traditional Parenting, Lessons of the Storyteller, Lessons of the Cradleboard, Harmony in Childrearing, Traditional Behavior Management, Lessons of Mother Nature, Praise in Traditional Parenting, and Choices in Parenting.

Further information about Positive Indian Parenting can be obtained from the

National Indian Child Welfare Association
5100 SW Macadam, Suite 300
Portland, OR 97239
(503) 222–4044
www.nicwa.org

SIBLINGS WITHOUT RIVALRY: A TOPIC-CENTERED PROGRAM

This six-session program by Adele Faber and Elaine Mazlish is devoted entirely to addressing the inevitable rivalries and conflicts of siblings.[27] It provides unique perspectives on these rivalries and a variety of creative ways to help parents manage them.

Session One: Helping Siblings Deal with Their Feelings About One Another

What would it feel like to have one's spouse bring home another wife or husband, and expect you to immediately love the intruder? This stunning analogy serves as a vehicle for helping parents appreciate the conflicted and powerful feelings children have for their siblings. They are also asked to recall their feelings for their own siblings.

A variety of ways are introduced for helping their children deal with negative feelings about a sibling, including acknowledging those feelings ("You feel he does it to irritate you" or "You don't like my spending so much time with her") rather than dismissing them, and helping children channel their feelings into symbolic or creative outlets ("No hurting your sister! You can show me your feelings with your doll," or, for an older child, "I think your sister needs to know how enraged you are in writing!").

Session Two: Keeping Children Separate and Unequal

Parents learn how children react to being compared unfavorably or favorably and how siblings feel about being treated equally. Ways to treat children unequally and still be fair are modeled and taught. Parents focus on each child's individual needs, instead of worrying about giving equal amounts. Also included are techniques for showing children how they are loved uniquely ("No one has your thoughts, your feelings, and your smile. I'm so glad you're my daughter!") instead of claiming equal love.

Session Three: Siblings in Roles

This session shows why brothers and sisters are often cast, and cast each other, into different roles, and how powerfully these roles affect their relationships with each other. Skills to help free each child to become his or her whole self are taught, such as how a parent helps a child who has been cast in the role of the "victim" to stand up for herself ("You can tell your brother, Daddy bought it for me. It's mine. I decide if I want to share!") or how a parent teaches a child who is a "bully" that he's capable of civil action ("No clobbering! You know how to get what you want without using physical force").

Session Four: When the Kids Fight

This session deals with the inevitable and sometimes dangerous impulse for siblings to fight each other. A step-by-step procedure to help children work out their problems themselves is suggested. Parents learn other skills to use when their children fight over property and when the fighting is heading toward hurting. Thus, a series of noninterventions and interventions are offered for parents to use, depending on the dangerousness of the conflict. The tactic of last resort, as in other programs such as *Confident Parenting*, is separation or time-out.

Session Five: Problem Solving

Here, a multistep approach is presented for helping children deal with problems they can't work out themselves. It enables parents to sit down with their young combatants and help them move toward resolving their conflicts by writing down each child's feelings and concerns without comment, then reading them aloud. The parents acknowledge the difficulty of the problem and ask everyone to come up with suggestions to solve the problem. Then all parties review each suggestion together and check those to which everyone can agree, shaking hands over the agreements and making plans to meet again.

Session Six: A Final Review

The last session is used to review and consolidate the skills learned. It includes applying all the skills in potentially explosive situations. Finally, parents are given a second opportunity to look at their own sibling relationships, and to see those relationships from the new perspectives they have gained through the program.[28]

More information about *Siblings Without Rivalry* can be obtained from the CICC website (www.ciccparenting.org) or from the website of the authors (http://fabermazlish.com).

THE *NURTURING* PROGRAMS

These programs by Dr. Stephen Bavolek represent *Age-Related Skill-Building* programs in the versions prepared for parents with different aged children, as well as *Family Skill-Building* programs in which all members of the family participate.

The origins of the *Nurturing* programs were very different from those of the other programs described thus far. They originated as educational interventions for abusive and dysfunctional families. At the time that the initial *Nurturing* program was designed, research with families who were abusive to their babies and young children showed that certain characteristic outlooks of parents in these families tended to contribute to the maltreatment of their children. These included:

1. *Inappropriate expectations* about the abilities of their children, where the parents assumed that their children could accomplish certain tasks long before their bodies and minds had developed sufficiently to accomplish them. The result was that there was always friction and disappointment, and the children were left feeling that they could never satisfy their parents.
2. *Lack of awareness of the child's emotional needs* and a related inability to respond appropriately. This lack of empathic understanding contributed further to the misunderstanding and poor nurturing of children.
3. *Strong belief in the value of using corporal punishment* to control and discipline children. Given these parents' misunderstandings of their children's abilities and their own difficulties with empathy, their belief in corporal punishment often got translated into severe beatings to keep children in line.
4. *A tendency to expect children to attend to and take care of the needs of the parents.* This reversal of the roles of parents and children fueled some serious and even fatal interactions between parents and babies, where the baby's incessant crying was interpreted to mean that the baby did not love the parent, or where a toddler's developmentally appropriate negativity was seen as deliberately making life miserable for an already overburdened parent.[29]

The originators of the *Nurturing* program chose to teach topics and skills specifically designed to address and counteract these harmful outlooks and attitudes. To counter inappropriate expectations, they included specific information about children's developmental stages and what realistically could be expected from children of different ages and stages, thus providing parents with solid information to offset their previously inappropriate expectations and help them become more aware of their children's needs for nurturance. In response to parental problems with being empathic, they provided skills for recognizing and identifying feelings and methods to expand self-awareness. To counter strong beliefs in corporal punishment, they provided conceptual tools for distinguishing between discipline and punishment, and they provided specific and nonviolent behavior-management skills for setting limits on children's behavior. Many of these behavior-management skills are similar to those taught in the CICC programs. Throughout the *Nurturing* program, it is reinforced that the parent's main role is that of a nurturer, thus counteracting the tendency to reverse this role.

In addition, the creators of the *Nurturing* program were also aware that many abusive parents were themselves maltreated as children and that they needed to be nurtured or reparented. Thus, special activities were included in the program to help nurture the parents, in addition to providing information and training to assist the parents in nurturing their children.

The program creators also realized that because the children of these parents were so poorly treated, the children themselves would need special help and training. This led them to design a program for the children to run concurrently with the program for the parents.

The result of all of these ideas is *Nurturing* programs that include all family members. The entire family comes to the class. The parents go into one group, and the children go into their own group. Both learn about nurturing ways of relating to themselves and to their family members. Halfway through the session, the parents and children come back together for some mutual nurturing and training, and for snacks and fun activities. Then they return to their individual groups for additional training. They end the session by coming back together for a group hug.

All versions of the program emphasize the *Nurturing* philosophy of developing empathy (the ability to be aware of the needs of others and to value those needs) among all family members and about the development of self-esteem (feeling good about themselves as men and women and boys and girls) within all family members. Each version also teaches a variety of skills to replace the use of corporal punishment.[30] A creative array of teaching methods are employed, including games, coloring books, videotaped presentations of concepts and skills, scary touch dolls, family logs, and videotapes such as *Shaking, Hitting and Spanking: What to Do Instead* and *Nurturing Touch*, where infant message techniques are demonstrated.

There now exist *Nurturing* programs for parents who are about to become parents (*The Prenatal Program*); program versions for parents of very young children, which are available in both English and Spanish; program versions for parents of elementary school–age children and for parents of adolescents; and a program for teenage parents and their families. Here's an example:

Nurturing **Program for Parents and Adolescents**

The often extraordinary intellectual, physical, and emotional developments that occur during the teenage years are presented and discussed, and specific strategies for relating to teenagers are taught.

Parents are told that two words best summarize the period of adolescence: *independence* and *autonomy*. All adolescents, to some degree or another, want to feel in control, want to make their own decisions, want to choose their own friends, and do not want to be told how to look, how to dress, or how to think. In short, adolescents want a piece of the action. They want to be included in making decisions, especially those that directly affect them.

The *Nurturing* program concludes that the key to living with adolescents is to let them exercise some autonomy and independence. The program informs parents that the adolescent's ability to think abstractly has grown by leaps and bounds. Instead of dealing with things "the way they are," adolescents begin to think about things "the way they could be." Statements by parents such as "This is my house and as long as you live under my roof, you obey my rules" simply are not accepted by teenagers. They want to know the logic or reasoning behind some action or rule. They do not want to follow a rule just because someone says so. Parents who do not realize the purpose behind all the "Whys" that teenagers ask can find life with their teenager to be one battle after another.

The program stresses that talking with, listening to, compromising, negotiating, and including adolescents as decision makers is the only way parents and teenagers can live together in harmony.

The program also helps parents and teenagers work together to arrive at livable family rules, with rewards for following rules as well as penalties for violating them. Rewards suggested for desirable, rule-following actions include praise, touch, privileges, allowance, and objects that money can buy. The penalties or punishments include loss of privileges, being grounded, restitution (paying for some misdeed with money or extra chores), and parental disappointment.

Issues such as pregnancy delay, sex, sexuality, HIV/AIDS, suicide, chemical use, and peer pressure are given special coverage. As in all *Nurturing* programs, the children have their own group in which to discuss these matters independently of their parents, adding opportunities for children to explore and successfully deal with these important issues on their own.

This *Nurturing* program consists of 12 3-hour training sessions. More can be learned about all of the *Nurturing* programs at both the author's website (www.nurturingparenting.com) and the CICC website (www.ciccparenting.org). As is probably quite obvious, although most of these programs were initially created for parents who had been maltreating their children, they are quite applicable and useful for any and all parents who want to do a good job raising their children.

STEPS TO INDEPENDENCE

This program by Drs. Bruce Baker and Alan Brightman is for teaching the parents of children with special needs how to teach their children basic self-help, play, and functional academic skills.[31] Parents learn a systematic, step-by-step teaching approach that involves knowing exactly what you want to teach to a child, how to do the teaching, and what types of rewards to use.

The range of skills that the program prepares the parents to teach their children includes:

> *Basic Attention Skills.* Looking when called, coming when called, identifying objects, following simple directions, and imitating
> *Basic Gross Motor Skills.* Sitting down, standing up from a chair, and going up and down stairs
> *Basic Fine Motor Skills and Activities.* Pushing, pulling, holding and turning, holding and releasing objects, water play, putting objects into a hole in a box, and pinching

Self-Help Skills. Drinking from a cup, eating with a spoon, eating
with a fork, spreading and cutting with a knife, removing and
putting on pants, putting on socks, threading a belt, zipping
up, buttoning, putting on shoes, hanging up clothes, brushing
teeth, washing face, bathing, making a bed, setting the table,
sweeping

Play Skills. For playing alone: stacking rings, stringing beads,
working puzzles, matching pictures. For playing with others:
beanbag toss, playing ball, art gallery, and dramatic play

Functional Academic Skills. Reading sight words, telling time, using
money[32]

The book for this program is called *Steps to Independence* and it is available on the CICC website.

STOP AND THINK SOCIAL SKILLS TRAINING PROGRAM

The *Stop and Think* program by Dr. Howard M. Knoof also teaches parents how to teach their children important skills, but this program is for all parents, not just those with children with special needs.[33] *Stop and Think* helps parents teach their children several basic and advanced social skills.

Survival Skills

These are the most basic skills that are needed in order to be successful with all of the other skills that are taught. These skills lay the foundation for all other skills and include:

Listening
Following directions
Using nice talk
Using brave talk
Rewarding yourself
Evaluating yourself

Interpersonal Skills

These skills help children interact successfully and get along with siblings, peers, older and younger students, parents, teachers, and other adults. Included here are:

Sharing
Asking for permission
Joining an activity
Contributing to discussions
Answering questions
How to interrupt
How to wait your turn
How to wait for an adult's attention
Beginning/ending a conversation
Giving/accepting compliments

Problem-Solving Skills

These skills help children solve or prevent individual, interactive, peer, or classroom problems, and include:

Asking for help
Apologizing
Accepting consequences
Setting a goal
Deciding what to do
Avoiding trouble
Understanding the feelings of others
Responding to failure

Conflict Resolution Skills

These skills help children deal with highly emotional situations and resolve existing intrapersonal and interpersonal conflicts. Included here are:

Dealing with teasing
Dealing with losing
Dealing with anger
Walking away from a fight
Dealing with accusations
Dealing with being left out
Dealing with peer pressure
Dealing with fear
Dealing with the anger of others[34]

This *Stop and Think Social Skill Training* program uses a five-step approach for teaching, reinforcing, or using any of the social skills mentioned above. The five steps are:

1. *Stop and Think!* This step is designed to condition children to take the time necessary to calm down and think about how they want to handle a situation.
2. *Are You Going to Make a Good Choice or a Bad Choice?* This step provides children with a chance to decide what kind of choice they want to make. With help from parents, along with the meaningful positive and negative consequences for various choices, children decide to make a "good choice."
3. *What Are Your Choices or Steps?* This step helps children develop a specific plan before implementing a social skill. Parents assist children by providing possible good choices or by teaching specific skills by breaking them into their component behavioral parts. This step helps children to "think before they act"—getting them ready to move into action.
4. *Just Do It!* Here is where children actually perform their "good choice" behavior. If the specific skill or choice works, that's great. If not, the child is either provided with additional choices by their parents, or they are taught a new skill to use. Sometimes, they are prompted to go over the steps of a previously taught skill to make sure that they are using it properly. Once successful, it's on to the last step.
5. *The Good Job!* This step prompts children to reinforce themselves for successfully using a social skill and successfully responding to a situation or request. This step is important because children—and adults—do not always reinforce themselves for making good choices and doing a good job. Thus, this step teaches self-reinforcement.[35]

PARENTS ON BOARD

The *Parents on Board* program by Drs. Michael H. Popkin, Bettie B. Youngs, and Jane M. Healy, is a parent-involvement-in-education program.[36] It is the program from which we drew many of the ideas about education for the guidelines in Chapter 4. The *Parents on Board* program is for parents of 4- to 14-year-old children, and it is based on the assumption that parents want their children to succeed in school, but aren't sure how they can help.

The program reinforces parents' motivation for their children's academic success by sharing some important facts from the research on children's academic achievement. The research is very clear that children whose parents are involved in their education:

Get better grades
Do more homework
Have better attendance
Have a higher graduation rate
Demonstrate a more positive attitude[37]

The program then goes on to teach parents a set of skills and attitudes on how best to be involved in their children's education. The three teaching sessions cover:

Session One: Preparing Your Child to Succeed

Learning styles
Learning habits
Social skills
Healthy bodies, healthy minds
Structuring the school-smart home
Start the year off right
Maintain a good relationship all year
Understanding information from the school
If you suspect a learning difference

Session Two: Encouraging Positive Behavior

Encouragement
Discipline
Beliefs build success
How to "teach" a positive belief

Session Three: Reinforcing Your Child's Academic Skills

Parent as coach
Coaching your child in reading
Coaching your child in writing, spelling, math, and science[38]

There are many other skill-building programs that now exist, each of which teaches a series of excellent skills and strategies. There are more such programs for the parents of young children and for the parents of teenagers. There are programs that focus on specific parenting issues and challenges, and similar programs for parents of children with special needs.

The following are brief descriptions of some of these fine programs. You can learn about them by going to the CICC website section on Parenting Skill-Building programs or going to the websites indicated.

ACTIVE PARENTING

There are several versions of this program, which was the first in the nation to make use of filmed vignettes of effective and ineffective ways of raising children.[39] These include versions for parents of different-aged children (*1, 2, 3, 4 Parents!* for parents of children 4 and under; *Active Parenting Now* for parents of elementary school–age children; and *Active Parenting for Teens*). There are also program versions for parents from Jewish and Christian backgrounds, and for parents who are raising children in stepfamilies. In addition, there are programs of different lengths, including single-topic programs that can be taught through *Lunch-and-Learn* presentations at work sites, and three- and seven-session versions.

These programs exemplify and use the Encouragement Approach that we learned in the guidelines chapter. Other parenting topics and skills that are taught include the use of logical and natural consequences, active communication, emotional intelligence, "I" Messages, the goals of misbehavior, and family meetings.[40] The program can be accessed at www.activeparenting.org.

CHILDREN IN THE MIDDLE

This is a program for parents who are going through a divorce. Communication skills are taught to help them learn how to avoid involving their children in loyalty conflicts, which are the most damaging aspect of divorce for children. The program can be accessed at www.divorce-education.com.

FAMILIES AND SCHOOLS TOGETHER (*FAST*)

FAST is program that brings parents, children, and schools together for a variety of activities, bonding, and togetherness. Ten to twelve families meet for eight weekly sessions for a family meal and a variety of social activities, including music, drawing, family games, children's games, a parent group, and a chance for parents to interact with each other. These activities are fun for the children and families. Participating families eat dinner together and participate in communication activities that improve their functioning as family units. The program can be accessed at www.wcer.wisc.edu/fast.

GUIDING GOOD CHOICES

This is a substance abuse prevention program that was previously known as *Preparing for the Drug Free Years*. It teaches parents the skills and information needed to reduce their children's risk for using alcohol and other drugs. Designed for parents of children in grades four to eight (ages 9–14), the program can be found at www.drp.org/prevention-programs/guiding-good-choices.

PARENTING WISELY

Parenting Wisely is an interactive CD-ROM program designed for parents of adolescents and preadolescents (ages 8–18). Nine typical problem situations are presented, including doing homework, chores, stepparent–youth relationships, monitoring "troublesome" friends, improving poor school performance, sibling fighting, and complying with parental requests over phone use and music volume.[41] Both effective and ineffective solutions are depicted for each problem, followed by comprehensive critiques and explanations of the parenting and communication skills viewed. The program's website is www.familyworksinc.com.

STRENGTHENING FAMILIES

This 14-session parenting and family skill-building program teaches parenting skills, children's life skills, and family life skills. Parents and children participate separately and together. There are special versions for parents with children of different ages, as well as versions for various cultural groups. The program can be accessed at www.strengtheningfamiliesprogram.org.

SYSTEMATIC TRAINING FOR EFFECTIVE PARENTING (STEP)

This program relies on the Encouragement Approach that was learned in the chapter on guidelines, as well as on the teaching of a variety of other skills and strategies, such as the goals of child misbehavior, logical and natural consequences, and family meetings. There are different versions for parents with young children (*Early Childhood STEP*) and parents of teenagers (*STEP Teen*); there is the basic *STEP* program for parents of elementary school children, and versions for use in religious settings. The program can be found at both www.ciccparenting.org or www.STEPPUBLISHERS.org.

THE INCREDIBLE YEARS

This parenting skill-building program is devoted to the particular challenges of raising children in the 4- to 8-year-old age range, and especially children who are experiencing behavior problems. It focuses on strengthening parenting competencies (monitoring, positive discipline, confidence) and fostering parents' involvement in children's school experiences in order to promote children's academic and social competencies and reduce conduct problems.[42] The program's website is www.incredibleyears.com.

Remember, if you can't find any of these programs being offered by your local organizations, give the leaders of those organizations information about the programs, and ask them to bring the program to the community. Recall that there are at least three ways that they can do that, each of which was indicated in the previous chapter.

CHAPTER EIGHT

More Parenting Resources

As has been mentioned, the 21st-century parent is at an advantage because there have never been as many parenting and family skill-building and other parenting education services available to help in raising healthy and happy children. The current generation of parents is also advantaged because it has never been easier to find the other types of community services that are available to assist you and your family. This is so because of the creation of the 2-1-1 telephone connecting number.

2-1-1 AND COMMUNITY SERVICES

This is an easy-to-remember telephone number that, where available, connects people with important community services and volunteer opportunities. The implementation of 2-1-1 is being spearheaded by the United Way and referral agencies in state and local communities.

Every hour of every day, someone in the United States needs essential services—from finding an after-school program to securing adequate care for a child or an aging parent. Faced with a dramatic increase in the number of agencies and help-lines, people often don't know where to turn. In many cases, people end up going without these necessary services because they do not know where to start. 2-1-1 helps people find and give help.

Although services that are offered through 2-1-1 vary from community to community, 2-1-1 provides callers with information about and referrals to human services for everyday needs and in times of crisis. For example, 2-1-1 can offer access to the following types of services:

Basic Human Needs Resources: Food banks, clothing closets, shelters, rent assistance, utility assistance.

Physical and Mental Health Resources: Health insurance programs, Medicaid and Medicare, maternal health, Children's Health Insurance Program (CHIP), medical information lines, crisis intervention services, support groups, counseling, drug and alcohol intervention and rehabilitation.

Employment Supports: Financial assistance, job training, transportation assistance, education programs.

Support for Older Americans and Persons with Disabilities: Adult day care, congregate meals, Meals on Wheels, respite care, home health care, transportation, homemaker services.

Support for Children, Youth, and Families: Child care, after-school programs, Head Start, family resource centers, summer camps and recreation programs, mentoring, tutoring, protective services.[1]

Volunteer Opportunities and Donations

As of January 2007, 2-1-1 serves over 193 million Americans—over 65% of the U.S. population. There were 209 active 2-1-1 systems covering all or part of 41 states (including 18 states with 100% coverage), plus Washington, D.C. and Puerto Rico.[2]

Most people will be able to find just about any type of service by calling 2-1-1. If you do not live in an area where 2-1-1 is operating, you can find a local Information and Referral Service by going to the website of one of the main organizations that is spearheading the spread of 2-1-1 (along with the United Way), the Alliance of Information and Referrals Systems (AIRS), located online at www.airs.org. AIRS is the professional association for more than 1,000 community information and referral providers.[3] Once you are on the AIRS homepage, click on the 2-1-1 logo. That will take you to a page that will guide you to find a local information and referral agency.

TELEVISION

The proliferation of cable and pay-per-view channels has made television an extremely helpful vehicle for learning about effective parenting and child development. Television always had some programming directed toward parents, and now there are more channels through which you can gain such education.

In addition, news broadcasts often have segments on "Tips for Parents," where the stations contact parenting experts to provide guidance and convey information on parenting through sound bites. The value of such programming is evidenced by the fact that these parenting news features often air during the times when the television stations have the most to gain from having as large a viewership as possible, the "sweep" periods when a larger audience can influence how much stations can charge for advertising time.

Specific programs that are devoted to effective parenting are excellent ways to learn. The various *Supernanny* shows are good examples. The wise nannies who are dispatched to do their special type of home-visiting parenting education employ methods and principles that are taught in many of the parenting skill-building programs that we have learned about. They are extremely creative practitioners who convey sophisticated ideas in ways that are easy to comprehend. They also have a high appreciation for the family dynamics that feed into problems in childrearing. Often, the families who are chosen for these types of programs are families in which chaos reigns, and the problems between the parents are major contributors to the chaos. The supernannies perform a great service by demonstrating how important it is to address those relationship issues. For families that are reaching the breaking point because of childrearing problems, a combination of wise counseling and parenting skill-training is the best mixture. The TV supernannies provide fine examples.

Another popular show that provides very personalized and dramatic examples of both ineffective and effective parenting is the *Dr. Phil Show*. Dr. Phil draws on his personal and professional experiences as a practicing psychologist to help parents and families that are in distress and hurting each other. He provides perspective on what these families are doing to perpetuate their problems and then offers guidance on how these problems can be better addressed. The guidance includes learning and using better parenting and human relations skills—the same types of skills that are taught in modern parenting and family programs.

PARENTING MAGAZINES AND NEWSPAPERS

In addition to the venerable *Parents Magazine,* there is now a great range of fine magazines that provide excellent articles and tips on parenting. There are also parenting magazines for specific populations of parents, such as *Working Mothers* magazine. These publications often have issues that focus on a specific parenting challenge and provide several different perspectives. For example, the October 2006 issue of *Parenting* was devoted to the issue of getting organized. It included the results of a survey of 1,000 mothers who "spilled their secrets." It provided guidance on matters such as organizing the family in the morning, cleaning and errands, preparing for dinner, making bedtime less stressful, and having weekends for enjoyment.

Other print media resources that are now available include parenting newspapers that you can obtain at newsstands and newspaper boxes in the front of markets and children's stores. These publications usually reflect their local nature, such as *LA Parent, Seattle Child*, or *New York Family*. Each of these publications provides a unique resource for parents, educators, professionals, and child-care providers, by supplying information on what to do and where to go with children in their own town, school district, and neighborhood.

Regular features include a monthly calendar of events for children and their parents, practical advice for parents, information about outings, and reviews of current plays, movies, books, and local restaurants. Feature articles discuss a range of important issues that affect families, from prenatal care to teenage parties.

These regional publications have their own organization, the Parenting Publications of America. You can search for the parenting newspaper in your area by going to the organization's website (www.parenting publications.org) and entering your state in the search section.

USING THE INTERNET

As we have already seen, 21st-century parents are fortunate because of the existence of the Internet. All of the top parenting and family skill-building programs have websites where you can learn about them and become connected. In addition, a few of those fine programs can actually be taken over the Internet. For example, it is now possible to participate in an Active Parenting program from home by visiting www.activeparenting.com.

The resources mentioned here barely scratch the surface of what is actually available on the Internet to assist you with raising your children. By going to a search engine such as google.com, you will find at least 63 million websites about parenting![4] Many of these websites are outstanding. They help answer just about any question you might have about parenting, and they include chat rooms and bulletin boards where you can correspond electronically with other parents and parenting experts. Websites of a comprehensive nature, such as www.babycenter.com and www.parentcenter.com, also allow you to receive a regular parenting newsletter that is geared to the specific age of your child.

However, many parenting websites are of minimal or little value. The challenge is to find those that are going to be most beneficial to you in your unique parenting situation.

Fortunately, several concerned individuals and organizations have taken the time and energy to evaluate the enormous number of parenting websites and recommend the ones they consider to be exemplary. Here are some of the places where you can go to find the results of these thoughtful and careful reviews:

> *"Best Bet" Parenting Websites (www.cyfs.org).* This list was compiled by a workgroup of parents and parent educators affiliated with the Children, Youth, and Family Services organization in Charlottesville, Virginia. To access their extensively annotated list, go to their website, scroll down to find "Best Parenting Websites" and click. The list is organized so you can find excellent sites for the parenting of children of different ages and sites on a variety of related topics, such as advocacy, stress management, and adoption advice.
>
> *Top Sites for Parents (www.topsitesforparents.com).* Dr. Vernon Brablam, a retired optometrist and father of four daughters, searched hundreds of thousands of parenting websites. He arrived at "200+ Fabulous, Fantastic and Informative Things for Parents to Learn on the Internet."[5] He has organized these fabulous sites into the following categories: General Parenting; Pregnancy, Infants, and Toddlers; Kid's Health; Adolescents and Teens; Spiritual; Disabilities and Special Needs; Divorce and Shared Parenting; and Adoptive Parenting. His entire list can be downloaded in the form of an e-book.
>
> *Parenthood.com (www.parenthood.com/links.html).* This is an excellent website that contains a directory of other very helpful sites, organized by topics, such as breastfeeding, caring for children, motherhood, fatherhood, health/medical, safety, starting a family, and so forth. Many of the other, more comprehensive sites, such as babycenter.com and parentcenter.com, also have these types of Internet parenting directories.

ForParentsOnly.com. This website provides a search engine that can connect you to any category of parenting websites you may want to explore.

Tufts University Child and Family WebGuide (www.cfw.tufts.edu). This web guide is a directory that evaluates, describes, and provides links to hundreds of sites containing child development research and practical advice. It was created and is operated by the Eliot-Pearson Department of Child Development at Tufts University. It was initiated because many parenting websites provide information that is not consistent with child development research. This resource guides viewers toward those sites that provide research-based parenting advice. It is based on parent and professional feedback, as well as support from noted child development experts such as David Elkind, Edward Zigler, and the late Fred Rogers. It includes major sections on Family/Parenting, Education/Learning, Typical Child Development, Health/Mental Health, and Resources/Recreation.

Let's move on to see what it means for our country when we are as effective parents as possible, and to find out what else we can use our power to accomplish for our own children and for all the children and families in America.

CHAPTER NINE

Conclusions

When you are effective as a parent, you are performing a tremendous service for your children, for your community, and for the entire nation. Your non-abused and non-neglected children are most likely to become healthy, happy, and productive citizens who eventually become good parents themselves. Your family and your children's families are also more likely to be the strongest and most stable families in your communities.

Your competencies and commitment to your children also make it less likely that your children will have the learning, health, and mental health problems that so often predispose children to failure in school and a desire to strike back at the community. You are, therefore, also helping to make communities safer and better places to live, and saving yourself and other taxpayers the expense of having to treat public problems such as juvenile delinquency, substance abuse, school dropout, gangs, crime, and violence.

You are also helping to make schools better by sending them students that are ready and capable of learning, and you are helping civic and religious institutions by bringing them young people who are comfortable helping others because of how well they have been cared for themselves. In addition, you are improving the economy of the nation because your effectively raised young people are the most likely to have developed both the technical and interpersonal skills and outlooks that are needed for success in the 21st-century workforce (see Figure 9.1).

However, it is not at all easy to be an effective parent during these fast-paced and turbulent times. There are internal and external forces that make parenting particularly daunting. These include difficulties that so many parents experience in getting along with each other within marriages and other relationships, as well as external forces that

FIGURE 9.1. Benefits of Effective Parenting

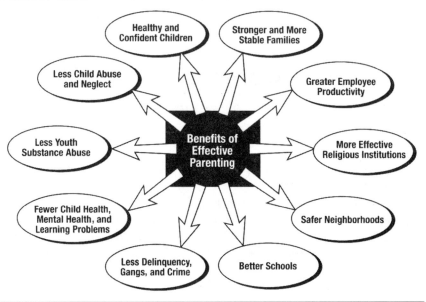

come from children being pressured to use drugs and to engage in adult sex at earlier ages than ever before, pressures that put them at risk for becoming teenage parents and contracting potentially deadly STDs. There is also the problem of gangs that can make leaving the house or apartment a treacherous undertaking, and the violence to which the omnipresent media expose our children. Indeed, parenting at the beginning of the 21st century could be thought of as parenting in the worst of times.

But, as we have learned, raising children today is also parenting in the best of times. Never before in history have there been as many parenting assistance services and programs than there are now. In addition, no prior generation of parents has had the Internet through which to learn about services and programs that can help, and in which they can enroll and receive assistance. The literally millions of websites about parenting afford a cornucopia of learning opportunities. And, although prior generations could call their local Information and Referral Service to find out where in their communities they could obtain various services, there now is one number that the vast majority of American parents can use to become connected with local services: 2-1-1.

In addition, we now have solid, research-based information about a productive pattern of parenting that best predisposes our children to become healthy, happy, and productive people. This pattern includes being warm, accepting, and respectful of our children; being firm and fair in providing discipline; making age-appropriate demands for mature behavior; being sensitive and responsive to children's cues and needs; and making children a priority in our lives. We now also know from research that there are other patterns and even specific practices, such as corporal punishment and verbal aggression, that are harmful to our children's growth and lives.

Best of all, there are now available many programs and resources to help us keep our parenting in line with the productive pattern, including the modern parenting and family skill-building programs that we have learned about. These programs are vehicles for helping to instill in our children the virtues and values that are most cherished in our society, such as fairness, honesty, humility, courtesy, mutual respect, empathy, compassion, hard work, responsibility, and self-discipline. The emphasis in these programs on relating to children without using corporal punishment also helps further the value of nonviolence.

The combination of knowledge about what is most helpful in raising children in a democratic society and the availability of numerous educational programs and resources to guide and assist us makes the seemingly daunting problems of raising children in the 21st century not only manageable but surmountable.

The challenge is how to make wise and efficient use of all the resources that are now so conveniently available. A related challenge is that we may have to advocate in our local communities to ensure that the full array of modern parenting resources, including modern parenting and family skill-building programs, is available for our own use and the use of our fellow parents. Reading and using the presentation and guidelines found in this book is a good starting point, so you are well on your way.

Underlying the numerous examples and recommendations for being a positive and effective parent that we have reviewed in this book are what might be called the "principles of positive parenting":

- The models we provide in our daily interactions with our children and in our interactions with our partners and spouses are important in determining what our children learn and how they behave.
- The consequences that we provide for our children when they behave well or poorly are critical to how they will behave in the future. The more frequently these consequences are of a positive and nurturing nature, the more likely it is that our children will grow positively. The more thoughtful and time-consuming the consequences that we provide when our children misbehave, the more likely it is that our children will become prosocial and productive community members.
- Assuming a non-hitting attitude and stance is necessary so that we do not model violence in the home. Such an attitude and approach stimulates and requires us to learn nonviolent problem-solving and conflict resolution methods, such as those that are available in the modern skill-building programs.
- Making children a priority in our lives requires time, patience, sacrifice, and a willingness to learn. But it is well worth the effort, as children who are priorities are the most likely to turn out to be fine citizens and good mommies and daddies themselves.

THE NATIONAL EFFECTIVE PARENTING INITIATIVE (NEPI)

There is more that we can do to help ourselves become better parents to our own children. There is also more that can be done to help all of the children in our communities be raised as effectively and skill-fully as possible. These personal and societal goals can be furthered and accomplished through involvement with a grassroots effort that I have played a role in creating—NEPI, the National Effective Parenting Initiative. NEPI addresses those aspects of our society where we can and must do better, such as preventing the abuse and neglect of our children and having children with special needs identified and properly helped as early in life as possible.

NEPI is a coalition of concerned individuals and organizations that is working toward the goal of having every child in our country effectively and humanely raised by parents who have received the best possible education, training, and support. Achieving this goal begins with each and every parent committing him- or herself to becoming the best parent possible and seeking out and receiving the best available parenting education. Having read this book makes you particularly well-qualified to become part of NEPI.

It is easy to become involved. Just go to NEPI's website, www. effectiveparentingusa.org. There, you will find an array of suggestions that you can use right now to help yourself be the best parent possible and to help all parents raise healthy and productive citizens. There are three interrelated membership programs: for parents, for professionals who educate and work with parents and children, and for agencies and organizations that provide parenting services. Each membership program has its own array of benefits and responsibilities, including access to and interaction with the nation's top parent experts and programs.

One of the things that you can do is make a public statement by signing an online *Effective Parenting Petition*. This lets the world and our elected officials know where you stand on these important matters. Here's what the petition says:

> Every child deserves to be raised sensitively and effectively by loving and skillful parents.
> When children are so raised, they are on a path to reach their full potential as human beings. They are best prepared to become healthy, peaceful and productive adults.
> Parents and others who assume the awesome responsibility of raising children deserve the best possible parenting education, guidance and support.
> Love is not enough. The dangers of childhood and the pressures of modern family life require parents to be especially knowledgeable and skillful.
> It is in the best interests of our children and our nation for all parents to be educated and supported as fully as possible.[1]

By signing this petition, you are affirming the importance of advocating, celebrating, and promoting effective parenting and parenting education.

Other actions that you can take are fully described on the NEPI website. Some of those actions include advocating that our elected officials, including the president and members of Congress, become champions of effective parenting and parenting education, and institute a federal government "Effective Parenting Initiative." There has already been progress in those areas through a White House briefing and through communications with different members of Congress.[2] Information about the proposed initiative and the briefing is also available on the NEPI website.

I strongly urge you to extend your desire to be the best parent possible by helping all parents do the same through participation in NEPI.

Finally, it is my sincerest desire that you use what I have shared with you in this book to help you do what is best for your children. Being an effective parent is both a difficult and time-consuming under-taking, but it is well worth the effort, energy, and sacrifice. Giving our children the gift of effective parenting is giving them the greatest gift of all. And, as my wife and I are finding out from all we have done to be the best parents possible for our daughters Lisa and Brittany, effective parenting is truly a gift that keeps on giving.

The CICC *Discovery Tool*— Sample Version

In this sample version of the *Discovery Tool*, you will be able to take and score the questionnaires for children in three age periods: birth through 3 months, 9 to 11 months, and children who are 3 years old. For the other age periods, use the Internet version of the tool, which can be found at www.ciccparenting.org. There is a modest fee for using that self-scoring version.

PART ONE:
THE AGE-SPECIFIC *DISCOVERY TOOL* QUESTIONNAIRES

Instructions: Except for the birth through 3 months of age period, all of the age-specific CICC *Discovery Tool* questionnaires include the six areas of child development. Within each area, you will usually find items that are referred to as "basic skills" and items that are referred to as "potential problem behaviors."

You are to indicate whether a skill or behavior item is either "true" or "false" for a particular child. By indicating that a basic skill is "true," you are indicating that the child *has actually shown or demonstrated that specific skill.* By selecting "false" in regard to a specific basic skill item, you are saying that the *skill has not been observed or demonstrated.* By indicating that a potential problem behavior is "true," you are saying that the particular problem behavior *has been observed.* (Note: In the case when the problem behavior is an *absence of a behavior*—e.g., the child doesn't speak, indicating "true" shows that the child has not or is not engaging in the particular behavior.) By selecting "false" as a response to a potential problem behavior item, you are indicating that this behavior *has not been observed.*

For the birth through 3 months of age period, you are provided with important childrearing information and are alerted to behaviors that should be of special concern and for which you should seek professional consultation.

As you complete the questionnaire, you may want to stop to observe or interact with the child to be sure about your answers. Or you may want to consult with a spouse or other person who is connected with the child regarding a particular item. As you will be able to tell, the questionnaires inquire about very specific skills and potential problems.

The results of your taking the CICC *Discovery Tool* questionnaire will be most useful to you when you fill it out as accurately as possible. Take your time. Have fun learning about the varied and numerous skills that most children your child's age develop. It's important to be honest about indicating potential problem behaviors.

Finally, in selecting which age-specific questionnaire to use, consider whether the child was born prematurely. If so, you will need to subtract the number of weeks that the child was born early, which may result in your having to use the questionnaire for a child who is "younger" than your child. For example, if your child was born 4 weeks premature and is currently 15 months old, your child's "adjusted age" would be 14 months old and, therefore, you would select the questionnaire for children 12 through 14 months of age.

BIRTH THROUGH 3 MONTHS OF AGE

You need not be concerned if your infant's developmental journey during these months is somewhat different from the route taken by a neighbor's baby. There are major events—such as a child being born premature, difficulties in the birthing process, medical conditions, environmental stresses, and other conditions—that may have a tremendous impact on development during this period of life, so babies of this age differ greatly from one another.

A newborn baby's main developmental task is to adjust to life outside the protected environment of the mother's womb. It is an important time of transition as he or she learns to become independent of what the mother provided automatically during the 9 months of prenatal development. During this period, the infant develops from a relatively helpless newborn taking his or her first breath to an individual who has mastered those developmental achievements usually seen in a 4-month-old child.

Generally, this is the time when babies develop the ability to suck proficiently for nourishment. They begin to become alert to their environment. As muscle strength increases, the infant gains head control and meaningful use of arms and hands.

A baby needs a lot of cuddling and social contact with its mother or other primary caregiver to maximize his or her development. It is wise to respond to a baby's cries to help him or her develop a sense of trust. You can't spoil a baby at this age by providing too much love and attention.

You need to talk to the baby and gaze into his or her eyes. All of these behaviors will help strengthen the attachment that is so necessary for healthy development. Many babies this age like to be swaddled, or wrapped snuggly, in a receiving blanket. This mimics the comforting feeling of being closely held inside the mother's uterus and helps them adjust to their new life.

Developmental Alert: If you are the baby's parent, you know your baby better than anyone else and you are often the first to notice a delay in an infant's development. Yet parents aren't always sure whether a behavior they observe is something to be concerned about. Although every child develops differently, the following uncommon behaviors may be a cause for concern and should be discussed with a health-care provider:

- Tic-like movements (sudden jerks or twitches) of the face and head
- Moving one side of the body significantly more than the other
- Looking unusually stiff
- Rarely moving arms and legs
- Not blinking when shown a bright light
- Not reacting to sudden, loud noises (for example, does not startle, blink, stop sucking, cry, or wake up when you clap loudly near him or her)
- Being difficult to hold (for example, arching the back when you try to hold him or her)

9 THROUGH 11 MONTHS OF AGE

Skills and Behaviors

Select "true" or "false" for each item as it applies to your child. We know that choosing "true" or "false" may be difficult because young children often change from day to day. However, please select the answer that best describes this child *at this time.*

Movement (physical development and motor skills)

A. Basic Skills

___True or ___False   Sits independently (without support)

___True or ___False   Can support most of his or her weight in a standing position (held or alone)

___True or ___False   Crawls, creeps, or scoots forward

___True or ___False   Moves toy from hand to hand

___True or ___False   Can scoop or pinch to pick up a small object (for example, a Cheerio or raisin)

B. Potential Problem Behavior

___True or ___False   Moves or uses one side of the body significantly more than the other (more than just favoring one hand over the other)

Thinking and Learning (cognitive development)

A. Basic Skills

___True or ___False   Explores with hands and mouth

___True or ___False   Repeats actions to experiment (for example, shakes, bangs, throws, or drops objects to make noise)

___True or ___False   Finds partially hidden objects (for example, uncovers toy that is half-covered by a blanket)

Communication (receptive and expressive language)

A. Basic Skills

___True or ___False   Responds to own name (for example, looks up when called)

___True or ___False   Understands a few words (such as *no, bye-bye, juice,* and *up*)

___True or ___False   Listens to or follows conversations of others

___True or ___False   Imitates some sounds you make (like a cough)

___True or ___False   Babbles (using sounds such as , "da da da," "ma ma ma," "ba ba ba")

___True or ___False   Uses vocal signals other than crying to gain assistance

B. Potential Problem Behavior

___True or ___False   Rarely makes sounds (such as cooing and babbling)

The Senses: Vision, Hearing, and Touch (includes sensory integration)

A. Basic Skills

___True or ___False   Looks at and follows a moving object or person (for example, will watch you move a toy from side to side or up and down)

___True or ___False   Turns head or eyes toward a sound

___True or ___False   Enjoys or puts up with different types of touch (such as being held, bathed, or having hair brushed)

Relating to Self and Others (social and emotional development)

A. Basic Skills

___True or ___False   Shows a full range of emotions (for example, smiles, cries, and shows angry facial expressions)

___True or ___False   Interested in mirror images (reaches out and pats his or her reflection in mirror)

___True or ___False   Enjoys watching (and may play) games like "peek-a-boo"

B. Potential Problem Behaviors

___True or ___False   Does not laugh or smile

___True or ___False   Avoids or rarely makes eye contact with others (for example, when trying to get the baby's attention, the baby avoids looking right at you)

___True or ___False   Is very difficult to calm down or comfort (on a regular basis, will continue to cry, fuss, or scream even after being held, rocked, talked to, changed, or fed)

Self-Care (daily living skills)

A. Basic Skills

___True or ___False   Sleeps for at least 4–6 hours during the night

___True or ___False   Feeds self with fingers

___True or ___False   Holds bottle by self

3-YEAR-OLD CHILDREN

Skills and Behaviors

Select "true" or "false" for each item as it applies to this child. We know that choosing "true" or "false" may be difficult because young children often change from day to day. However, please select the answer that best describes this child *at this time.*

Movement (physical development and motor skills)

A. Basic Skills

___True or ___False   Runs easily, falling rarely

___True or ___False   Jumps in place (with both feet off the ground)

___True or ___False   Kicks a ball forward

___True or ___False   Walks up stairs without help

___True or ___False   Rides a tricycle or a bicycle with training wheels

___True or ___False   Enjoys movement (such as climbing, going down slide, swinging, and running around playground)

___True or ___False   Throws a small ball overhand

___True or ___False   Turns pages of a book one page at a time

___True or ___False   Holds crayon or pencil with fingers rather than in fist

___True or ___False   Copies a circle (when shown how)

___True or ___False   Tries to cut paper with children's scissors (may not be able to cut the paper, but can get scissors to open and close)

B. Potential Problem Behaviors

___True or ___False   Falls a lot when walking or seems unusually "clumsy"

___True or ___False   Rocks body a lot

___True or ___False   Uses unusual hand movements on a regular basis (for example, flaps hands in front of face or flaps like a bird)

___True or ___False   Walks on tiptoes a lot

___True or ___False   Uses one side of the body more than the other (other than being right- or left-handed)

___True or ___False   Looks unusually stiff

___True or ___False   Looks floppy, like a "rag doll"

Thinking and Learning *(cognitive development)*

A. Basic Skills

___True or ___False   Knows that he or she is a boy or a girl

___True or ___False   Can tell you his or her age

___True or ___False   Knows what common household things are used for (for example, knows the telephone is for calling Mommy or Daddy at work)

___True or ___False   Can match things by their shape and/or color

___True or ___False   Understands some simple math ideas (for example, can count to 2 and knows the difference between "more" and "less" and "big" and "little")

___True or ___False   Can repeat back to you at least part of some common rhymes (such as "Twinkle, Twinkle Little Star" and "Itsy Bitsy Spider")

___True or ___False   Follows two-step directions (such as "pick up the toy and put it on the table")

___True or ___False   Plays make-believe with dolls, animals, and people

___True or ___False   Can play one game or activity for at least 3–5 minutes without getting up to go to another activity

Communication *(expressive and receptive language)*

A. Basic Skills

___True or ___False   Can tell you his or her first name (or nickname) and last name

___True or ___False   Can name four or more different objects in a picture book (such as "ball," "kitty," "doll," or "doggy")

___True or ___False   Asks "what" and "where" questions (for example, "What's that?" or "Where's Mommy?")

___True or ___False   Uses words that describe things (such as "It's icky" or "I'm hungry")

___True or ___False   Uses sentences with three or more words (such as "Give me juice" or "Mommy go bye-bye")

___True or ___False   Uses words that strangers can understand most of the time

___True or ___False   Can describe what people are doing (for example, "The girl is running" or "Daddy's eating")

B. Potential Problem Behaviors

___True or ___False   Talks mostly by "parroting" or repeating what others say or what he or she hears on television

___True or ___False   Does not respond to conversation (for example, talks at you, or doesn't really answer your question)

___True or ___False   Used to talk, but now has stopped talking or uses only one or two words

___True or ___False   If child talks, has speech that is mostly difficult to understand, even by family members

___True or ___False   Does not speak at all

___True or ___False   If child talks, cannot say certain sounds in words, or changes the sounds in words (like "tar" for "car"), or drops sounds from words (like "ca" for "cat") making the child's speech difficult to understand much of the time

___True or ___False   Child's voice is not clear; voice sounds hoarse or raspy much or all of the time

___True or ___False   Cannot communicate either by words or pointing (for example, will only cry when needing something)

___True or ___False   Does not seem to understand what is said

The Senses: Vision, Hearing, Taste, and Touch
(includes sensory integration)

A. Basic Skills

___True or ___False   Enjoys or puts up with different types of touch (such as hugging and hair or tooth brushing)

___True or ___False   Responds when name is called (for example, looks up or says something)

___True or ___False   Moves to or hums along with music

B. Potential Problem Behaviors

___True or ___False   Often holds head awkwardly or closes one eye to look at something

___True or ___False   Turns one ear toward the sound he or she wants to hear

___True or ___False   Is bothered by noises that don't seem to bother others (for example, holds hands over ears, cries, or runs away when the vacuum is turned on)

___True or ___False   Will only eat a few foods and reacts strongly to other foods (for example, will gag, vomit, or spit out food)

___True or ___False   Can't stand how certain textures feel (such as clothing tags or getting sand on hands)

Relating to Self and Others *(social/emotional development)*

A. Basic Skills

___True or ___False   Enjoys humor (for example, laughs at silly faces or voices)

___True or ___False   Shows affection (for example, gives hugs and/or kisses)

___True or ___False   Plays with (not just next to) other children at least a little

___True or ___False   Has at least one special friend (where other children are available to be friends)

___True or ___False   Understands ideas such as "mine" and "his" or "hers"

___True or ___False   Can take turns in games

B. Potential Problem Behaviors

___True or ___False   Shows no interest in playing with other children

___True or ___False   Avoids looking people in the eye most of the time

___True or ___False   Stares into space or talks to self a lot

___True or ___False   Has no fear or awareness of danger (for example, runs into the street over and over)

___True or ___False   Shows anger or intense frustration almost every day (for instance, throws tantrums, fights, screams, or hits other children)

___True or ___False   Breaks or destroys things a lot

___True or ___False   Hurts other people or animals a lot

___True or ___False   Hurts self repeatedly (for example, bangs head, hits self, or bites hand)

Self-Care *(daily living skills)*

A. Basic Skills

___True or ___False   Can feed self, spilling a little (for example, can use a spoon and/or a fork, and can drink from a cup)

___True or ___False   Washes and dries his or her hands without help

___True or ___False   Brushes his or her teeth with or without help

___True or ___False   Can put on and take off simple clothes pretty much without help (such as sweatpants or a T-shirt)

___True or ___False   Is mostly toilet trained (may still have some accidents during the day and/or wet at night)

B. Potential Problem Behaviors

___True or ___False   Has sleeping problems (for example, usually wakes
                             up many times during the night, has serious difficulty
                             falling asleep, or only sleeps 2–3 hours at a time)

PART TWO: MEDICAL, BIRTH, AND FAMILY CONDITIONS

A wide range of medical conditions, birth complications, and family
background characteristics are known through hundreds of research
studies to predispose and/or cause children to develop mild, moderate, or severe developmental, behavioral, and health needs or difficulties. It is important that every parent become aware of these predisposing or causative conditions, as their presence should alert parents
that they must seek out and receive professional assistance for their
child.

Predisposing or causative conditions are often referred to by professionals as "risk factors" for childhood disorders and problems. They
include biological, medical, and hereditary causes that affect the parent and/or the child; problems that may have occurred at the hospital
while the baby was being delivered; neighborhood conditions where
children are exposed to violence and react by developing problems or
regressing to earlier stages of functioning; and living in poverty, where
the absence of healthy and stimulating surroundings may depress a
child's development. These are matters over which parents have little
or no control.

Some predisposing conditions are the direct result of harmful actions on the part of parents, caregivers, or others toward the developing child. Some of these are intentional, such as when an adult physically, emotionally, or sexually abuses a young child. At other times,
development is negatively impacted unintentionally, such as when a
mother abuses alcohol and other drugs while she is pregnant.

Regardless of the reasons that these conditions exist, it is important that once parents understand the potential harm that can be
done to their children, they must seek out professional assistance. It
is equally important for other family members, friends of the family,
and child-care workers to respond similarly to the presence of these
conditions.

In order to help determine whether or not the child for whom you
completed the *Discovery Tool* questionnaire has experienced any of these

risk factors, you are asked to provide information about the child's history or current status. Again, you may want to consult with your spouse or other persons who are knowledgeable about this child.

It may be a little uncomfortable for you to share some of the necessary information, but your honesty in providing the medical, birth, and family condition information is critical for determining the most accurate results.

If you just completed the questionnaire for a child under 2 years of age, you need to answer the following set of 16 questions. If you just completed the questionnaire for a child 2 years or older, you need to answer the three questions about children 2 years and older.

Questions About the Child Under 2 Years of Age for Whom I Answered the Skills and Behaviors Questionnaire

___True or ___False — Was born significantly premature (born more than 8 weeks early)

___True or ___False — Had a very low birth weight (weight at birth under 3 pounds or 1,500 grams)

___True or ___False — Used a breathing tube for more than 2 days within the first month of life

___True or ___False — Had or has failure to thrive (severe weight loss or significant lack of weight gain and growth)

___True or ___False — Has been previously admitted to a neonatal intensive care unit

___True or ___False — Has had seizures (not due to a fever)

___True or ___False — Has had a brain injury, anomaly, or infection

___True or ___False — Has had a serious injury, accident, or illness that may affect development

___True or ___False — Has a genetic disorder or syndrome (such as Down Syndrome)

___True or ___False — Has a severe hearing, visual, or orthopedic problem

___True or ___False — Has been diagnosed with an ongoing and serious medical condition (such as a heart valve disorder)

___True or ___False — Had prenatal exposure to drugs, alcohol, medications, or toxic chemicals known to affect the unborn baby

___True or ___False — Is unusually stiff or floppy (like a "rag doll")

___True or ___False — Has a parent who is developmentally disabled

___True or ___False — Has been the victim of child abuse and/or neglect

___True or ___False — Was previously, or is currently being, served by a program for children with special needs

Questions About a Child 2 Years or Older for Whom I Answered the Skills and Behavior Questionnaire

___True or ___False   Has seizures (not fully controlled by medication)

___True or ___False   Has a severe hearing or visual problem

___True or ___False   Has a diagnosed syndrome or ongoing medical
                          condition (for example, serious asthma)

Now you are ready to score the questionnaires. Here's the scoring sheet:

Discovery Tool Scoring Sheet

Name of Person Completing Tool: _____

Date: _____

Birthdate of Child: _____

Age Range of *Discovery Tool* Questionnaire: _____

❑ Premature? (Number of Weeks Early: ____)

The Six Areas of Development

	Movement (Physical and Motor Development)	Thinking and Learning (Cognitive Development)	Communication (Receptive and Expressive Language)	The Senses (Vision, Hearing, Taste, and Touch)	Relating to Self and Others (Social and Emotional Development)	Self-Care (Daily Living Skills)	Total
How many Basic Skills are missing in each area of development? ("false" responses)							
How many Potential Problem Behaviors are present in each area of development? ("true" responses)							

Family, Birth, and Medical Conditions

How Many Conditions Are Present? ("true" Responses)	Circle the Number of Conditions That Are Present
	0 1 2 3 4 5 6 7 8 9 10 11 12 13 14 15 16

Scoring System

Child may have special needs if

> Four or more basic skills are missing overall ("false" responses)
> Two or more basic skills are missing ("false" responses) from any
>   one area of development.
> Three or more potential problem behaviors are present ("true"
>   responses) from all areas of development.
> Two or more medical, birth, and family conditions are present
>   (two or more "true" responses).

Remember, if these results suggest that this child may have special needs, it is wise to have the child examined by a pediatrician, psychologist, or team of professionals to conduct a developmental assessment to determine whether the child does indeed have special needs, and, if so, to work with those professionals to find a good early intervention program for the child and the family. Chapter 5 provides the relevant information on developmental assessments and early intervention programs.

If the results suggest that this child does not have special needs—i.e., the child does not show the numbers of delayed skills, potential behavior problems, and predisposing conditions that warrant being alerted to the possibility of special needs—then it seems that the child is developing in a fine, age-appropriate fashion. That's great news! It is wise, however, to use the tool again in a few months to see if the child is still developing well. Sometimes, special need patterns do not develop right away, so it is good to do a little checking up on that possibility. In any case, using the tool again can give you more things to enjoy about this child's development as you learn more about the various developmental milestones that he or she is achieving.

Notes

Chapter 1

1. Alvy (2002a)

Chapter 2

1. Child Trends Data Bank. (n.d.). The number of children under age 18 in the United States has grown from 47.3 million in 1950 to 73.5 million in 2005. By the year 2030, that number is expected to grow to 85.7 million.
2. O'Hare (2001)
3. Kreider & Flekis (2002)
4. U.S. Department of Health and Human Services (n.d.)
5. U.S. Department of Health and Human Services (n.d.)
6. Casper & Schultz (1999)
7. Center for Nutrition Policy and Promotion (2005)
8. Center for Nutrition Policy and Promotion (2005)
9. Center for Nutrition Policy and Promotion (2005)
10. Jump Start Coalition for Financial Literacy (2005)
11. The College Board (2004)
12. Kids Count Census Data Online (n.d.)
13. National Center for Children in Poverty (n.d.)
14. The White House (n.d.)
15. Institute of Medicine (2004)
16. Institute of Medicine (2004)
17. Institute of Medicine (2004)
18. National Alliance on Mental Illness (n.d.a)
19. National Alliance on Mental Illness (n.d.b)
20. El Nazar (2006)
21. U.S. Census Bureau (2000)
22. El Nazar (2006).
23. El Nazar (2006).
24. El Nazar (2006).
25. Children's Partnership (2005)
26. Children's Partnership (2005)

27. Kaiser Family Foundation (2005b)

28. Lenhart, Rainie, & Lewis (2001)

29. Wikipedia (n.d.)

30. Foehr (2006)

31. Finklehor, Mitchell, & Wolek (2000)

32. Kaiser Family Foundation (2003a, 2003b, 2004, 2005a); American Academy of Pediatrics (1999)

33. Center for Media Literacy (n.d.)

34. Bushman & Huesmann (2001); Kirsh (2006)

35. Nicoli & Keiffer (2005)

36. The multitasking generation (2006)

37. The multitasking generation (2006)

38. Foehr (2006)

39. Weil & Rosen (1997)

40. Centers for Disease Control and Prevention (n.d.a)

41. Centers for Disease Control and Prevention (n.d.b)

42. American Academy of Pediatrics (n.d.)

43. SAMHSA's National Clearinghouse for Alcohol and Drug Information (n.d.)

44. National Institute on Drug Abuse (2002)

45. National Institute on Drug Abuse (2002)

46. Substance Abuse and Mental Health Services Administration (2002a)

47. Substance Abuse and Mental Health Services Administration (2002a)

48. Substance Abuse and Mental Health Services Administration (2002a)

49. Substance Abuse and Mental Health Services Administration (2002b)

50. Substance Abuse and Mental Health Services Administration (2002b)

51. National Campaign to Prevent Teen Pregnancy (2003)

52. Centers for Disease Control and Prevention (2006a)

53. Centers for Disease Control and Prevention (2006a)

54. Office of Population Affairs, U.S. Department of Health and Human Services (2004)

55. Weinstock, Berman, & Cates (2004)

56. Loeber & Farrington (1998, 2001)

57. Reston, Therolf, & Smith (2006)

58. Egley & Major (2003)

59. National Clearinghouse on Child Abuse and Neglect (2002); Centers for Disease Control and Prevention (2006b)

60. Alvy (1994)

61. U.S. Department of Health and Human Services & Administration on Children, Youth and Families (2007)

62. Alvy (1975); Centers for Disease Control and Prevention (2006b); Feindler, Rathus, & Silver (2003); Flowers (2000); Heyman & Slep (2002); Institute of Medicine Staff Board (2002); Malley-Morrison & Hines (2003); Stark (2000)

63. Centers for Disease Control and Prevention (2006b)

64. Centers for Disease Control and Prevention (2006b)

65. Bigner (2006)

Chapter 3

1. Alvy (1994)
2. The White House (n.d.)
3. Bornstein (1995)
4. Martin (1975); Maccoby & Martin (1983)
5. Coopersmith (1967)
6. Martin (1975)
7. Martin (1975)
8. Martin (1975)
9. Martin (1975)
10. Maccoby & Martin (1983)
11. Alvy (1994)
12. Bandura (1986)
13. Bandura (1986)
14. Bandura (1986)
15. Bandura (1986)
16. Kumpfer & Alvarado (2003); Kumpfer (1987); Alvy (1991)
17. Vissing, Straus, Gelles & Harrop (1991); Straus & Stewart (1999); Straus (2005); Gershoff (2002)
18. Vissing, Straus, Gelles & Harrop (1991)
19. Vissing, Straus, Gelles & Harrop (1991)
20. Straus & Stewart (1999)
21. Gershoff (2002)
22. Gershoff (2002)
23. Straus (2005)
24. Alvy (2007)
25. Project No Spank (n.d.)

Chapter 4

1. Center for the Improvement of Child Caring (2001b)
2. Center for the Improvement of Child Caring (1996)
3. Center for the Improvement of Child Caring (2001a)
4. Popkin (2002)
5. Dinkmeyer, McKay, & Dinkmeyer (1997)
6. Alvy (2002b)
7. Center for the Improvement of Child Caring (2001b)
8. Center for the Improvement of Child Caring (2001b)
9. Center for the Improvement of Child Caring (2001b)
10. Bavolek (2003)
11. Bavolek (1990)
12. Elovson (1993)
13. Popkin, Youngs, & Healy (1995)
14. Popkin, Youngs, & Healy (1995)
15. Popkin, Youngs, & Healy (1995)

16. Popkin, Youngs, & Healy (1995)

17. Popkin, Youngs, & Healy (1995)

18. Popkin, Youngs, & Healy (1995)

19. Popkin, Youngs, & Healy (1995)

20. Popkin, Youngs, & Healy (1995)

21. Popkin, Youngs, & Healy (1995)

22. Mellin (2003)

23. Mellin (2003)

24. Alvy (1991), pp. 11–26; Office of Substance Abuse Prevention (1991); Center for Substance Abuse Prevention/Office of Juvenile Justice and Delinquency Prevention (2000)

25. National Clearinghouse for Alcohol and Drug Information (n.d.)

26. Centers for Disease Control and Prevention (n.d.c)

27. Sexuality Information and Education Council of the United States (SIECUS) (2002); Carlson (2006); Chrisman & Couchenour (2002); Lefkowitz, Sigman, & Au (2002)

28. Office of Population Affairs, U.S. Department of Health and Human Services (2004)

29. Office of Population Affairs, U.S. Department of Health and Human Services (2004)

30. Office of Population Affairs, U.S. Department of Health and Human Services (2004)

31. National Campaign to Prevent Teen Pregnancy (2000)

32. Office of Population Affairs, U.S. Department of Health and Human Services (2004)

33. Mackey (2004)

34. Prosperity 4 Kids (n.d.)

35. Thoman & Jolis (2003)

36. Commonsense Media (n.d.b)

37. Commonsense Media (n.d.a)

38. Southern Poverty Law Center (n.d.b)

39. Southern Poverty Law Center (n.d.a)

Chapter 5

1. Center for the Improvement of Child Caring (n.d.d)

2. Alvy (2002b)

3. Alvy (2002b)

4. Alvy (2002b)

5. Alvy (2002b)

6. American Psychiatric Association (2000)

7. Alvy (2002b)

8. Alvy (2002b)

9. Child Find (n.d.)

10. Centers for Disease Control and Prevention (n.d.a)

11. Centers for Disease Control and Prevention (n.d.a)

12. National Dissemination Center for Children with Disabilities (n.d.a)
13. National Dissemination Center for Children with Disabilities (n.d.a)
14. National Dissemination Center for Children with Disabilities (n.d.a)
15. National Dissemination Center for Children with Disabilities (n.d.a)
16. National Dissemination Center for Children with Disabilities (n.d.a)
17. National Dissemination Center for Children with Disabilities (n.d.a)
18. National Dissemination Center for Children with Disabilities (n.d.b)
19. National Dissemination Center for Children with Disabilities (n.d.b)
20. National Dissemination Center for Children with Disabilities (n.d.b)
21. Barrett (2000)
22. American Academy of Pediatrics (n.d.)
23. Alvy (2002b)
24. Center for the Improvement of Child Caring (n.d.c)
25. Forepath (n.d.)
26. Administration for Children, Youth, and Families (n.d.)
27. Shonkoff & Meisels (2000)

Chapter 6

1. Alvy (1994); Center for the Improvement of Child Caring (n.d.b).
2. Gordon (2000)
3. *Nurse–Family Partnership* (n.d.)
4. *Nurse–Family Partnership* (n.d.)
5. *Healthy Families America* (n.d.)
6. *Parents as Teachers* (n.d.)

Chapter 7

1. Gordon (2000)
2. Gordon (2000); Alvy (1994)
3. Gordon (2000); Alvy (1994)
4. Gordon (2000); Alvy (1994)
5. Gordon (2000); Alvy (1994)
6. Gordon (2000); Alvy (1994)
7. Gordon (2000); Alvy (1994)
8. Gordon (2000); Alvy (1994)
9. Center for the Improvement of Child Caring (2001b)
10. Center for the Improvement of Child Caring (2001b)
11. Center for the Improvement of Child Caring (2001b)
12. Center for the Improvement of Child Caring (2001b)
13. Center for the Improvement of Child Caring (2001b)
14. Center for the Improvement of Child Caring (2001b)
15. Center for the Improvement of Child Caring (1996)
16. Alvy (1987)
17. Center for the Improvement of Child Caring (1996)
18. Center for the Improvement of Child Caring (1996)

19. Center for the Improvement of Child Caring (1996)
20. Center for the Improvement of Child Caring (n.d.a)
21. Center for the Improvement of Child Caring (2001a)
22. Center for the Improvement of Child Caring (2001a)
23. Northwest Indian Child Welfare Institute (1986)
24. Northwest Indian Child Welfare Institute (1986)
25. Northwest Indian Child Welfare Institute (1986)
26. Northwest Indian Child Welfare Institute (1986)
27. Faber & Mazlish (1998)
28. Faber & Mazlish (1987)
29. Family Development Resources (n.d.)
30. Bavolek (2003)
31. Baker & Brightman (2002)
32. Baker & Brightman (2002)
33. Knoff (2005)
34. Knoff (2005)
35. Knoff (2005)
36. Popkin, Youngs, & Healy (1995)
37. Popkin, Youngs, & Healy (1995)
38. Popkin, Youngs, & Healy (1995)
39. Popkin (1998a, 1998b, 2002)
40. Popkin (1998a, 1998b, 2002)
41. Family Works (n.d.)
42. Incredible Years (n.d.)

Chapter 8

1. Alliance of Information and Referral Systems (n.d.)
2. Alliance of Information and Referral Systems (n.d.)
3. Alliance of Information and Referral Systems (n.d.)
4. Google (n.d.)
5. Top Sites for Parents (n.d.)

Chapter 9

1. iPetitions.com (n.d.)
2. National Effective Parenting Initiative (n.d.)

References

Administration for Children, Youth, and Families. (2006). *Child maltreatment 2004.* Washington, DC: U.S. Government Printing Office.

Administration for Children, Youth, and Families. (n.d.). *About Head Start.* Retrieved April 29, 2007, from http://www.acf.hhs.gov/programs/hsb/about/index.htm

Alliance of Information and Referral Systems (AIRS). (n.d.). *2-1-1: Transforming access to human services.* Retrieved May 9, 2007, from http://www.airs.org/lookingfor211.asp

Alvy, K. T. (1975). Preventing child abuse. *American Psychologist, 30,* 921–928.

Alvy, K. T. (1987). *Black parenting: Strategies for training.* New York: Irvington Publishers.

Alvy, K. T. (1991). Parent training as a prevention strategy. In *Parent training is prevention: Preventing alcohol and other drug problems among youth in the family* (pp. 11–27) [DHHS Publication No. (ADM) 91-1715]. Rockville, MD: Alcohol, Drug Abuse and Mental Health Administration.

Alvy, K. T. (1994). *Parent training today: A social necessity.* Studio City, CA: Center for the Improvement of Child Caring.

Alvy, K. T. (2002a). *The power of positive parenting: 10 guidelines for raising healthy and confident children.* Studio City, CA: Center for the Improvement of Child Caring.

Alvy, K. T. (2002b). *The CICC discovery tool: A practical guide to help parents understand their children's development, identify any special needs and become connected to helpful resources.* Studio City, CA: Center for the Improvement of Child Caring.

Alvy, K. T. (2007, February 22). *Banning corporal punishment: What the arguments tell us about our character regarding the treatment of children* [Center for the Improvement of Child Caring]. Retrieved April 23, 2007, from http://ciccparenting.org/NewsLetters/BanCorpEssay.htm

American Academy of Pediatrics. (1999). Media education. *Pediatrics, 104,* 341–343.

American Academy of Pediatrics. (n.d.). *Definition of children with special health care needs.* Retrieved April 21, 2007, from http://www.medicalhomeinfo.org/about/def_cshcn.html

American Psychiatric Association. (2000). *Diagnostic and statistical manual of mental disorders* (4th ed.), *Text revision* [DSM-IV-TR]. Washington, DC: Author.

Baker, B. L., & Brightman, A. J. (2002). *Steps to independence: Teaching everyday skills to children with special needs.* Baltimore, MD: Paul H. Brooks.

Bandura, A. (1986). *Social foundations of thought and action: A social cognitive theory.* Englewood Cliffs, NJ: Prentice Hall.

Barrett, S. W. (2000). Economics of early childhood intervention. In J. P. Shonkoff & S. J. Meisels (Eds.), *Handbook of early childhood intervention* (2nd ed.; pp. 560–582). Cambridge, UK: Cambridge University Press.

Bavolek, S. J. (1990). *Shaking, hitting, spanking: What to do instead, Leader's guide.* Park City, UT: Family Development Resources.

Bavolek, S. J. (2003). *Nurturing skills for parents.* Park City, UT: Family Development Resources.

Bigner, J. J. (2006). *Parent–child relations: An introduction to parenting* (7th ed.). Upper Saddle River, NJ: Pearson/Merrill, Prentice Hall.

Bornstein, M. H. (Ed.). (1995). *Handbook of parenting: Volume 1, Children and parenting.* Mahwah, NJ: Lawrence Erlbaum.

Bushman, B. J., & Huesmann, L. R. (2001). Effects of televised violence on aggression. In D. G. Singer & J. L. Singer (Eds.), *Handbook of children and the media* (pp. 223–254). Thousand Oaks, CA: Sage.

Carlson, F. M. (2006). *Essential touch: Meeting the needs of young children.* Washington, DC: National Association for the Education of Young Children.

Casper, V., & Schultz, S. B. (1999). *Gay parents/straight schools: Building communication and trust.* New York: Teachers College Press.

Center for Media Literacy. (n.d.). *Advertising/consumerism.* Retrieved April 22, 2007, from http://www.medialit.org/focus/adv_home.html

Center for Nutrition Policy and Promotion. (2005). *Expenditures on children by families, 2004* [Miscellaneous Publication Number 1528–2004]. Washington, DC: U.S. Department of Agriculture.

Center for Substance Abuse Prevention/Office of Juvenile Justice and Delinquency Prevention. (2000, April). *Strengthening America's families: Model family programs for substance abuse and delinquency prevention.* Salt Lake City: University of Utah, Department of Health Promotion and Education.

Center for the Improvement of Child Caring. (1996). *Effective Black parenting: Parent handbook.* Studio City, CA: Author.

Center for the Improvement of Child Caring. (2001a). *Los niños bien educados: Parent handbook.* Studio City, CA: Author.

Center for the Improvement of Child Caring. (2001b). *Confident parenting: Parent handbook.* Studio City, CA: Author.

Center for the Improvement of Child Caring. (n.d.a). *Affiliations of persons trained as parenting instructors through CICC-sponsored training events.* Retrieved May 1, 2007, from http://ciccparenting.org/cicc_tfp_30.asp?f=cicc

Center for the Improvement of Child Caring. (n.d.b). *Parenting skill-building programs.* Retrieved February 23, 2007, from http://ciccparenting.org/ParSkill BuildingPrograms.aspx

Center for the Improvement of Child Caring. (n.d.c). *Welcome to the CICC Discovery Tool.* Retrieved April 29, 2007, from http://www.ciccdiscoverytool.org/ Welcome.aspx

Center for the Improvement of Child Caring. (n.d.d). *What is a special need?* Retrieved February 23, 2007, from http://www.ciccparenting.org/cicc_What_Is.aspx

Centers for Disease Control and Prevention. (2006a, April). *A glance at the HIV/ AIDS epidemic.* Retrieved April 22, 2007, from http://www.cdc.gov/hiv/ resources/factsheets/At-A-Glance.htm

Centers for Disease Control and Prevention. (2006b). *Child maltreatment fact sheet.* Retrieved February 23, 2007, from http://www.cdc.gov/ncipc/factsheets/ cmfacts.htm

Centers for Disease Control and Prevention. (n.d.a). *Autism: What are the symptoms?* Retrieved April 29, 2007, from http://www.cdc.gov/ncbddd/autism/ symptoms.htm

Centers for Disease Control and Prevention. (n.d.b). *How common are autism spectrum disorders?* Retrieved August 30, 2006, from http://www.cdc.gov/ ncbddd/autism/asd_common.htm

Centers for Disease Control and Prevention. (n.d.c). *Sexually transmitted diseases.* Retrieved February 23, 2007, from http://www.cdc.gov/node.do/id/ 0900f3ec80009a98

Child Find. (n.d.). *IDEA Child Find project.* Retrieved April 29, 2007, from http:// www.childfindidea.org/

Child Trends Data Bank. (n.d.). *Number of children.* Retrieved February 18, 2007, from http://www.childtrendsdatabank.org/pdf/53_PDF.pdf

Children's Partnership. (2005). *Measuring digital opportunity for America's children: Where we stand and where we go from here.* Santa Monica, CA: Author.

Chrisman, K., & Couchenour, D. (2002). *Healthy sexual development: A guide for early childhood educators and families.* Washington, DC: National Association for the Education of Young Children.

The College Board. (2004). *Trends in college pricing.* New York: Author.

Commonsense Media. (n.d.a). *Communicating: Common sense tips.* Retrieved April 24, 2007, from http://www.commonsense.com/internet-safety-guide/ communicating.php

Commonsense Media. (n.d.b). *Keeping your kids internet safe and smart: A survival guide for parents.* Retrieved April 25, 2007, from http://www.commonsense. com/ooframe/news/email/subscribe.php

Commonsense Media. (n.d.c). *Violence.* Retrieved April 24, 2007, from http:// www.commonsensemedia.org/resources/violence.php

Coopersmith, S. (1967). *The antecedents of self-esteem.* San Francisco, CA: W. H. Freeman.

Dinkmeyer, D., Sr., McKay, G. D., & Dinkmeyer, D., Jr. (1997). *The parent's handbook: Systematic training for effective parenting.* Circle Pines, MN: American Guidance Service.

Egley, A., Jr., & Major, A. K. (2003). *Highlights of the 2001 national youth gang survey.* Washington, DC: U.S. Department of Justice, Office of Juvenile Justice and Delinquency Prevention.

El Nazar, H. (2006, July 5). A nation of 300 million. *USA Today*, p. 1.

Elovson, A. (1993). *The kindergarten survival handbook: The before school checklist and a guide for parents.* Santa Monica, CA: Parent Education Resources.

Faber, A., & Mazlish, E. (1987). *Siblings without rivalry: Group workshop kit.* Rye, NY: Faber/Mazlish Workshops.

Faber, A., & Mazlish, E. (1998). *Siblings without rivalry.* New York: Avon Books.

Family Development Resources. (n.d.). *Research and validation.* Retrieved May 7, 2007, from http://nurturingparenting.com/research_validation/index.htm

Family Works. (n.d.). *Welcome to Family Works, Inc., home of parenting wisely.* Retrieved May 8, 2007, from http://familyworksinc.com/index.html

Feindler, E. L., Rathus, J. H., & Silver, L. B. (2003). *Assessment of family violence: A handbook for researchers and practitioners.* Washington, DC: American Psychological Association.

Finklehor, D., Mitchell, K. J., & Wolak, J. (2000). *Online victimization: A report on the nation's youth.* Alexandria, VA: National Center for Missing and Exploited Children.

Flowers, R. B. (2000). *Domestic crimes, family violence, and child abuse: A study of contemporary American society.* Jefferson, NC: McFarland and Company.

Foehr, U. G. (2006). *Media multitasking among American youth: Prevalence, predictors and pairings.* Menlo Park, CA: Kaiser Family Foundation.

Forepath. (n.d.). *Welcome to the PEDS child development screening test.* Retrieved April 29, 2007, from http://www.forepath.org/

Gershoff, E. T. (2002). Corporal punishment by parents and associated child behaviors and experiences: A meta-analytic and theoretical review. *Psychology Bulletin, 128*(4), 539–579.

Google. (n.d.). *Parenting: Google search.* Retrieved May 9, 2007, from http://www.google.com/search?hl=en&ie=ISO-8859-1&q=Parenting&btnG=Google+Search

Gordon, T. (2000). *Parent effectiveness training: The proven program for raising responsible children.* New York: Three Rivers Press.

Healthy Families America. (n.d.). Retrieved April 31, 2007, from http://www.healthyfamiliesamerica.org/home/index.shtml

Heyman, R. E., & Slep, A. M. S. (2002). Do child abuse and intergenerational violence lead to adulthood family violence? *Journal of Marriage and Family, 64,* 864–870.

Incredible Years. (n.d.). *The incredible years.* Retrieved May 8, 2007, from http://incredibleyears.com/

Institute of Medicine. (2004, September). *Childhood obesity in the United States: Facts and figures.* Retrieved April 20, 2007, from http://www.iom.edu/Object.File/Master/22/606/Finalfactsandfigures2.pdf

Institute of Medicine Staff Board. (2002). *Confronting chronic neglect: The education and training of health professionals on family violence.* Washington, DC: National Academy Press.

iPetitions.com. (n.d.). *Effective parenting petition.* Retrieved May 9, 2007, from http://www.ipetitions.com/petition/effectiveparentingusa/index.html

Jump Start Coalition for Financial Literacy. (2005). *Making the case for financial literacy: A collection of personal finance statistics gathered from other sources.* Retrieved April 20, 2007, from http://www.jumpstartcoalition.com/upload/Personal%20Financial%20Stats%202005%20Letterhead.doc

Kaiser Family Foundation. (2003a, December). *A teacher in the living room? Educational media for babies, toddlers, and preschoolers.* Menlo Park, CA: Author.

Kaiser Family Foundation. (2003b, Fall). *Zero to six: Electronic media in the lives of infants, toddlers and preschoolers.* Menlo Park, CA: Author.

Kaiser Family Foundation. (2004). *The role of media in childhood obesity.* Menlo Park, CA: Author.

Kaiser Family Foundation. (2005a, January). *The effects of electronic media on children ages zero to six: A history of research.* Menlo Park, CA: Author.

Kaiser Family Foundation. (2005b, March). *Generation M: Media in the lives of 8–18 year olds.* Menlo Park, CA: Author.

Kids Count Census Data Online. (n.d.). *Table 22: Own children by family type and employment status of parents by age group in the 2000 census.* Retrieved April 20, 2007, from http://www.kidscount.org/cgi-bin/aeccensus.cgi?action=profiler esults&area=00N&areaparent=00N&printerfriendly=0&section=6

Kirsh, S. J. (2006). *Children, adolescents and media violence.* Thousands Oaks, CA: Sage.

Knoff, H. M. (2005). *The stop and think parenting book: A guide to children's good behavior.* Longmont, CO: Sopris West Educational Services.

Koplan, J. P., Liverman, C. T., & Kraak, V. I. (Eds.). (2005). *Preventing childhood obesity: Health in the balance.* Washington, DC: Institute of Medicine of the National Academies, The National Academies Press.

Kreider, R. A., & Flekis, J. M. (2002). *Number, timing and duration of marriages and divorces: 1996* (Current Population Reports; pp. 70–80). Washington, DC: U.S. Census Bureau.

Kumpfer, K. L. (1987). Etiology and prevention of vulnerability to chemical dependency in children of substance abusers. In B. Brown & A. Miles (Eds.), *Youth at high risk for substance abuse* [DHHS Pub. No. (ADM) 87-1537]. Rockville, MD: Alcohol, Drug Abuse and Mental Health Administration.

Kumpfer, K. L., & Alvarado, R. (2003, June/July). Family-strengthening approaches for the prevention of youth behavior problems. *American Psychologist, 58*(6/7), 457–465.

Lefkowitz, E. S., Sigman, M., & Au, T. K. (2002). Helping mothers discuss sexuality and AIDS with adolescents. *Child Development, 71*(5), 1383–1394.

Lenhart, A., Rainie, L., & Lewis, O. (2001). *Teenage life online: The rise of the instant-message generation and the Internet's impact on friendships and family relationships.* Washington, DC: Pew Internet and American Life Project.

Loeber, R., & Farrington, D. P. (1998). *Serious and violent juvenile offenders: Risk factors and successful interventions.* Thousand Oaks, CA: Sage.

Loeber, R., & Farrington, D. P. (2001). *Child delinquents: Development, intervention, and service needs.* Thousand Oaks, CA: Sage.

Maccoby, E., & Martin, J. (1983). Socialization within the context of the family. In M. E. Heatherington (Ed.), *Handbook of child psychology* (Vol. IV; pp. 1–102). New York: Wiley.

Mackey, L. (2004). *Money mama and the three little pigs.* Agoura Hills, CA: P4K Publishing.

Malley-Morrison, K., & Hines, D. (2003). *Family violence in a cultural perspective: Defining, understanding and combating abuse.* Thousand Oaks, CA: Sage.

Martin, B. (1975). Child–parent relations. In F. Horowitz (Ed.), *Review of child development research* (Vol. 4; pp. 463–540). Chicago: University of Chicago Press.

Mellin, L. M. (2003). *Shapedown parent's guide: A guide for supporting your child.* San Anselmo, CA: Balboa.

The multitasking generation. (2006, March 26). *Time,* pp. 48–55.

National Alliance on Mental Illness. (n.d.a). *Anorexia Nervosa.* Retrieved April 21, 2007, from http://www.nami.org/PrinterTemplate. cfm?Section=By_Illness&template=/ContentManagement/ContentDisplay. cfm&ContentID=7409

National Alliance on Mental Illness. (n.d.b). *NAMI fact sheet on Bulimia Nervosa.* Retrieved April 20, 2007, from http://www.nami.org/Template. cfm?section=Search/SearchDisplay.cfm

National Campaign to Prevent Teen Pregnancy. (2000, April). *The cautious generation? Teens tell us about sex, virginity and "the talk."* Available at www. teenpregnancy.org

National Campaign to Prevent Teen Pregnancy. (2003). *14 and younger: The sexual behavior of young adolescents.* Washington, DC: Author.

National Center for Children in Poverty. (n.d.). *Basic facts about low-income children: Birth to age 18.* Retrieved February 23, 2007, from http://www.nccp.org/pub_ cpt06a.html

National Clearinghouse for Alcohol and Drug Information. (n.d.). *Parents/caregivers.* Retrieved April 24, 2007, from http://ncadistore.samhsa.gov/catalog/ facts.aspx?topic=14

National Clearinghouse on Child Abuse and Neglect. (2002). *Child maltreatment 2002: Summary of key findings.* Washington, DC: Author.

National Dissemination Center for Children with Disabilities. (n.d.a). *AD/HD 101.* Retrieved April 29, 2007, from http://www.nichcy.org/enews/foundations/ ADHD101.asp

National Dissemination Center for Children with Disabilities. (n.d.b). *NICHCY connections . . . to learning disabilities.* Retrieved April 29, 2007, from http:// www.nichcy.org/resources/LD1.asp

National Effective Parenting Initiative. (n.d.). *White house briefing.* Retrieved May 9, 2007, from https://www.effectiveparentingusa.org/White_House_Briefing. html

National Institute on Drug Abuse. (2002, September). *NIDA InfoFacts: Cigarettes and other nicotine products.* Washington, DC: U.S. Government Printing Office.

Nicoli, J, & Keiffer, K. M. (2005, August). *Violence in videogames: A review of the empirical research.* Paper presented at the annual meeting of the American Psychological Association, Washington, DC.

Northwest Indian Child Welfare Institute. (1986). *Positive Indian parenting: Honoring our children by honoring our traditions.* Portland, OR: Author.

Nurse–family partnership. (n.d.). Retrieved April 31, 2007, from http://www.nurse-familypartnership.org/index.cfm?fuseaction=home

Office of Population Affairs, U.S. Department of Health and Human Services. (2004). *Parents, speak up! A guide for discussing abstinence, sex, and relationships.* Washington, DC: Author.

Office of Substance Abuse Prevention. (1991). *Parent training is prevention: Preventing alcohol and other drug problems among youth in the family* [DHHS Publication No. (ADM) 91–1715]. Washington, DC: U.S. Government Printing Office.

O'Hare, B. (2001). *The rise—and fall?—of single parent families* [Population Reference Bureau]. Retrieved February 18, 2007, from http://www.prb.org/Articles/2001/The RiseandFallofSingleParentFamilies.aspx

Parents, The Anti-Drug: The National Youth Anti-Drug Media Campaign. (n.d.). *Drug information.* Retrieved February 23, 2007, from http://www.theantidrug.com/drug_info/

Parents as Teachers. (n.d.). Retrieved April 31, 2007, from http://www.parentsasteachers.org/site/pp.asp?c=ekIRLcMZJxE&b=272091

Popkin, M. H. (1998a). *Active parenting of teens: Parent's guide.* Atlanta, GA: Active Parenting Publishers.

Popkin, M. H. (1998b). *Parenting your 1- to 4-year-old.* Atlanta, GA: Active Parenting Publishers.

Popkin, M. H. (2002). *Active parenting now.* Atlanta, GA: Active Parenting Publishers.

Popkin, M. H., Youngs, B. B., & Healy, J. M. (1995). *Helping your child succeed at school: A guide to parents of 4 to 14 year olds.* Atlanta, GA: Active Parenting Publishers.

Project No Spank. (n.d.). *Countries where spanking is prohibited by law in the home, at school, everywhere!* Retrieved April 23, 2007, from http://www.nospank.net/totalban.htm

Prosperity 4 Kids. (n.d.). *Chore charts, allowance & children.* Retrieved April 25, 2007, from http://prosperity4kids.com/allowance.shtml

Reston, M., Therolf, G., & Smith, D. (2006, August 8). As L.A. violent crimes drop, the desert becomes a hot spot. *Los Angeles Times*, p. A1.

SAMHSA's National Clearinghouse for Alcohol and Drug Information. (n.d.). *Welcome to prevention online, PREVLINE.* Retrieved February 18, 2007, from http://ncadi.samhsa.gov/

Sexuality Information and Education Council of the United States (SIECUS). (2002). *Innovative approaches to increase parent–child communication about sexuality: Their impact and examples from the field.* New York: Author.

Shonkoff, J. P., & Meisels, S. J. (Eds.). (2000). *Handbook of early childhood intervention* (2nd ed.). Cambridge, UK: Cambridge University Press.

Southern Poverty Law Center. (n.d.a). *10 ways to fight hate.* Retrieved April 24, 2007, from http://www.tolerance.org/10ways/resources.htm

Southern Poverty Law Center. (n.d.b). *Parenting for tolerance.* Retrieved April 24, 2007, from http://www.tolerance.org/parents/index.jsp

Stark, E. (2000). *Everything you need to know about family violence.* New York: Rosen.

Straus, M. A. (2005). *Beating the devil out of them: Corporal punishment in American families.* New Brunswick, NJ: Transaction Publishers.

Straus, M. A., & Stewart, J. H. (1999). Corporal punishment by American parents: National data on prevalence, chronicity, severity and duration, in relationship to child and family characteristics. *Clinical Child and Family Psychology Review, 2*, 55–70.

Substance Abuse and Mental Health Services Administration. (2002a, September 4). *Results from the 2001 national household survey on drug abuse: Volume I. Summary of national findings.* Washington, DC: U.S. Government Printing Office.

Substance Abuse and Mental Health Services Administration. (2002b, February 14). *Summary of findings from the 2000 national household survey on drug abuse.* Washington, DC: U.S. Government Printing Office.

Thoman, E., & Jolis, T. (2003). *Literacy for the 21st century: An overview and orientation guide to media literacy education* [Center for Media Literacy]. Available at www.medialit.org

Top Sites for Parents. (n.d.). *Top sites for parents: 200+ fabulous, fantastic and informative things for parents to learn on the Internet.* Retrieved May 9, 2007, from http://topsitesforparents.com/

U.S. Census Bureau. (2000). *All across the U.S.A.: Population distribution and composition, 2000* [The Population Profile of the United States: 2000 (Internet Release)]. Retrieved February 23, 2007, from http://www.census.gov/population/www/pop-profile/profile2000.html

U.S. Department of Health and Human Services. (n.d). *Benefits of healthy marriages.* Retrieved February 18, 2007, from http://www.acf.hhs.gov/healthy marriage/benefits/index.html

U.S. Department of Health and Human Services & Administration on Children, Youth and Families. (2007). *Child maltreatment 2005.* Washington, DC: U.S. Government Printing Office.

Vissing, Y. M., Straus, M. A., Gelles, R. J., & Harrop, J. W. (1991). Verbal aggression by parents and psychological problems of children. *Child Abuse and Neglect, 15,* 223–238.

Weil, M. M., & Rosen, L. D. (1997). *Technostress: Coping with technology at work, home and play.* New York: Wiley.

Weinstock, H., Berman, S., & Cates, S., Jr. (2004). Sexually transmitted diseases among American youth: Incidence and prevalence estimates, 2000. *Perspectives on Sexual and Reproductive Health, 36*(1), 6–10.

The White House. (n.d.). *Fact sheet: America's workforce: Ready for the 21st century.* Retrieved April 20, 2007, from http://www.whitehouse.gov/news/releases/2004/08/20040805-6.html

Wikipedia. (n.d.). *MySpace.* Retrieved April 22, 2007, from http://en.wikipedia.org/wiki/Myspace

Index

About the Author

Dr. Kerby T. Alvy, a clinical child psychologist, is the founder and executive director of the Center for the Improvement of Child Caring, and a founding board member of the National Effective Parenting Initiative. He is the author of many books and articles on parenting, child development, and child abuse, as well as authoring and co-authoring parenting education programs and seminars. His other books include *Parent Training Today: A Social Necessity*, one of the most comprehensive and authoritative books ever written on parent training, and *Black Parenting: Strategies for Training*, a groundbreaking book of research on African American parenting and implications for culturally specific parent training. The parenting education programs and seminars that Dr. Alvy has authored and co-authored include the Center's trio of national model programs: *Confident Parenting: Survival Skill Training*, *Effective Black Parenting*, and *Los Niños Bien Educados*. The latter two programs have become the most widely used, culturally specific parenting skill-building programs in the United States. His competencies as a researcher and scientist have been acknowledged through research and demonstration grants from a variety of federal government agencies, and from his being selected to serve on scientific review committees.

Dr. Alvy was previously affiliated with Kedren Community Mental Health Center in South Central Los Angeles for 7 years, where he served as director of Children's Services, and with the California School of Professional Psychology for 17 years, where he was a professor and dean for Academic Affairs. He has also taught at other institutions, including UCLA and the California State University at Los Angeles.

Dr. Alvy has received numerous awards for his and CICC's accomplishments in improving the quality of childrearing in America, including being honored at the White House in 1994 as part of the First National Parent's Day Celebration. He received the Distinguished Alumni Award in 1997 from the State University of New York at Albany, where he received his doctorate in psychology, and earned the "Illuminating the Way to the New Millennium Award" from the Parenting Coalition International and the U.S. Center for Substance Abuse Prevention in 1999.